*The foe claims in vain a philosopher I am.
God knows I am not what* he says *I am.
But, having endured this sorrow's nest, I ask:
Why should I not know at least what I am?*

—Omar Khayyam

HUMAN ARCHITECTURE
Journal of the Sociology of Self-Knowledge

Editor:
M.H. (Behrooz) Tamdgidi
Assistant Professor of Sociology
UMass Boston

Human Architecture: Journal of the Sociology of Self-Knowledge (ISSN # 1540-5699) is published by the Okcir Press, tel/fax: 781.874.1448, website: www.okcir.com, e-mail: journal@okcir.com. Okcir Press is an imprint of Ahead Publishing House (APH), 6 Hobbs Road, Medford, MA, 02155, U.S.A.
Copyright © by Ahead Publishing House, 2002-4. All rights reserved.

Submissions: *Human Architecture* publishes both submitted and invited manuscripts as well as working papers of the Omar Khayyam Center for Integrative Research (OKCIR) in Utopia, Mysticism, and the Academy—an independent research and educational project associated with the Okcir Press. Contributors extend permission to *Human Architecture* for the publication of their work in the journal. They retain copyrights to their work and may publish them elsewhere. If the submitted manuscript has been published elsewhere before, written permission from both the author(s) and publication(s) where it earlier appeared should accompany submission to *Human Architecture*.

Editorial decisions: Selection of papers from submitted manuscripts will be based on their substantive relevance to the mission of the journal. Views expressed in the journal by contributors are those of their authors and may not necessarily coincide with one another, or with the views of the editor or members of the Editorial Advisory Board. Authors are responsible for the accuracy and integrity of factual, bibliographic, and referential materials used in their own articles. Empirical, historical, theoretical, as well as methodological discourses relevant to the mission of the journal are all encouraged. The primary language used is English, but material in other languages may be included if relevant to the purpose of the journal.

What to submit: All manuscripts should be submitted in electronic format. They should preferably be double-spaced in Times 12 typeface., with 1 inch margins all around. In general, please follow a consistent bibliographic and citation style throughout the manuscript, following the ASA (American Sociological Association), MLA, or the University of Chicago style guides.

Where to submit: The Editor, *Human Architecture*, Okcir Press, 6 Hobbs Road, Medford, MA, 02155, U.S.A., tel/fax: 781.874.1448, e-mail: journal@okcir.com

Subscriptions: Individual and institutional rates for single issues of *Human Architecture* are $15 and $30 respectively. Individual and institutional subscription rates for four consecutive issues beginning from the current issue (when subscription order is received) are $48 and $96 respectively—reflecting a 20% discount per single issue rate. Rates include domestic shipping and sales tax, where applicable. For international or bulk orders please inquire for special rates & shipping charges. Make checks payable in U.S. dollars to Ahead Publishing House, and send payments to the Okcir Press, 6 Hobbs Road, Medford, MA, 02155, U.S.A. Back issues or additional copies of the journal are available upon request at the same per single issue rates as indicated above. Contributors each receive one free copy of the issue in which their articles appear. Contributors and Editorial Advisory Board members receive a 20% discount on individual single issue rates.

Advertisements: Current rates and specifications may be obtained by contacting the Okcir Press, 6 Hobbs Road, Medford, MA, 02155, U.S.A., tel/fax: 781.874.1448, e-mail: journal@okcir.com

Inquiries: Address all correspondence and requests to *Human Architecture*, Okcir Press, 6 Hobbs Road, Medford, MA, 02155, U.S.A., tel/fax: 781.874.1448, e-mail: journal@okcir.com

Changes of address: Six weeks' advance notice must be given when notifying change of address. Please include both the old and the new address in your written/e-mailed request. **Postmaster:** Send address changes to the Okcir Press, 6 Hobbs Road, Medford, MA, 02155, U.S.A.

ISBN 1-888024-19-4

Human Architecture:
Journal of the Sociology of Self-Knowledge
Volume II, Number 2, Fall '03/Spring '04
ISSN: 1540-5699
ISBN: 1-888024-19-4

Editorial Advisory Board

Ayan Ahmed
B.A., Sociology
UMass Boston

Bart Bonikowski
Doctoral Student of Sociology
Duke University

David Baronov
Assistant Professor of Sociology
St. John Fisher College

Keilah Billings
Undergraduate Student of Sociology
UMass Boston

Milton Butts Jr.
Assistant Professor of Sociology
UMass Boston

Jorge Capetillo-Ponce
Assistant Professor of Sociology
UMass Boston

Arlene Dallalfar
Professor of Sociology & Women's Studies
Lesley College

Alicia Dowd
Assistant Professor of Higher Education Administration and Leadership
Graduate College of Education
UMass Boston

Estelle Disch
Professor of Sociology
UMass Boston

Bryan Gangemi
Student/Activist
UMass Boston

Tu Huynh
Doctoral Student of Sociology
SUNY-Binghamton

Glenn Jacobs
Associate Professor of Sociology
UMass Boston

Emily Margulies
B.A., Sociology
SUNY-Oneonta

Jonathan Martin
Assistant Professor of Sociology
Framingham State College

Martha Montero-Sieburth
Associate Professor of Higher Education Administration and Leadership
Graduate College of Education
UMass Boston

Siamak Movahedi
Professor of Sociology
UMass Boston

Anthony Nadler
Assistant Coordinator
Office of Service-Learning and Community Outreach
UMass Boston

Donna M. Rafferty
Undergraduate Student of Sociology
UMass Boston

Jesse Reichek
Professor Emeritus of Architecture
U.C. Berkeley

Annie Roper
Undergraduate Student of Sociology
UMass Boston

Khaldoun Samman
Assistant Professor of Sociology
Macalester College

Emmett Schaefer
Adjunct Assistant Professor of Sociology
UMass Boston

Ingrid Semaan
Doctoral Candidate of Sociology
UMass Amherst

Tim Sieber
Professor of Anthropology
UMass Boston

Rajini Srikanth
Associate Professor of English
UMass Boston

Shirley Tang
Assistant Professor of Asian American Studies and American Studies
UMass Boston

Rika Yonemura
Doctoral Student of Sociology
U.C. San Diego

Samuel Zalanga
Assistant Professor of Sociology
Bethel College

Contents

HUMAN ARCHITECTURE
Journal of the Sociology of Self-Knowledge

Volume II   Number 2   Fall 2003/Spring 2004

---

vii   *Editor's Note: "A Welcoming Statement to the Editorial Advisory Board"*

Ayan Ahmed
1   **The Complexity of Naive Acceptance of Socially Manipulated Beliefs**

Elizabeth J. Schumacher
10   **Alice in the Gendered Sports-Fan Wonderland: A Sociological Inquiry**

Chris DaPonte
18   **Will I Marry Her?**

Guadalupe Paz
25   **The Effect of Immigrant Experiences on the Bifurcation of Women's Consciousness**

Marie Neuner
33   **Who are "I"?: A Sociology of My Traditional, Modern, and Postmodern Selves**

D. M. Rafferty
41   **My Life's Tapestry: Casting Theoretical Lights on the Social Threads That Tie Me Down**

Annie Roper
48   **From Alienation to Exploration: Breaking Free from the Iron Cages of My Life**

M. D.
58   **Body Image: A Clouded Reality**

Michelle B. Jacobs
66   **Obsessed with Impression Management: A Critical Sociology of Body Image in Capitalist Society**

Jennifer M. Kosmas
74   **The Roots of Procrastination: A Sociological Inquiry into Why I Wait Until Tomorrow**

Lynne K. Marlette
82   **Honesty, Trust, and Love—In *That* Order: A Sociology of My Emotional Kaleidoscope**

Keilah Billings
91   **Questioning Motherhood: A Sociological Awakening**

Contents

HUMAN ARCHITECTURE
Journal of the Sociology of Self-Knowledge

Volume II   Number 2   Fall 2003/Spring 2004

Nancy O'Keefe Dyer
99 **Durkheim, Mead, and Heroin Addiction**

Buddi Osco
105 **Anomie or Alienation?: A Self-Exploration of the Roots of Substance Ab/use**

Savvas Fetfatsidis
109 **Just Live: The Trick Is, You Have A Choice**

Kuong C. Ly
116 **"Asian": Just A Simple Word**

Jorge Capetillo-Ponce
122 **Defining the Other**

M. H. (Behrooz) Tamdgidi
125 **De/Reconstructing Utopianism: Towards a World-Historical Typology**

143 **Contributors & Abstracts**

Editor's Note:
A Welcoming Statement to the Editorial Advisory Board

The present issue of *Human Architecture* includes a collection of excellent undergraduate student essays written in various courses offered at UMass Boston during the 2003-4 academic year. The diversity of issues explored by students in these essays, and the richness of the applied ways in which they critically incorporate theoretical concepts and insights into the fabric of their everyday lives in social context, can hardly be summarized in a short editorial note. So I invite the readers to read these essays forthwith. In many ways, principally because of the courage of these students in exploring the interlinkages of their personal troubles with public issues, but also because of their decisions to share them with others through the public medium of this journal, the present issue of *Human Architecture* marks another important step towards establishing this journal as a useful academic forum.

The encouragement for the continued publication of this journal has come from other quarters as well. The sources of these encouragements have ranged from the warm and supportive sociology faculty at UMass Boston whose ranks I joined in Fall 2003, to the wonderful community of scholars, students, and staff across the disciplines on this campus whom I met at numerous meetings and conferences during the past year, and finally to the kind acceptance by several faculty, staff, and students both on this and other campuses to join the forum provided by this journal as members of its new Editorial Advisory Board. Spearheading such encouragements was that kindly offered by Professor Jorge Capetillo-Ponce, of the Sociology Department, who participated together with me in organizing a CIT (Center for the Improvement of Teaching) workshop on "Classroom Publishing as a Liberating Pedagogical Strategy" in January 2004 at UMass Boston. Capetillo later encouraged several of his students to submit their papers to the present issue and contributed a short piece himself, hopefully as a beginning for many more to come. I thank him for his kind and friendly support.

I would like to take the opportunity of this space to appreciate and welcome the joining of the members of the Editorial Advisory Board to this forum. For this purpose, it may be helpful to take a step back and provide a brief overview of the purpose and goals of this journal, and the ways in which it can be made useful to the academic community across rank, disciplinary, university, and on/off-campus boundaries.

I began this journal when I was still a doctoral graduate student at SUNY-Binghamton, while teaching undergraduate sociology as a full-time faculty at SUNY-Oneonta for two years. Being a hybrid student/faculty journal with a welcoming emphasis on undergraduate learning, teaching, and research, therefore, goes to the heart and the very origins of this journal. I would like to maintain this diversity in terms of both paper submissions as well as composition of the Editorial Advisory Board, as I believe such a diversity can only help enrich this forum and fill in a gap in existing journals which often limit their constituencies to one or another set of academic ranks.

One need that gradually arose upon the publication of the previous three issues of the journal was that of finding ways to keep more continuous contact among those the journal linked with one another. Perhaps the most important need the Editorial Advisory Board will meet will be its networking function—helping those contributing to and interested in the mission of the journal to keep in touch across its multiple issues. The establishment of the Board has already served this good purpose of renewing contacts, the number of which will hopefully grow and deepen in the future. Creatively building new spatiotemporal contacts among those sharing an interest in the mission of the journal is one of the important practical goals of *Human Architecture*.

Substantively, the journal aims to publish works in what may be called *liberating (or critical) autobiographical research and practice* genre, inspired by C. Wright Mills's "sociological imagination"—seeking to explore (and perhaps help transform) the interplay between private troubles and public issues through critical personal self-explorations in an increasingly global and world-historical contexts. As may be noted, the "sociology of self-knowledge" subtitling this journal seeks to extend the sociological imagination on both ends of the dialectic, emphasizing on one hand the need for personal self-reflexivity (in contrast to the study only of *others'* personal troubles), and, on the other hand, the increasingly global and world-historical scopes of the "public" landscape which constitutes, and is constituted by, our everyday personal lives. Substantively, "human architecture" is meant to also convey the creative spatiotemporal work involved in understanding and transforming the dialectics of micro/macro social forces shaping our everyday lives.

I understand that such a lofty goal as restated above is not realized overnight in each essay published, or in each issue of the journal as a whole. This may give an added meaning to the term "journal" as it aims to chronicle ongoing personal journeys of self discovery and change, welcoming papers that demonstrate commitments along that path even though each piece may constitute only a small (but important) step in that direction. I feel the student papers published in the four (including the present) issues of the journal provide good examples of works done in this genre. Borrowing from the words of the Persian poet Hafez who was humbly speaking of the scale of his own travels compared to the mystical journeys of his spiritual mentor Attar in the *Conference of the Birds*, we know it will take the visiting of all the seven cities of love to make the final journey, but first we can only hope to begin with making the first turn of the first alley. The journey of a thousand miles begins with a first step—says a similar Chinese proverb.

The "sociological imagination," or its sister concept, "the sociology of self-knowledge," does not have to—nor should it—be interpreted as a property of sociology. Aside from sociology itself as a "discipline" being an interdisciplinary mode of social inquiry, I strongly believe, and I think the academia-eschewing C. Wright Mills also believed, that such an imagination can best be nourished in a cross-disciplinary framework that cuts across the sciences (both natural and social) and the humanities. If anything, I think the other social sciences and the humanities can only help balance the dialecticity of the imagination in terms of emphases on not only how society shapes personal selves, but also how personal selves shape inner and broader social realities. For this reason, I certainly hope that the joining of members of the Editorial Advisory Board to this forum, coming from diverse disciplinary backgrounds and affiliations, will contribute to enriching the imaginations pursued and chronicled through this journal with an ever broadening and deepening interdisciplinary spirit.

The Editorial Advisory Board members and readers will hopefully find in this journal a useful forum to direct their own or others' papers which more or less echo the mission of the journal. The journal articles are currently used as required or recommended readings in several courses taught at UMass Boston, acquainting students' works with one another while providing some excellent examples of how various theoretical perspectives can be used in critical and applied autobiographical research. In fact, references made across student essays and voices previously published in this journal are apparent in the essays of this volume. The journal provides a wonderful opportunity for the meeting of various undergraduate, graduate, faculty, and hopefully off-campus activist voices committed to liberating social theory and praxis. The journal, which is committed to at least one issue per academic year, is meant to serve primarily the use-value of a communication medium that brings people of same interests together to share and enrich one another's learning, teaching, research, and practical endeavors.

In short, this journal:
- provides a publishing channel for chronicling critical and scholarly growth in self-knowledge in increasingly global and world-historical frameworks;
- is a cross-rank, cross-disciplinary, and cross-campus reading resource which may be used as required/recommended text available through library, e/reserve/Prometheus, and bookstore;
- as a publishing option in instructional pedagogy, encourages students' communication and writing proficiency as potential authors;
- empowers students as published authors, enriching their professional portfolios in further pursuit of their academic, career, and other pursuits;
- builds networks and encourages communications within and across academic ranks, disciplines, and campuses—locally and globally;
- builds networks and communications across on/off-campus learning, teaching, research, and activism—locally and globally.

Human Architecture: Journal of the Sociology of Self-Knowledge has been framed since its beginnings as a utopistic publishing outlet of an imagined research center that seeks to establish a critical dialogue across the world-historical utopian, mystical, and academic discourses on the good society and whether and how it can be achieved despite all past failures. For those familiar with my work, and the issues raised in my perspective of the journal and the research agenda of its imagined research center, it should suffice to point out here briefly that the dialogue is meant to be one concerned with critical and liberating theory and practice beyond all ideological frameworks impeding creative efforts made in the past towards better selves and worlds. The use of Omar Khayyam as a motif for the imagined research project and for the journal—given the critical stance Khayyam seemed to have had taken with respect to all philosophical, religious, and scientific knowledges and circles of his time while still entertaining a deep thirst for the true, the good, and the beautiful—is meant to convey a similar attitude adopted by this journal to all knowledges of past and present with regards to whether and how human liberation may be sought.

The liberation itself, and the necessity of endeavors along its path, however, seems to me to be the one and only agenda we can claim as what gives meaning and a mission to this journal. I sincerely hope that the Liberal Arts missions of various campuses represented by the submissions and Advisory Board members of this and future journals will only help reinforce and enrich the spatiotemporal—self and global, here-and-now and world-historical—liberal arts mission of *Human Architecture* as well.

Behrooz Tamdgidi
UMass Boston

The Complexity of Naive Acceptance of Socially Manipulated Beliefs

Ayan Ahmed

UMass Boston

Every society has traditions and routines that define its realities. Its members hold these **values** with high esteem and pass them down to the following generation. The recipients, in turn, become hesitant to embrace major changes to those norms that they consider defining the very essence of who they are. Each generation therefore derives its principals and beliefs from the one that preceded it. It follows, then, that the influences the children in these societies obtain are social in nature.

I moved to the United States several years ago laden with my own share of **beliefs** and traditions that were handed to me by my Somalian society. Needless to say I was at complete odds with the American culture, tradition, and beliefs. **Ethnocentricity** ran wild both in me and the Americans I interacted with. They too were responding to the influential social **norms** and realities that were constructed to fit their lifestyles. The western **social structure** was at work in me, diluting the non-western social structure that had until then shaped my identity. These **conflicting** realities created a need in me to search for who I was becoming, or who I initially was before being transformed into this stranger who wasn't sure of what was happening to her. Confusion set in after an initial period of confidence achieved by ridiculing the strange **culture** that I got exposed to.

A notable crisis in me occurred when I started to question the social manipulation of religious teachings or principals that were previously passed down as a matter of fact. The more questions my mind created, the more I believed I was damned and doomed. Never had thoughts of that nature occurred to me back when I happily lived among my society. I even considered leaving the United States at one time and going back to my familiar routine and beliefs. All that which the scholars decreed were firmly curved out of stone.

Plato's metaphor of the three men in the cave comes to mind to illustrate how closed-minded I was. The metaphor is about three people who were tied to their seats in a cave. There was a light source (fire) behind them such that shadows of what was paraded in front of the fire and behind them reflected on the front wall they were facing. These people had never left the cave since they were born and could not even turn around to see the fire. One of them was finally grabbed and dragged out of the cave while he was kicking and screaming. Finally when he was brought out of the cave and into the real world, he was completely torn apart. His realities were of shadows and images, but came to discover the moon, the sun, and the stars, rivers and birds of different feathers, and lush gardens of flowers and fruits. His reality completely changed and when time came to be put back in to the cave, he resisted and was dragged back while kicking and screaming. Finally when he was tied to his seat, the others questioned him about the shadows that were being reflected on the wall. Since in this cave community, one received more status by how well one interpreted the shadows, the others were terrified that they too might one day be dragged out and come back in an idiotic state like

---

Notice: Copyright of *Human Architecture: Journal of the Sociology of Self-Knowledge* is the property of Ahead Publishing House (imprint: Okcir Press) and its content may not be copied or emailed to multiple sites or posted to a listserv without the copyright holder's express written permission. However, users may print, download, or email articles for individual use.

their friend. Little did they know that the friend was no longer interested in the shadows:

> Plato can hardly have meant that the ordinary man can not distinguish between shadows and real things. But he does seem to be saying, with a touch of caricature (we must not take him too solemnly), that the ordinary man is often very uncritical in his beliefs, which are little more than a "careless" acceptance of appearance. (Lee 1978:256)

As a Muslim, and coming from a country that is 100% Muslims, I noticed that Christians too had as much a conviction in their faith as I did in mine. They went to church, like I went to the Mosque. They prayed to their God with as much humility as I did. They strongly believed that Christianity was the only true religion as much as I believed that Islam was. They would try to save me from eternal hell fire by preaching to me, as much as I did try to save them.

Apparently the longer I stayed and studied in the U.S. the more I came to realize that the same conviction is held not only by Muslims and Christians, but by any other faith as well, across the world. *"How different was I from the rest?" "Did the scholars and the Imams not teach me that Islam was the only acceptable religion?—that if one died before accepting Islam as one's religion, then one goes to hell?" "So what if the others believed so about their faiths too?"* This reminded me of the lady at work who said that Jesus was God and that if I died before accepting Jesus Christ as my savior then I will go hell. *"God! How could she believe that? Can't she see she is wrong?" "How much of the Bible does she personally know other than what was preached to her?" "And how much do I know about the Quran?"* By now, I had formed a **habit** of having a part of me acting as the devil's advocate while the other threatened the first and warned it of the dire consequences that will face this soul by corrupting it with blasphemous thoughts.

Underlying all this was my newfound knowledge of sociology, especially **Symbolic Interactionism,** which emphasized the interactions humans have with each other and how we don't just respond to one another's actions, but rather define or interpret these actions in terms of the meanings they hold for the actors involved. The responses we make are not directly related to the actions of one another but instead are based on the meaning which we attach to such actions. Thus, human interaction is mediated by the use of symbols, interpretations, or simply by determining the meaning of one another's actions. For instance, culture and religion in my case set the conditions for my actions, but culture and religion do not determine my actions. I did not or society does not act toward these social systems but rather we act toward situations. According to George Herbert **Mead**, as described by Wallace and Wolf (1999),

> ... individuals act on their own environment, and in doing so they create the objects that people it. He distinguishes between "things," or stimuli that exist prior to and independent of the individuals, and the "objects," which exist only in relation to acts. "Things" are converted to "objects" through the acts of individuals. (198)

Despite this, my righteous **self** would not barge from its deeply held norms and beliefs. This newly found knowledge of sociology provided me with an experience which is similar to what Peter **Berger** would refer to as **Secondary socialization**—i.e., "any subsequent process that inducts an already socialized individual into new sectors of the objective world of his society" (Wallace and Wolf 1999:281).

This was a period of hardship for me. I

was looking hard at myself and what I was becoming. The same question kept on popping in my head: *"How was I different from the millions of the faithful of different religions?"* In short, everything that could be said about my feeling toward my religion was true with theirs. It even occurred to me that if I were born in the United States to Christian parents, then I would have been a Christian by faith. The devil's advocate self in me kept on shouting, *"It follows from this logic then that I am a Muslim because I was born to a Muslim family and society."*

Although I was having these thoughts, never did I think of becoming a Christian or a Jew or a Hindu or anything. I was simply being torn apart by the similarities all people of faith exhibited, and the irony with which each faith believed they were the true and undisputed legitimate entity. Like Neo in the movie *The Matrix*, I wanted to know how deep the rabbit hole went. I was questioning what **reality** was. The need for me to know was so overwhelming that I became a little braver and realized that searching for the truth or reality itself was a noble cause to pursue.

True, in Islam there is a saying that "All new born babies are born with the inclination of knowing who their true God is, and it is only their parents that either make them Christians or Jews" or Hindu or any other faith for that matter. But this did not negate the fact that all I knew about Islam was based on **derivative beliefs**. I had never set on a course to verify beyond doubt that what I was taught was in true accordance with actual Islam as was revealed to the prophet Muhammad (peace be upon him). In further evaluation of my situation I could not help but come to the same conclusion that I was not well educated about my faith that is Islam.

I was simply (like many people today) programmed to follow a set of rules that were not open to discussion. Unlike others, I did not have any flexibility. In her essay "Religion in an Individualistic Society"(2003) Jillian Sloan acknowledged the flexibility of her beliefs and their societal construct:

> Lutherans are not very strict or formal in their practice. In my experience I have had every opportunity to develop my own beliefs, both by my Church and my mother. (73)

I admire the way people profess what they believe in. For instance, the movie *Billy Elliot* illustrates how Billy goes against what the class and gender norms were in his community by following his heart and becoming a ballet dancer as opposed to a boxer, which is the "masculine" thing to do, as his father shouted "lads do boxing, football, and wrestling—not *ballet*." Not only does Billy remain true to himself and to his mother's wish but he also breaks the **stereotypes** that society tries to impose on him.

The Iranian Muslim scholar and philosopher Imam Ghazali (1058-1111), in his article *"From That Which Delivers From Error"* expresses his understanding of religion relative to the different ideological norms prevalent at the time, particularly the view of philosophy in relation to Islamic thoughts. He writes:

> I therefore said within myself: 'To begin with, what I am looking for is knowledge of what things really are, so I must undoubtedly try to find what knowledge really is.' Thus, I know that ten is more than three. Let us suppose that someone says to me: 'No, three is more than ten, and in proof of that I shall change this rod into a serpent'; and let us suppose that he actually changes the rod into a serpent and that I witness him doing so. No doubts about what I know are raised in me because of this. The only result is that I wonder precise-

ly how he is able to produce this change. Of doubt about my knowledge there is no trace. (McNeil 1973:209-210)

Although I have not reached a conclusion about what the "knowledge" of religion really is (as Ghazali says), I could not talk about this inner conflict and evaluation for a long time for the erroneous fear that my fellow Muslims would shun me and label me names. These conflicts that I had are somewhat similar to what M. Goltry writes about in her essay "Theoretical Reflections on Peer Judgements" (2003). According to Goltry the need for social approval engenders group conformity. In my case I was conditioned by the will of those around me and was eager to get along with them and not create a conflict. I did not want to lose my **status** within the community or as Emile **Durkheim** and later **Functionalists** would have had it, I did not want to break off from our commonly held **value system**.

However, and right after September 11, 2001, I became extremely scrutinized by weary eyes of the masses of which some thought Islam to be evil. I was readily identifiable because of my head coverings. I once traveled to Atlanta, Georgia, for a wedding and I was isolated from the others to be given a thorough exam to make sure I was not hiding anything in my hair that would jeopardize the safety of the passengers.

I became increasingly self-aware and felt **alienated** at those times and I found myself even leaning to the view that these ethnic or religious profilers were right. Again, here I was trying to fit in and accept the judgement passed down by the masses. I have realized that in the Christian world, particularly in the U.S., little is known about Islam. Most Americans I have met and discussed religion with didn't know much about Islam. My *hijaab* (head covering) would often bewilder them, and they would wonder why I had it on. The *hijaab* I wear has in recent years stood out like a sore thumb particularly since in the media Islam has become synonymous with terrorism.

Society has a funny way of making individuals **conform** to certain norms and cultural beliefs. Richard E. Rubenstein in his book, *Aristotle's Children. How Christians, Muslims, and Jews Rediscovered Ancient Wisdom and Illuminated The Dark Ages,* talks about modernity and cultural bias. He writes:

> We continue to tell the story of modernism as if it began with the 16th century Renaissance, and with scientists like Copernicus, Galileo, and Isaac Newton. Why? One reason involves the myth of cultural authenticity: the notion, common to many cultures, that a particular civilization developed on its own from original sources rather than being borrowed from or imposed by outsiders. 'Our' culture is authentically native, the partisans of every nation insist, while 'theirs' is merely derivative or imitative. (Rubenstein 2003:6)

In the movie *Twelve Angry Men* the character played by Henry Fonda was constantly encouraging others to put themselves in the convict's shoes. That is how we should conduct ourselves in today's world. I could easily see why some of my friends in the U.S. always think of my *hijaab* as a form of **oppression** for women. But why is it that they can't see that Pakistan (a Muslim country) had a woman president who still wore a *hijaab*—or Khaleda Zia who was the Prime Minister of Bangladesh, or Megawati Sukarnoputri President of Indonesia which has the largest Muslim population in the world? How could that be a form of oppression? And when was the last time United States had a woman president, anyway? I would encourage people to practice a **phenomenological** attitude towards their everyday life—that is, not to take learned notions and traditions for granted but to question them and view societies and cultures from the point of view of their actors and how they have been socially and historically constructed. I understand how hard that might be, for I personally tried it and encountered tremendous objections and restrictions that were unsaid but yet present in the form of societal disapproval.

Although it took me several years to analyze the predicament I was in—for I could not ask anyone for fear that they would spread a rumor that I was questioning my faith—I can now speak out without any fear and with confidence that unless one can personally know oneself one can not understand how what they feel—as far as personal conflict is concerned—is not just an experience limited to oneself but is a universal experience that crouches up on each individual within all societies worldwide, and across all cultures and faiths.

Now, after gaining some insight into who I am, I am capable of critically setting aside others desire to intimidate me in the name of a **communal tradition.** In fact, I have noticed that the more you take a firm stand on an issue that is collectively ruled upon, the more you will be shunned initially and respected later. This contradiction, I believe, stems from the fact that others are initially scared to be rejected and they prefer not to make their beliefs public and hence join the common voice of the society. Later when they become capable of analyzing the situation sincerely, they respect you for making a choice they would have probably made but were too scared to do so. In his essay "Defying the Sweatshop, Sociologically Speaking" (2003), Steve Sacco clearly demonstrated how through what he called "Commercial Disobedience," he intended to make a difference by boycotting companies that use sweatshop labor. I on the other hand intend to use "Intellectual Disobedience," by refusing to submit to these derived beliefs and instead opt to do a serious learning of what I believe in and accept no second hand information or interpretations. I understand that for this end, I have a long way to go.

I am concerned that the blind following of a few scholars (few relative to the masses) that dictate the entirety of what any religion is all about will have a major social impact on communities throughout the world. Killings in the name of religion were and are still rampant. "My God is better than yours" is said through many different religious actions. I believe **fanaticism** in any religion is caused by the fact that people are extremely eager to rely on others' explanations and interpretations of the very religion they profess to be part of but do little to study and understand it. Since when have humans been so flawless that the accuracy of their interpretations is to be considered divine?

The beliefs that we each have are a product of the societies we lived in. That is why we have different realities more so in this global society than ever. For instance if I was to borrow Emile **Durkheim's** premise—that the needs and self interests of humans are shaped by **social facts** external to the individual, among which he included the **collective conscience**, i.e., the shared moral norms and values in a society—one will see that the **global society** we live in is far from the harmonious picture of **"organic solidarity"** that Durkheim promised for the modern life. The movie *The Big One*, directed by Michael Moore, clearly illustrates the nature of capitalism in this so-called modern society where corporations like Nike are getting richer and richer at the expense of their foreign and underpaid workers thereby reproducing the antagonistic **working** and **bourgeoisie** classes **Karl Marx** wrote about, or the oppressor and the oppressed classes as **Paulo Freire** would put it. The PBS documentary *Affluenza* clearly establishes how this idea of "collective conscience" is a far cry from what we have been reduced to as a society where materialism and consumerism is becoming a poor substitute for common social values while (what **Simmel** would call) **blasé attitudes** take root in deep recesses of our minds towards poverty and neglect of the have-nots.

Ironically we each believe that our set of realities are firmly grounded on the absolute truths that exist universally. Little do we understand that most of us are operating on purely derivative belief that originated from our parents and society at large. Only those of us who set their biased selves aside and try to investigate the social reality will arrive at an independent understanding free of blind dilution from societal influences and manipulations.

For instance, if one were to pick those beliefs that were imprinted on their psyche as infallible truths, exposed them to logical and factual knowledge, and realized that those principles or beliefs did not hold water, then one should become dissatisfied with explanations based solely on alleged declarations by a saint or a religious authority. If such explanations go against the grain of one's knowledge and understanding, one should easily, without guilt, refute such notions.

In essence—using Christianity and then Islam as examples—both Catholicism and Protestantism can not be right. Only one of them must be right with regards to the teachings of the Bible. Similarly, only one of either Shia or Sunni sects must be true with regards to the teachings of the Quran. Similar considerations will have to be made across the mentioned religions as well, i.e., between the holy Bible and the holy Quran. Some might claim that it is not that one of them has a firmer handle on the truth than the other but both are telling different aspects of the truth. But we all know that is not the belief of those who profess these faiths. For them, the belief that each professes is the only truth.

Another useful way of looking at the issue at hand is by analyzing the complexity of how the subconscious mind works, especially with regards to the hypnotic effect of religious beliefs. Regarding the subconscious mind, my inquiry has deepened to include far-reaching effects that religion plays in our minds. More so, religion (which exist in multiple and different forms) has in some ways caused, consciously and subconsciously, rifts both among diverse religious groups *and* those who simply view religion as spiritual nonsense.

When analyzing the conscious disparity between individuals in matters relating to religion as a whole or in part, it is inevitable that one will see two distinct groups—those that find something inherently wrong with religious devotion (in whichever form it may be practiced, i.e., Christianity, Islam, Hinduism, etc.), and those who have been conditioned by religious hypnotism to such a degree that in some cases medication are shunned in favor of the healing power of prayers. A good example here is (and to just pick one among the numerous examples available from each faith) the Jehovah Witnesses who refuse blood transfusion even when it means a matter of life or death. Even then it is a fallacy to consider that religious devotion is senseless spirituality. An equal erroneous belief would be when one would see it wrong to substitute medication for the healing power of prayer or any other form of unconscionable and unduly oppressive custom that limits the freedom of one being a fully critical and reflective being that preserves life.

The wrestler later turned governor of Minnesota, Ventura, once said that religion is for people with weak minds. I don't think he is alone (at least in the U.S.) in coming to this conclusion. Religion is seen as something that thoughtful individuals would be better off staying away from. Stephen L. Carter, in his book *The Culture of Disbelief* refers to a book written by two therapists who argued that anyone who puts aside the needs of his or her family in order to serve his or her religion was suffering from an illness the authors called "toxic faith." Carter continues to wonder how those therapists would have judged the toxicity levels of faith in say people like Moses, Jesus, or Mohammed. Carter seems to be saying this in a tongue-in-cheek fashion alluding to the reader that these therapists are far from making any logical statements. I disagree with his statement and I am using this example to simply illustrate the opposite "conscious" positions in the spectrum these two different groups of people hold as I previously stated. Carter's comparison lies in gauging the levels of faith between say an unknown regular person trying to be faithful in extreme ways and faith levels of prophets such as Moses or Jesus or Mohammed, (peace be upon them). But the actual issue at hand is whether putting aside the needs of one's family in order to serve one's religion is right or wrong. In as far as Mohammed's teachings are concerned, it is wrong to put aside the needs of one's family and pursue serving one's religion only. (Proving this point is not the focus of my paper and I am using this example just to show the rhetoric used to discredit ones opponents).

In chapter two of his book *The Culture of Disbelief* Carter accurately posits that a good way to "end a conversation or start an argument" among a group of "well educated professionals" is to say that your religious belief and the will of "God" forbids you to see issues like pornography or abortion as been right! He is of the view that in the unlikely event that anyone hangs around you, if there are any, then you will be accused of "imposing your religious beliefs on others." Whether "toxic faith" is present or not, or whether you will be accused of imposing "religious belief on others," we see the gap in thought between those who believe in religion and those who at least see it as a fad. The above paragraphs are a summary of the extreme and opposite positions held by those who, at least consciously, are either for or against religion—however strange their words or actions might be.

Complicating the issue of the differences in positions held at the conscious level, however, is the significance of seeing how people on both sides of the argument are in many ways acting on **subconscious** impulses. Not delving any further, look even at me writing this essay as the best example. I started this inquiry by questioning what I call "socially manipulated beliefs" and now I can not help but admit that I and most of us are also subconsciously influenced by social forces. A constructive criticism I received while writing this paper read, "Notice how even in the midst of your argument you used religious symbols and phrases, interaction, and rituals that reinforce one or another belief whether or not you question "manipulation" at the conscious level."

Sociologists like Emile **Durkheim** have gone to the extent of suggesting that society is an entity of its own. Society, in his view, is a phenomenon that exists independently of individuals who conform to its needs. Only when one resists the **social facts** or forces does one become aware of their presence, and the constraints they impose in the course of socialization:

> This unremitting pressure to which the child is subjected [is] the very pressure of the social milieu which tends to fashion him in its own image, and of which parents and teachers are merely the representatives and intermediaries. (Farganis 1999:61)

Since social pressures have become second nature to us (allegedly, as Durkheim suggests) then one sees the complexity of not only submitting to (let alone resisting) social manipulation, but recognizing the "manipulation" in the first place. In his *The Elementary Forms of Religious Life* Durkheim goes to the extent of suggesting that "Society" and "God" are one and the same thing. That 'God' is a social construct and that society, since it has its own needs, permeates the human mind and controls it to responds to its liking:

> Since it [society] has a nature which is peculiar to itself and different from our individual nature, it pursues ends which are likewise special to it, but as it cannot attain them except through our intermediacy, it imperiously demands our aid. (Farganis 1999: 74)

Tamdgidi, in his paper "Freire Meets Gurdjieff and Rumi" (2004) interprets **Freire's** view of world history as a process of humanization in which "unfinished humanity" seeks becoming "fully human." For Freire here, "fully human" means becoming a being of praxis, as Tamdgidi explains—that is to say "an integrated being of critical reflection and practical action." This in essence (the interplay of critical reflection and practical action) is what I am seeking. But as I found out, the density of ideas involved in analyzing the **oppressed self** and how this self is catapulted into becoming the **oppressor self**, not to mention the collective societal requirement to educate one another on eliminating oppression, is far reaching and complex. The context in which oppression was used in Freire's a writings according to Tamdgidi's comparative study, is one in which oppression is seen as a form of manipulation resulting from social forces that mold or shape one's thoughts and actions according to social requirements and not in accordance with what an individual sees as right.

Some, a majority, are prevented from developing their critical-reflective powers and thereby reduced to beings of isolated and alienated unreflective and mechanical action, anesthetized into living as things and objects serving to perpetuate and reproduce their oppressive social structures. ... dehumanized and alienated "beings for another", and not "beings for themselves ... (Tamdgidi 2004:6)

The point here is that when we as individuals accept and not question beliefs that were simply taught to us by scholars, teachers, ministers, priests, or imams, then we are in essence "beings for another." Therefore, in order for one to become fully critical and reflective one has to engage in educating oneself to eradicate or break the shackles of oppression.

G. I. **Gurdjieff's** ideas, as discussed by Tamdgidi in the same paper, were eye openers in my analysis of 'social manipulation.' Gurdjieff's idea of the nature of oppression is focused internally on the individual. This was apparent in his analogy of the carriage, the horse and the driver all constituting the individual, i.e. the three centers (emotional, physical and intellectual) which need to communicate with each other so as to make possible an integrated self. Gurdjieff argues that if the centers are alienated from each other, we don't learn the proper way of using our intellect and this separation influences us to conform to oppressive social forces. It is this fragmentation of the centers and selves that prevents us from being fully human.

What necessitates the urge to believe in any faith is the fear of damnation, be it in this world or the hereafter. Given that this is an issue that really matters to most people of faith, I have tried in this paper to take steps in better knowing myself and acquiring a base on which I can conduct my life not based on what society dictates but in accordance with what I personally prove to be true—free of bias, superstitious beliefs, or erroneous claims that have been passed down from our forefathers.

I will not be perfect, or perhaps there are no absolute truths or realities that humans can touch or experience. However, this should not prevent me from at least making an effort to investigate, learn, and search for that which is right in accordance to my achieved intellect. This will in turn tell others in society that I am an independent person making efforts to free myself of manipulation or oppression by others and, through previous social conditioning, by myself. In other words, each of us require a a declaration of independence in words and deeds, which alone can set the conditions for changing the inherited social mold.

Few among us indulge in independent verification of their derived beliefs.

REFERENCES

Farganis, J. (2000). *Readings in Social Theory: The Classic Tradition to Post-Modernism.* Third edition. McGraw Hill College Divison.

Goltry, M. (2003). "Theoretical Reflections on Peer Judgements". *Human Architecture: Journal of the Sociology of Self -Knowledge.* Volume 2, Number 1 Spring.

Lee, Desmond. (1978). *Plato The Republic.* Second Edition. Penguins Books.

McNeil, H. William. (1973). *The Islamic World.* Oxford University Press, Inc.

Rubenstein, E. Richard. (2003). *Aristotle's Children: How Christians, Muslims, and Jews Rediscovered Ancient Wisdom And Illuminated The Dark Ages.* Harcourt Books.

Sacco, Steve (2002). "Defying the Sweatshop: Sociologically Speaking", *Human Architecture: Journal of the Sociology of Self -Knowledge.* Volume I, Number 2, Fall.

Sloan, Jillian E. (2003). "Religion in an Individualistic Society". *Human Architecture: Journal of the Sociology of Self- Knowledge.* Volume 2, Number 1, Spring.

Stephen, Carter. (1994). *The Culture of Disbelief: How American Law and Politics Trivializes Religious Devotion.* Anchor Books.

Tamdgidi, Mohammad H. (2004). *Freire Meets Gurdjieff and Rumi: Towards the Pedagogy of the Oppressed and Oppressing Selves.* Presented to Social Theory Forum, 2004, Umass Boston.

Wallace, R and Wolf, A. (1999). *Contemporary Sociological Theory: Expanding the Classical Tradition.* Fifth Edition. New Jersey: Prentice hall.

Films:

"Affluenza". (1997). Bullfrog Films

"Billy Elliot". (2000). Universal Pictures.

"The Big One". (1999). Miramax Home Entertainment.

"The Matrix". (1999). Warner Brothers.

"Twelve Angry Men". (1957). MGM.

Alice in the Gendered Sports-Fan Wonderland: A Sociological Inquiry

Elizabeth J. Schumacher

UMass Boston

C. Wright Mills encouraged people to develop a **sociological imagination** in order to "place themselves in social context and identify how public issues affect them at the personal level, arguing that people need to know the source of their difficulties in order to make sense of their lives" (Disch 2). I believe that gender is often the context in which such difficulties arise. Disch goes on to stress the importance of empowerment through the challenging of the patriarchal system. She states that, "without seeing the complexity of human experience and the complexity of human oppression, we cannot begin to address the real needs of human beings caught in systematically oppressive social structures" (Disch 14).

Though the feminist movement has vastly improved the situation of women, many challenges and obstacles still endure. Over the past century, substantial progress has been made in the opportunities afforded to women in voting rights, education, and job possibilities, but many social issues still need to be improved. In this paper I will discuss the obstacles women continue to face in their efforts to be seen as equals in the sports world as fans.

In her paper, "Theoretical Reflections on Peer Judgments" (2003), M. Goltry speaks of how society plays a crucial role in how we view ourselves. She states, "It is through our interactions with others that we form opinions of ourselves" (Goltry 19). In my opinion, society plays a crucial role not only in how we view ourselves but also in how we behave, as well as how we seek to influence how others view us as well. Some things just aren't fully under our control, gender being one of these. I took a class on the Sociology of Gender, and found the readings on embodiment to be the most interesting part of the class. In particular, "Beauty is the Beast: Psychological Effects of the Pursuit of the Perfect Female Body" (1995), by Elayne A. Saltzberg and Joan C. Chrisler, went into great details concerning the differences between men and women and how they are viewed by society in relation to their appearance. The reading begins by quoting Ambrose Bierce (1958), "To men a man is but a mind. Who cares what face he carries or what he wears? But woman's body is the woman" (Saltzberg & Chrisler 167). Though there have been great steps forward for women since this time, this idea can still be felt in the present day. The authors go on to point out that men are considered "handsome," while women are "beautiful." The term handsome being derived from the word hand and referring to qualities of strength, action, and achievement, while beauty simply refers to decoration. "Men are instrumental; women are ornamental" (Saltzberg & Chrisler 167).

This idea, I believe, translates into how we are expected to act as sports fans: men should be cheering loud and active, while women are expected to just "sit and be pretty." This has been especially apparent to me this year, as the Red Sox and Patriots both had such amazing seasons. It is now, however, during March Madness, that I realize it has bothered me year after year. I attended the University of Maryland for four years, including the 2001 season in which the Terrapins went to the Final Four for the first time in school history and the 2002 season in which they won their first National Championship. In my case, being a Maryland sports fan is an important part of my **identity.**

A long-time misconception is that only men care about such sports as football, baseball, and basketball. For example, when a television show portrays the Super Bowl, it usually has something to do with men watching the game and their wives receive the **stigma** of being upset with their husbands regarding their watching the game. It seems that television still follows the **traditional gender roles** most of the time when it comes to sports. However, in the real world, women have become much more interested in "traditionally male" sports over the past few decades. The film *Twelve Angry Men* seems to be illustrative of this perspective. While the film concerned a jury rather than a sporting event, I find it interesting that back in the 1950s, just as sporting events are still considered today to be male-dominated places, men were portrayed to be as best suited for jury positions. It seems as though the movie was making a statement that some places, such as a jury room, were meant only for men—just as I believe many men feel today that sporting events are not appropriate places for women, at least not for more than ornamentation.

I also believe that a woman's **anticipatory socialization** in sports differs greatly from the consequences that she actually encounters once she makes the "positive orientation to the values of a group other than one's own" (Wallace and Wolf, 50). I believe that most women think that they will receive **intrinsic rewards** for their "love of the game." They believe that they will earn the respect of men as they will be impressed with their knowledge and passion; but many times this is not the case. While the film *Affluenza* portrays Americans as striving for increase in **status** through the purchase of symbolic material goods that they neither need nor always even want, I believe some men think that the majority of women only "pretend" to like sports in an attempt to achieve a higher status in the eyes of men.

I consider the world of sports and sports fans to be a good example of the **patriarchalism** in our society, which also relates to Dorothy Smith's **Feminist Standpoint Theory.** The sports world demonstrates women's experience with a "**line of fault** between what they know and experience in their everyday/everynight lives and what is official knowledge as expressed in the symbols, images, vocabularies, and concepts of the patriarchal culture" (Wallace and Wolf, 286). As a result, female fans must accept a **bifurcated** consciousness. They must show their interest in the game, but do so in such a manner as to not upset the traditional female gender roles they are expected to follow.

I also consider the belief that women should not be vocal or aggressive fans relates to Max Weber's concept of *traditional authority*—authority enjoyed because it has been handed down from the past; "patriarchalism is by far the most important type of domination the legitimacy of which rests upon tradition. Patriarchalism means the authority of the father, the husband, the senior of the house" (Wallace and Wolf, 73). I think the idea that women should simply sit and be silent is an utter and deplorable form of domination and deprecation.

I believe that traditional authority and patriarchalism also relate to the concept of **symbolic interaction**, as it is our appearance, many times, that defines how others will treat us and how they believe we should behave. I have dealt with this issue many times during Maryland basketball games. The men in the room yell loud, jump around, and high-five each other after every good play, but if I, or another female, acted in any of these ways, the men would look at us like we had two heads. I believe that they just didn't expect us, as women, to be physically into the game.

I also consider this to be an example of the **objectification** of women. Most men expect women to be quiet and dainty, not loud and rambunctious fans like themselves. They enjoy watching the female cheerleaders with the short skirts and bare midriffs, but comment whenever a woman is dressed, cheering, and acting like a "man." I also believe that this objectification can lead to the **internalization** by women of this "objectivated social reality," thus legitimizing it. George Herbert Mead's concept of the **generalized other**, in which "individuals internalize the norms and values generated by the dominant institutions," also explains this phenomenon (Wallace and Wolf, 202). Samara Cohen describes this idea by stating, "Our personalities are shaped by interactions we have with people as individuals, and as groups in society (2003:9)." These concepts have to do with the **social construction of reality** that is displayed throughout the film *The Matrix*. A person comes to accept as true what society tells them is true. Though a woman may want to cheer and behave in the same manner as her male fan counterparts, she will accept as true the idea that she should not behave in this manner since women must remain "feminine" at all times, and this behavior is simply unacceptable.

Rational choice theory states that the values that women hold help explain the rationality of their behavior. I believe this to be very true. While I am a true Maryland fan and hold great passion for my team, I also value my womanhood greatly. I have come to prefer watching games on television by myself, or with other female Maryland fans, as an attempt to keep up my appearance as a "lady" to as many people as possible. While, "the [Rational Choice] theory does not ... explain how women come to hold these values in the first place (Wallace and Wolf, 420)," I believe that this particular value is something that is internalized in us from the time we are born.

Charles Cooley's concept of the **looking-glass self** can be observed at work in the behavior of female fans such as myself. I believe that it is very true that we judge ourselves based on our perceptions of others' opinions of us. I also believe that we let this affect our behavior in certain situations. With regards to this idea, I also believe that women cannot see past their femaleness when they consider themselves as fans. Personally, I find it easier to understand W.E.B. DuBois's race-related concept of **double-consciousness** when I apply it to issues of gender in sports. I do not see myself simply as a fan, but first as a female and then as a fan. Personally, I am aware of my behavior during a basketball game, and, at times, make an effort to keep my behavior in check, mindful of how I believe others think I should be acting. I do not think that this affected me as much when I was in Maryland, but it has recently been an issue. My boyfriend made a comment to me, and then later to others, about how I am so loud when I watch Maryland basketball games. Since then, I have noticed this, and made attempts to change this behavior during any sports game that I watch. I believe this change in behavior may be due, in part, to *latent function*, a consequence neither recognized nor intended, of my boyfriend and others' comments to me regarding how I should behave as a women while expressing my excitement during Maryland games.

This idea of women changing their behavior in order to guide and control the impressions others form of them is akin to **impression management.** Erving Goffman describes the idea of **front-stage,** or personal front, and how the standards are stricter for women than they are for men. He uses the example of clothing and appearance, but I believe the things that come into play in the case of watching a sporting event are posture, speech patterns, facial expressions, and body gestures. There are certain traditional **norms** for women regarding these issues, and when a woman does not follow these norms, she is criticized. Personally, I know that when I watch a Maryland basketball game, I am not exercising good posture—I may swear, I may make strange faces, and I may make body gestures such as jumping up and down that are not typical, or acceptable, for women.

I believe that men cannot see beyond a woman's *ascribed status* when it comes to sports. Even if a woman has proven, through her past performance in March Madness bracket pools for example, most men still have a hard time accepting their *achieved status*. My college roommate and I have proven time and again that we know what we are talking about with respect to college basketball, but our male friends still refuse to take us seriously. When they put together Fantasy Football Leagues, they still would not let us join, saying that women know nothing about football. According to Parsons modern societies are supposed to adjudicate others based on what they can do or have done, their achievement status, but this is obviously not the case in many situations regarding women and sports (Wallace and Wolf, 32).

Another observation I have made recently is that it seems to be more acceptable for men to react to sports with more *affectivity*, while women are expected to react with more *affective neutrality*. When the Red Sox were competing for the ALCS in October, my boyfriend spent hundreds of dollars to go to two of the home games, though he had gone to only one game all season, on a ticket I gave him for his birthday, and watched none on television. On the other hand, I went to quite a number of games and watched many on television throughout the season. Still, my boyfriend truly believed that he cared more about the Red Sox and that he deserved to be out celebrating their wins simply because he was a man while I should not be as exultant.

However, if the roles were reversed, I, or any other woman, would never be taken seriously and would be seen as a "fair weather fan" or "jumping on the bandwagon." Men, however, use the excuse that they are just too busy with work and other obligations in order to maintain their status as dedicated fans throughout the entire season—and it is accepted.

According to the *Functionalist* perspective, "boys who are aggressive and girls who are nurturing have learned the 'appropriate' gender role behavior: the socialization process worked" (Wallace and Wolf, 420). While I believe that many men consider most female fans to be "fake," I also believe that there are men who themselves are fans simply due to *socialization*. The process of socialization involves societal values being internalized by members of society, making society's values their own. It is a common societal perception that men are sports fans. Therefore, I believe that there are men in the U.S. who, while they don't really care much either way, act as if they are avid fans of the local teams simply to "fit in" with their friends. Also, if one were to follow this view on the other side, they would consider women who were aggressive fans themselves to be guilty of engendering *role conflict*, since they would be clearly deviating from the traditional female norm.

The film *Billy Elliot* depicts this idea of role conflict in the opposite circumstance. While behaviors and actions taken by a female fan are often seen as a threat to her femininity, Billy's desire to dance was viewed as a threat to his masculinity. Throughout the film, Billy's father was reluctant to accept his son's yearning for and love of ballet, and attempted to coerce him into a "masculine" sport. I see this as being equivalent to the male's attempt to exclude women from the "masculine" sports of basketball and football except in the circumstance of decoration, as cheerleaders. I believe men view the role of the fan as a masculine sport in itself, and are only comfortable when females in the vicinity are objectified or disregarded.

Conflict theory is based on the view that people and groups in society are in a constant struggle for power. Conflict theorists emphasize power as the core of social relationships. They view power are scarce, unequally divided, and essentially coercive. They also believe that people develop values and ideas that suit their own interests. I see this idea displayed in the fight for maintaining men as the only "true" sports fans. I believe men view the situation as if women's being fans somehow takes something away from men, as if being a fan is imbued with power, and if women are fans too, men lose some of their power.

I believe that womanhood is one example of a *status group*, as described by Max Weber. According to his definition, status groups are those "whose distinctiveness lies not in their shared economic position but either in their shared mode of life (often founded on a common education) or in the prestige attached to their birth and family" (Wallace and Wolf, 74). In the case of sports, I believe that being labeled as part of the female status group causes the person to lose the right to be taken seriously as a fan.

The film *Erin Brockovich* also depicts the challenges women face. I compare the reactions Erin receives from the other women because of how she is dressed to the reactions of both men and women to a woman who is an "aggressive" fan. People act like there is something wrong with being who you are and behaving (or dressing) the way you choose to behave. They act as if that one choice completely defines who you are and do not recognize it as simply one expression of your personality and preferences.

Elite Theory posits that "only a small number of people in any organization can hold authority and that their occupation of these positions automatically places them at odds with those subjected to it" (Wallace and Wolf, 75). The athletic world does not seem to be exempt from its own elite dynamics. I view the situation as being a similar one in which men believe they hold all of the knowledge and authority on the subject of sports, and therefore women should simply "sit and be pretty" and not offer any opinions or encouragements.

I believe that the concept of **esteem** may play into the disjuncture between male and female fans. According to Thorstein Veblen, people eagerly desire the esteem of others. Also, esteem is essentially a competitive matter as not everyone can enjoy high status. "A large part of people's behavior, Veblen argued, especially styles of consumption and leisure, can be explained by the struggle for high standing in the eyes of one's neighbors" (Wallace and Wolf, 76). While I believe that there are a few women who simply pretend to enjoy sports more than they actually do in an attempt to gain esteem, I believe that many men consider this to be a more frequent occurrence than it actually is. It seems that a lot of times men do not truly believe that women actually know or care about "male" sports, but act like women are only pretending to care in an attempt to gain the esteem of men.

It is as if there is what Emile Durkheim called a *collective conscience*, "the totality of beliefs and sentiments common to average citizens of the same society," (Wallace and Wolf, 21) regarding sports and sports fans in America. The general belief, it seems, is that sports fans are male. Men act as if all other men should follow and be fans of the local football, basketball, baseball, and hockey teams, but seem to be very surprised when women join the conversation regarding any of these sports. In my experience, after this surprise subsides, it seems that men do not really listen to anything I or other women say. They seem to either argue that all of our opinions are wrong, or disregard what we have to say completely if it is obvious that we are right and do know what we are talking about.

In his paper, *Freire Meets Gurdjieff and Rumi: Towards the Pedagogy of the Oppressed and Oppressing Selves*, Tamdgidi uses Paulo Freire to define a being of praxis as, "an incessantly liberating organism in that it is capable and in need of constantly changing both the objective and subjective conditions of its existence in order to survive (Tamdgidi 4)." I believe that female sports fans are example of beings deprived of what they deserve as beings of *praxis*. I view the notion that only men are true fans as an oppressive subjective condition which female fans are continuously striving to change just as women struggled in the past to change economic and social conditions relevant to the feminist movement.

Tamdgidi also speaks of the problem of **subconsciousness**. Citing Gurdjieff, he states that "one may be critically awakened, say to an oppressive situation within or without, but continue, given the force of subconsciously conditioned habits, to mechanically act as if such critical awareness never even existed" (Tamdgidi 12) I can relate this idea to my own experience, in particular when I am reminded of how my boyfriend and his friends act towards me and other women when we talk about or cheer for the Patriots or Red Sox. Though he acknowledges that I do know what I am talking about at the time, but he continues to act as if he does not think that I do. I believe this may be due to his conditioned subconscious thinking that women do not know about sports.

Tamdgidi's paper also describes the concept of **intra-personal oppression** and how a person "may actually oppress him or her self, through practices which *may*, theoretically speaking, have relatively little to do with interpersonal social rationalities" (23). He continues to infer that, "a 'looking-glass self' dynamic may be at work, for instance, where the person continues to demean him or her self simply because of a misinterpretation or misimagination of a comment ..." (Tamdgidi 23). I believe that this idea can clearly be recognized in the case of female fans with regard to their bifurcated consciousness. Personally, I have become aware of my behavior during games, and do change my behavior when others are present as I am uncomfortable and attempt to avoid the embarrassment of being perceived as an over-eager female fan. I had never before considered this reflection and subsequent change in my behavior as an instance of intra-personal oppression, but contemplating on the foregoing I do believe that it is.

In his article, "The Myth of the Sexual Athlete" (1994), Don Sabo speaks of the connection between sports and male sexuality. To make the connection, Sabo discloses stories of his and other men's attempts at gaining and/or maintaining the appearance of masculinity through "locker room sex talk." Sabo continues by stating, "to be manly in sports, traditionally, means to be competitive, successful, dominating, aggressive, stoical, goal-directed, and physically strong. Many athletes accept this definition of masculinity and apply it in their relationships with women. Dating becomes a sport in itself, and 'scoring'... is a mark of masculine achievement" (Sabo 264). I believe this idea may be related to *why* men do not view women as equals in being sports fans. Perhaps in the male mind, if a woman is as much of a fan as he is, he loses some of his sexual power, some of his masculinity—as if a woman who is a sports fan steals some of the competitiveness, domination, and aggressiveness that are supposed to be reserved for the male.

Furthermore, I view the lack of what Jürgen Habermas calls **communicative actions** between men and women during sports games to be another example of women being excluded as fans. During the 2004 Super Bowl, I and another female watched the game with three men and were utterly disregarded throughout the game. My boyfriend did not even hear me when I commented on Janet Jackson's "wardrobe malfunction" because, I believe, he had just tuned me out completely for the entire game. During the final minutes of the fourth quarter, the men were all standing around in a circle, and participated in communicative actions such as high-fiving, playfully hitting each other, and jumping up on each other, while the other female and I were left out. It was as if they thought we were not as excited as they were about our home team Patriots winning the Super Bowl. Habermas argues, "Communicative actions are not only processes of interpretation in which cultural knowledge is 'tested against the world'; they are at the same time processes of social integration and socialization" (quoted in Wallace and Wolf, 175). I believe this to be true, and feel that we, as females, were prevented from being socially integrated and socialized into the sports world due to our gender.

In order to begin to change the current circumstance of the role of women in sports, the concept of *inclusion* must be applied. It should no longer be acceptable for women to be treated differently or excluded from certain aspects of being a fan simply due to their gender. "Society must recognize that groups that have been excluded are capable of contributing to the functioning of the system" (Wallace and Wolf, 166), and by this I mean more than the function of decoration provided by cheerleaders. According to Wallace and Wolf, "[Miriam] Johnson ... argues that the inclusion of educated women into the occupational world outside the home on an equal basis with men has led to ***adaptive upgrading*** because it released more trained capacity into the system" (167). I believe the same can be true of the sports world if women are only given a chance to be taken seriously and seen as equals.

Judith Lorber, in her article, "The Social Construction of Gender" (1994), contends that gender is "constantly created and recreated out of human interaction, out of social life, and is the texture and order of the social life" (Lorber 96). She also asserts that,

> for the individual, gender construction starts with assignment to a sex category on the basis of what the genitalia look like at birth... A sex category becomes a gender status through naming, dress, and the use of other gender markers. Once a child's gender is evident, others treat those in one gender differently from those in the other, and the children respond to the different treatment by feeling different and behaving different. (Lorber 97)

I believe this notion is evident in the treatment of female fans and their subsequent emotional and behavioral responses. As discussed above, I have had many experiences in which I was looked at and treated differently (than a man would be) during a football, basketball, or baseball game, because of my gender. And, in further support of Lorber's assertion, I then began to feel being different and consequently began to behave differently. I believe that Judith Lorber's idea of the social construction of gender is true and evident in the case of female fans.

References

Bierce, A. (1958). *The Devil's Dictionary*. New York: Dover.

Cohen, S. (2002). "I Only *Thought* I Knew It All: Society and the Individual." *Human Architecture: Journal of the Sociology of Self-Knowledge*, Vol. I, No. 1, p. 9-17.

Disch, E. (2003). *Reconstructing Gender: A Multicultural Anthology*. Boston: McGraw-Hill. p. 1-25.

Goltry, M. (2003). "Theoretical Reflections on Peer Judgments." *Human Architecture: Journal of the Sociology of Self-Knowledge*. Vol. II, No. 1, p. 19-26.

Farganis, J. (2000). *Readings in Social Theory: The*

Classic Tradition to Post-Modernism. Third Edition. Boston: McGraw-Hill.

Lorber, J. "The Social Construction of Gender." (1994) *Reconstructing Gender: A Multicultural Anthology.* Boston: McGraw-Hill. 2003. p. 96-103.

Margulies, E. (2002). "From Anti-Man to Anti-Patriarchy." *Human Architecture: Journal of the Sociology of Self-Knowledge.* Vol. I

Margulies, E. (2003). "Why I Smoke: Sociology of A Deadly Habit." *Human Architecture: Journal of the Sociology of Self-Knowledge.* Vol. II, No. 1.

Sabo, D. "The Myth of the Sexual Athlete." (1994). *Reconstructing Gender: A Multicultural Anthology.* Boston: McGraw-Hill. 2003. p. 263-267.

Saltzberg, E.A. and Chrisler, J.C. (1995). "Beauty is the Beast: Psychological Effects of the Pursuit of the Perfect Female Body *Reconstructing Gender: A Multicultural Anthology.* Boston: McGraw-Hill. 2003. p. 167-177.

Tamdgidi, Mohammad H. (2004). *Freire Meets Gurdjieff and Rumi: Towards the Pedagogy of the Oppressed and Oppressing Selves.* Presented to Social Theory Forum, 2004, Umass Boston.

Wallace, R.A. and Wolf, A. (1999). *Contemporary Sociological Theory: Expanding the Classical Tradition.* Fifth Edition. New Jersey: Prentice Hall.

Films

"Affluenza." (1997). Bullfrog Films.

"The Big One." (1998). Miramax Home Entertainment.

"Billy Elliot." (2000). Universal Pictures.

"Erin Brockovich." (2000). Universal Pictures.

"The Matrix." (1999). Warner Bros.

"Twelve Angry Men" (1957

Will I Marry Her?

Chris DaPonte

UMass Boston

A Barbie and a Ken doll—complete with their two babies and a dog from my favorite aunt when I was seven years old—are the Christmas presents I most vividly remember from my childhood. This image of family influenced my vision of the future for many years to come. I believed that by the time I was twenty-five, I would look like Barbie and have her "two- kids-and-a-dog" life.

This is hardly a paper about a ruined life and image because of a plastic, yet beautiful, doll; rather, it is a look at how the image of family, even Barbie's family, has shaped my reality. Even as late as this year, I bought a dog shortly after my twenty-fifth birthday. Something is still missing, and although I am glad that I finally know that it is not Ken I long for, I struggle with the issue of how to realize my image of family.

At the age of eighteen, while visiting a friend in college, a remarkable turning point occurred in my life. During a short walk with my friend she explained that she wanted me to meet a friend of hers, but she wanted to "warn" me about her first. She had to warn me, she explained, because the girl that I would be meeting was gay. I considered myself very open-minded but I had never met anyone that was gay, so my **stereotyping** of her began instantly, without even realizing it. I wondered what she would look like, what she would be like, and I was a little scared of the unfamiliar that I would soon encounter. In *Twelve Angry Men*, we meet a juror who comments, "You know how 'those people' are!" In the film, this stereotype may have sent someone to death because the juror had a **prejudice** against a group of people they did not know. This was my fist thought upon hearing that I would be meeting someone that was gay: 'those people.' This prejudice did nothing but distort the truth and place an unfair label on someone. If I hadn't overcome it, my life would be very different today.

On the walk back to my friend's apartment, she explained to me that "the gay girl" thought that I was beautiful. I cringed and suddenly became extremely uncomfortable about the prospect of seeing her again. How could another girl look at me that way? When she explained that I should take it as a compliment and nothing more, I realized how unfair and even closed-minded I was being. When I saw "the gay girl" that day and again the next day, we spent some time together and seemed to connect in a way I hadn't ever connected with anyone. That night, I couldn't figure out why I was still there, still spending time with her, inexplicably drawn to her; she was gay. I began getting feelings I had never had before; suddenly wondering what my feelings were, what they meant and if it was okay to feel them. All of these thoughts were ringing in my head so much that when "the gay girl" kissed me I did absolutely nothing in return; I continued thinking about all the whys, whats, and hows. Worried about how I might become someone or something else. Fortunately, I finally kissed Nikki in return. I was not supposed to fall in love with a girl, but I did, and doing so has taught me more about love, acceptance, society and myself than any other experience in my life.

Recently, the issue of gay couples' rights to marry has raised much controversy. Over 60% of the population does not believe that gay couples should have the right to marry, but those that agree and disagree with gay marriage are all voicing loud protests against one another. President Bush is currently attempting to pass a Constitutional Amendment defining marriage as a union between a man and a woman. Most proponents of this amendment hold marriage as a sacred religious ceremony. *Ritual*, as defined by *Randall Collins* is a "'stereotyped sequence of gestures and sounds'... that make emotions more intense, and commit them more strongly to views of reality..." (Wallace and Wolf, 148). Those who are against gay marriage hold this view of a sacred ritual with family and friends. It is something that little girls spend years longing for. What they are not seeing, however, is that marriage does not end after the ceremony, and that the ceremony doesn't have to be about a white dress and a church.

According to the *functionalist* perspective, as stated by Farganis, "the reason people obey rules, follow codes of behavior, and abide by the laws of society, is that they accept the fundamental values of their society and see its authority structures as legitimate expressions of this consensus" (225). Individuals in society want to follow the laws of society. When others have strong arguments against gay marriage and oppose it, they trust the *institution*, or the "beliefs and modes of behavior instituted by the collectivity" (Wallace and Wolf, 22). Such institutional realities are seen by *Emile Durkheim* as a *social fact*, a set of "laws, moral, beliefs, customs standing external to the individual and shaping his or her life" (Wallace and Wolf, 22). Many trust the norms and past customs of society and try to turn them into their laws because they believe that is the way to induce what Durkheim's called social *integration*, "the incorporation of individuals into the social order [is]...important for the maintenance of social equilibrium" (Wallace and Wolf, 21). This concept can be looked at much differently, however, if we integrate homosexual couples into society, fostering equal relationships for all individuals.

Ralf Dahrendorf believes "that the distribution of *power* is the crucial determinant of social structure ... the essence of power is the control of sanctions, which enables those who possess power to give orders and obtain what they want from the powerless. Power is a 'lasting source of friction'" (Wallace and Wolf, 120). *Rae Lesser Blumberg* believes that "the most important of many factors... influencing women's overall equality is economic" (Wallace and Wolf, 144). She goes on to state that "the greater a woman's economic power... the greater her control over 'marriage, divorce, sexuality, household, authority, and various types of household decisions" (Wallace and Wolf, 144). In terms of the *stratification by gender*, whoever brings more income into a marriage will have more control over life decisions concerning the relationship. This may unfortunately hold true in heterosexual relationships, but in regards to relationships between two women, at least in my experience, it is never a question of who has more control, but rather one of equality between two individual who are oppressed in terms of gender and sexual orientation. In addition, marriage should never be about power and control, especially economically; it should always be about a shared and equal relationship between two people.

In the future, however, I see a different image forming, especially in regards to lesbian marriages. In the film *The Big One* Michael Moore, touring city by city, uncovers corporate greed in the United States. Company after company make millions, or even billions of dollars, lay off people, shut down entire factories, and move their facilities to other countries so that they may pay individuals in countries with no minimum wage law considerably lower sums of money. In the movie, we also meet Phillip

Knight, the CEO of the Nike Corporation. The Nike Corporation has absolutely no shoe-making factories in the U.S., but has factories in Indonesia among others. There, girls as young as 14 years of age work for as little as $2 a day to make sneakers for Nike. Mr. Knight is aware of this and the fact that Indonesia is an extremely exploited country with a regime that during some protests had killed over 200,000 of its own people. Mr. Knight, however, and so many other CEO's just like him, is not concerned with these conditions. Their goal is to make as much money as possible and they do not care who is negatively affected while they are doing it. In the film *Affluenza*, we learn of businesses, like Nike, subconsciously influencing our minds through advertisements. Although gay marriage is only fully accepted by about 25% of the population, gay magazines are already filled with advertisements aimed at the homosexual lifestyle. Not only are beer advertisements changed to sell the sexiness of two women rather than a heterosexual couple, but businesses such as hotels, cruise ships, and even sections of cities and towns are advertising specifically for the gay lifestyle so that they may cash in on gays' feeling more comfortable by helping gather their "group" in one particular location.

Norms "are established and maintained… by power, and their substance may well be explained in terms of interests of the powerful... established norms are nothing but ruling norms" (Dahrendorf, as cited in Wallace and Wolf, 121). Norms are established by the economically powerful. *Social stratification* "is caused by norms, which categorize some things as desirable and other as not" (Wallace and Wolf, 121). Society has always had norms; it is the image of desire, or undesirable, norms that causes conflict. Through social stratification, individuals in society, including myself, see a heterosexual marriage, and all that comes along with it, as desirable. When this happens, homosexual relationships and its conflicts, struggles, and negative images formed by society, become undesirable. Why have all that conflict when you can have the desirable vision?

Homosexual couples who are hoping to someday marry may be aided by what *Randall Collins* calls *mutual surveillance*—"the more people are in the physical presence of others—the more they accept the culture of the group and expect precise conformity in others" (Wallace and Wolf, 147). In addition, according to *Peter Blau*, *social exchange* "creates *trust* between people and integrates individuals into social groups" (Wallace and Wolf, 331). He believes that social exchanges

> ... tend to start small and evolve slowly. ... *Reciprocation* and expanded exchange are 'accompanied by a parallel growth of mutual trust. Hence, processes of social exchange, which may originate in pure self interest, generate trust in social relations through their recurrent and gradually expanding character. (Wallace and Wolf, 331)

Recently, when Nikki and I were out with a married couple, I realized how differently they viewed our relationship from theirs. It wasn't until later on in the evening when we talked about plans to visit family the following day—a family wedding planned for the summer that we had to attend, and a battle over who was going to walk the dog when we got home—that I think they finally realized that Nikki and I were almost exactly like them. Individuals need to spend more time with those that are different from them so that they will feel better about fully accepting them. I have always believed that no one who spent time with Nikki and I would really believe that we don't belong together.

I was forever looking at myself wondering how I could now be this person that I was not supposed to be. **George Herbert**

Mead explains that there are "two 'phases' of the self," the "**I**" and the "**me**" (Wallace and Wolf, 198). The self is the determining factor in an individual's behavior, split into the "I," or the creative, active self of you, and the "me," or society's version. Mead believed that individuals can "adjust, adapt, and control behavior based on self-reflection" (Farganis 12) through **symbolic interaction**. In "Theoretical Reflections on Peer Judgments" (2003), M. Goltry explains that her self-awareness and her focus on how others viewed her shaped her self-identity. Mead believed in individualism, and gave individuals tremendous faith in their own individuality. Based on his views, there is a "**fixed-entity**" in human beings that allows us to govern ourselves. He seems to suggest that we rely on our predictability and values as we increase our creativity and interests. This notion gives the individual tremendous personal power, if we use it in a positive and confident way. It is through symbolic interactionism that I accepted the fact that I was in love and that was okay. It took a tremendous amount of personal strength however, to keep reminding myself of that, of the meaning in love in new symbolic forms.

Phenomenology approaches the world from a stranger's point of view with no presumptions. "People who question the way their world is ordered or who are members of a *subordinate group*... like ... gays and lesbians... will acquire many insights into their situation if they put on the lens of this perspective... the 'bracketing' or suspending of taken-for-granted assumptions by oppressed groups makes sense in such situations... phenomenology took shape through political unrest. (Wallace and Wolf, 253, 254). It "challenges our culturally learned ideas... to question our way of looking at our way of being in the world" (Wallace and Wolf, 253). Unknowingly, I used phenomenology when questioning if it would be okay to have my relationship with Nikki. Questioning our way in the world opened my mind to a possibility I had never thought of before; it allowed me to be the person that I am today. I began this paper with another struggle, however, one about my images of family and marriage conflicting with the person that I am today, realizing that I was no longer a stranger to the concept.

Sociobiology is the study of "the biological basis of behavior." Sociobiologists "believe that biological factors and genetic influences set limits to the range of possible behaviors. These limits and behavioral tendencies, they argue, result from evolution, just as does the behavior of other species, and they must be understood in the context of natural selection" (Wallace and Wolf, 383). In contrast, **sociology of the body** is the study of a "social construction of our behavior" (Wallace and Wolf, 373). The question of why it felt okay to have my relationship is one related to the controversy between sociology of the body and sociobiology (Wallace and Wolf, 383). I personally believe that I was not born gay. On the other hand, I give no credit to the alternative concept of *social construction*. I truly believe that I simply fell in love and that what society would think played no part in how I fell in love. When I begin to think of marriage, however, I am consciously aware that society is playing a big part in how to live with my relationship.

Emile Durkheim explains that due to the **dualism of human nature** individuals have two sides. They have an egoistic side and the social side stems from the characteristics of society (Hurst 43). Individuals are constantly functioning through biological and societal impulses. When Nikki and I first met, I had an inner battle with the societal disapproval and my natural feelings. This conflict continued for years and is the reason why our society has the term "in the closet." For those who do not possess a strong sense of themselves in a society that fears difference, the societal impulses win over the individuals' personal feelings and cause them to conform themselves to a traditional society. **Georg Simmel** believed that conflict was good for society because it brought about change. Simmel also believed that "social action involves harmony and conflict, love and hatred" (Wallace and Wolf, 77). In my view this approach to **conflict theory** also holds true for individuals as well. "Individuals possess rationality, intellect, and a mind, they also possess a 'soul,' a nonrational dimension" (Hurst 44). On that fateful night I experienced inner conflict, when my soul (and heart) presided to change my life. Now I struggle with how to have the Barbie doll family and stay happy in my relationship with Nikki. Since there is currently no harmony between those battling for or against the issue of gay marriage, I hope that the conflict will eventually bring about a change that will be more equal for everyone.

When we imagine how we appear to others, how we imagine they see us and then allow that to affect our feelings about ourselves, we are experiencing what **Charles Horton Cooley** termed the **looking glass self**. In his own words, Cooley identifies three moments of the process as follows: "the imagination of our appearance to the other person; the imagination of his judgment of that appearance; and some sort of self-feeling, such as pride or mortification" (Wallace and Wolf, 195). These feelings, based solely on your imagination of someone else's judgment, can be positive or negative. Kristy Canfield, in "Repairing the Soul: Matching Inner with Outer Beauty" (2002), talks of "setting up a plan of protection against the cruelties of the world" after feeling no acceptance due to her speech impediment. Since all too often I assume that people are looking at me negatively causing feelings of low self-esteem about my physical characteristics, I decided to change my looking glass self in regards to my relationship. Believing that everyone who observes the interactions between Nikki and me is actually jealous of our relationship has made my relationship easier when faced with possibly uncomfortable situations. In the issue of marriage, however, I believe that everyone views it in a negative sense. Since I struggle with my future image of having a family, my looking glass self gives me a more negative view.

Ethnomethodology is the process in which we as people make sense of the world around us in everyday life. **Harold Garfinkel** believed that we should begin "to treat as problematic what is taken for granted in order to understand the commonsense of the everyday world." This concept becomes quite humorous for me when questioning heterosexual marriages. We take it for granted because it is the norm but if society began to treat it as a problem the way that homosexual marriages are currently being treated, it may be understood more that it is common sense that when two people are in love, they're in love. In *The Matrix*, Neo "struggles to overcome the opposing images of his life, the one in "the Matrix" and the one in the real world." (Danahay and Rieder 221). Neo's situation is especially complex, however, because he must attempt to make sense of the entire concept of life itself. When struggling with the issue of marriage, I cannot see heterosexual marriages as a problem because the image of Barbie's family was impressed on my views to be a perfect family.

According to Charles Hurst, for **Karl Marx** "much of what we become is determined by our relationships in society" (Hurst 44). He defines this as one aspect of our **species being**. Hurst further suggests that in Marx's view, individuals and society are in a "love-hate relationship of necessity." Marx believes that the capitalist society suppresses individuals' personal expressions. This proves true today in relation to the controversy of gay marriage. Seven years ago I never thought that anyone would be so much against simple expressions of a love that can only make people happier. My relationship to society, in my opinion, has always been very positive. If I am in a homosexual marriage, however, my relationship to society will be negative in the eyes of many.

Erving Goffman believed that "to interact with others successfully to achieve individual or collective objectives involves the ability to play a variety of roles and to manipulate the self in order to get from others the desired reactions, responses, or rewards" (Farganis 351). **Dramaturgy**, as he coined it, involves viewing "our actions and those of others through the prism of a dramatic stage play." Preparation for our interactions, the act itself performed in the **front stage**, took place **back stage**, hidden from the audience. Often I need to use this concept because I am forced to shield my relationship. I cannot see myself doing this, however, if I marry another woman.

C. Wright Mills's concept of **sociological imagination** "allows us to understand our personal predicaments by reference to wider events and institutions. It forces us to look around us for broader social conditions and processes" (Hurst 7). This concept took shape for me especially when studying the social movements in history and their similarities to the Civil Rights Movement. Currently, many people are claiming that the debate over gay marriage should be put to a popular vote. What they are forgetting is that not that long ago, millions were against civil rights for blacks, and that if left to a popular vote, there might still be segregated schools today. Fighting with myself about why it is not always okay to be who I am is always less painful when I realize that I am not alone and that society, and the events that shape it, take time for change.

Collective conscience is "underlying common beliefs and attitudes that exist independent of particular individuals and across generations, and that tie a society together" (Hurst 32). These beliefs, once socially constructed, however, acquire "their own life," and are not open to individual variations. We allow this to happen because society does not allow us to question the rules. When we step outside of this we are destroying the image. That is how some of my friends made me feel after I told them about my relationship with Nikki. I was suddenly this flawed character because they could no longer have the same image of me that they had before. When they question my future with her, it involves statements about who will wear the white wedding dress and who is more in charge in our relationship. When they ask questions like this, they are using what **Alfred Schutz** calls the "common sense" **stock of knowledge:** "Social recipes of conceptions of appropriate behavior that enable them to think of the world as made up of 'types' of things" (Wallace and Wolf, 255). This is when I realized how much we were being pressured to define ourselves in terms of our sexual orientation. Individuals, and society, form our society through **labels** and "types" without regard for its effects. A marriage may soon be defined as a union between a man and a woman, simply because society expects a white wedding dress and a black suit.

The world around us, including ourselves, is shaped by society. It tells us how we should look to fit society's "okay" image. **Ralf Dahrendorf** questions **deviance**, or deviant behavior, as the "failure of the socialization process rather than an expression of difference and dissent" (Farganis, 265). If we continue to label and stigmatize differences, society and the individuals in society will continue to fear these differences, or alter what is deviant with no regard for the individual. This is explored in Emily Margulies' "Why I Smoke: Sociology of a Deadly Habit" (2003). Society played the largest part in causing her smoking habit. When it became an addiction, however, society—which now had become intolerant of smoking—saw her as a deviant. Deviance is used to label anything that is different from the norms of society. In the film *Erin Brockovich*, Erin is portrayed as a deviant not only because of the way she dresses, but because the way she dresses conflicts with the image of who she really is. One of the negative responses I have heard upon telling someone else about my relationship with Nikki was, "Why, you're such a pretty girl?" What that person was ignorant about is that looks do not define who a person is and their life choices, and that those two are not always in perfect sync with society's expected relationship between the two.

Lewis Coser believes that "a group's position to and conflict with 'deviants' makes apparent to group members what they ought to do" (Wallace and Wolf, 131). "In this sense *internal conflict* is central to defining a group's identity, which is embodied in norms that define correct behavior. ... Coser also argues that internal conflict can increase a group's survival, cohesion, and stability" (Wallace and Wolf, 131). *Georg Simmel* believes that "opposition gives us inner satisfaction, distraction, relief" (Wallace and Wolf, 131). Although I struggle with many, trying to show them that gay marriage is okay even when they do not change their views instantly, I am relieved knowing that I can defend myself, my relationship, and the homosexual marriages of others with pride, in myself and in my group.

Billy Elliot, in a motion picture of the same name, grows up as a young boy in England, hiding his ballet slippers and sneaking to ballet class so that he may be able to dance without condemnation from his father. When his father does catch him, Billy's response—"What's wrong with ballet, it's perfectly normal"—is also a reflection of his own insecurities in a society that wants 10 year old boys go to boxing class. Eventual acceptance from his father causes Billy great joy, while still causing his father embarrassment. When Billy dances all along the street while walking with his father, his father replies "Is that absolutely necessary?" This scene reminded me a lot of my relationship with my father after he finally accepted my relationship with Nikki. Seven years later, my dad still refers to Nikki as his "other daughter," fielding the uncomfortable questions. The end of Billy Elliot gives me great hope as Billy's father and brother rush to see a ten-year-older Billy's performance of *The Swan Lake*. The pride that Billy's father feels can be felt. This was so important to me because I constantly struggle with how my father will feel if I do decide to marry Nikki. I hope that one day, when I am not looking, my father feels this same sense of unconditional pride over who I have become. Maybe this will happen after he walks me to my bride in my white wedding dress.

References

Canfield, Kristy. (2002). "Repairing the Soul: Matching Inner with Outer Beauty." *Human Architecture: Journal of the Sociology of Self-Knowledge*, I, 2, 20-26.

Danahay, M. and Rieder, D. (2002) "The Matrix, Marx, and the Coppertop's Life." *The Matrix and Philosophy: Welcome to the Desert of the Real*, 3, 18, 216-224.

Farganis, James. (2000). *Readings in Social Theory: The Classic Tradition to Post-Modernism*. Third Edition. Boston: McGraw Hill.

Goltry, M. (2003). "Theoretical Reflections on Peer Judgments." *Human Architecture: Journal of the Sociology of Self-Knowledge*, II, 1, 19-26.

Hurst, Charles E. (2000). *Living Theory: The Application of Classical Social Theory to Contemporary Life*. Massachusetts: Allyn and Bacon.

Margulies, Emily. (2003). "Why I Smoke: Sociology of a Deadly Habit." *Human Architecture: Journal of the Sociology of Self-Knowledge*, II, 1, 1-12.

Wallace, R. and Wolf, A. (1999). *Contemporary Sociological Theory: Expanding the Classical Tradition*. Fifth Edition. New Jersey: Prentice Hall.

Films:
"Affluenza" (1997). Bullfrog Films.
"Billy Elliot" (2000). Universal Studios.
"Erin Brockovich" (2000). MCA.
"The Big One" (1997). Walt Disney Video.
"The Matrix." (2000). Warner Bros.
"Twelve Angry Men." (1957). MGM.

The Effect of Immigrant Experiences on the Bifurcation of Women's Consciousness

Guadalupe Paz

UMass Boston

---

*Marx believed that through labor, human kind would be able to realize its "**species-being**," i.e., its potential for creative and purposeful activity through work. What Marx envisioned was the use of labor for the enhancement of human life beyond material necessity, for the creation of a society in which aesthetic as well as material needs could be fulfilled. Labor could potentially provide such an opportunity, for it allowed persons to display creative and purposeful activity through their work under the right conditions.* (Farganis 24)

Thinking back to my childhood, I remember observing my mom getting up early in the morning to make sure my brother and sister were ready for school. She would check their school uniforms to make sure they were clean and neatly ironed. In the same way she would check their shoes to make sure they were clean and shiny. The previous night, before going to bed, she would check their homework for errors and neatness. I was off the hook for a while, since I was younger than my brother and sister by four and five years respectively, but eventually I became part of the checking routine.

My mom was not a stay at home mom like many Latin American women. She was a working mother, partly for necessity and partly to fulfill her dream of being a professional as she used to say. For her, work was more than a means to gain a salary; it was a way to demonstrate her potential. Before, I didn't understand what my mom meant when she said she felt "fulfilled" by her work. Marx, as remembered by James Farganis in the quote above, knew exactly what this feeling is, it's the feeling that we are creative beings and that we have potential for something great. In the same way, it's the feeling experienced deep inside us, of having a purpose in life, knowing that we are here in this world not just by a random error but because we are meant to be here.

My mother would not have been able to do what she did, had she been born a couple of decades earlier. For example, my grandmother, a very intelligent woman, was not able to finish high school because she had to take care of her younger siblings while her parents managed the family business. The movie *Billy Elliot* shows a similar situation. Billy, a young teenage boy, has to assume the responsibility of taking care of his elderly grandmother while his father and brother work. In a way, this makes me think that in times of great need and uncertainty common attitudes are put aside. Billy's father was going through a strike situation where his older son was also involved. This was not a time to be considerate towards his younger son who should have been enjoying his childhood, instead of taking care of his grandmother.

My great grandparents were also going through a difficult time with their business and both had to work. It didn't matter that my grandmother was just a teenage girl;

she had to assume the responsibility of taking care of her siblings even if that meant giving up school. A couple of years later she got married and wanted to go back to school and later find a job but her husband told her that as long as he was alive she would never have to work, therefore, school was not a priority. For him her most important job was at home taking care of their children. My grandfather was not a mean, controlling man; he was very gentle and loving towards my grandmother and their children. He just expressed and followed the **social norms** that he had learned while growing up. It was customary that women stayed home taking care of their children. Sometimes we forget that society is all around us, influencing and shaping who we are. This brings to mind, what **Durkheim**, so eloquently said, "we know of its existence because society exercises control over our behavior, as rules of conduct, as laws, as customs, and as norms and values that we believe in and that shape our conscience and make us part of a collectively" (Durkheim, in Farganis 55). At the time when my grandparents married, women worked only if it was extremely necessary and usually the male was seen as a failure for not being able to provide sufficiently for his wife and family.

My grand parents' situation also exemplifies **Parsons' theory of action**, which includes the **pattern variables** to account for the categorization of expectations and the structure of relationships. According to Parsons, people are like actors who are oriented towards goals but have to fulfill certain conditions defined by established expectations. Parsons labeled relationships in traditional societies, for example the society my great grandparents lived in as **expressive** because they were personal and informal. In the same way, he labeled relationships in modern society as **instrumental** because they are impersonal and formal for the most part. So, when he analyzed **sex roles** in the family he concluded "the instrumental leadership role must be accorded to the father-husband, on whom the reputation and income of the family depend" (Wallace and Wolf, 31). In the same way, "because of the occupational responsibilities of the father, the mother must take on the expressive leadership role in the socialization of the children" (Wallace and Wolf, 31). Personally, I would say Parsons' idea of expressive and instrumental relationships related to sex roles in the family are outdated and untrue. Women are very capable of finding jobs that will support the whole family and men are also able to take in their hands the responsibility of taking care of their children. But, putting myself in the shoes of my grandparents when they were young back then, I would say that it perfectly illustrates what people thought the roles of men and women were. It's important to say that this point of view holds true for some cultures in our present time and the Hispanic culture is a good example. The Hispanic culture is basically still a **patriarchal** society. Men can do whatever they want and women can't. Men have economic and political power and women have to conform to low paying jobs, which results in a low **socioeconomic status**.

But fortunately those behaviors, rules of conduct, customs, norms, values and so forth are open to change and not etched in stone. This means that as human beings change, society is shaped accordingly. When my mother was young, my grandmother encouraged her to go to college and become a professional. My mother married my father just a year after she finished high school. Pretty soon, their first child was on the way, my sister and later my brother. Even with two babies at home and a full time job, my mother tried to go to evening classes at a nearby college. She did this for a semester, but soon she realized she could not do it any more. We lived in a big city but in the neighborhood everybody knew everybody's business. All of a sudden, people started talking about my mom and how she left her two infants alone with my grandmother the whole day. Jennifer Dutcher in her essay "A precarious Balance: Views of a Working Mother Walking the Tightrope" (2003), uses **Simmel's** idea that "small town life rests upon more deeply felt and emotional relationships" to illustrate that she felt compelled to satisfy her family and community with her actions (82). My mother also felt compelled to please her community, her neighbors, people who had seen her grow up and who expected her to be a good mother even if that meant giving up her idea of a career. She decided to dedicate her time to her family and children and thought of eventually resuming her education. Five years later when I was born, it seemed even more difficult for my mother to go back to school but still she had to try. My father is a good man who helped her and was very patient, but unfortunately people started talking about my mom and how little time she dedicated to her family. Once again, she had to give up her dream of becoming a professional.

We migrated to this country mainly for political reasons and partly because my parents wanted us to have a better future in a free country, where we would not fear for our safety. My older sister was fifteen years old, my bother was fourteen and I was ten when we arrived. At first, it was very difficult for my brother and sister to learn a new language, **adapt to a new culture** and change their social behavior. Gradually, they learned that what was "cool" in our country was old fashioned in this country. In the same way, they had to readjust their wardrobes in order to "fit in." For me, the change went more smoothly. I was still a young girl and using my, what George Herbert **Mead** calls, the **emergent self** it was easier for me to create new **selves** that adapted to the new society in which I was living. My brother and sister had already created their selves or the sense of who they were; therefore, it was more difficult for them to readjust. Failure to readjust to the new culture could have resulted in a feeling of **alienation.** P. Heim described this feeling of separation in her essay, "Alien Nation" (2002). She says "there were times in high school when I felt like an outsider and had low self-esteem" (36). According to her essay, I would say she felt alienated because she had different points of view or attitudes among people with whom she nevertheless shared a similar cultural background. But, if my brother and sister didn't conform to the new society they would feel alienated because they were from a different cultural background, which adds issues of racism and discrimination to the sense of alienation.

Although we never experienced **racism** or **discrimination** like William Wang recounts in his essay, "My Asian American Experience" (2002), we knew of its existence. William Wang related an episode when his father "arrived at the store to open it and found graffiti all over the front gate of the store... racial epithets were scattered throughout .... Remarks such as, "Get out chinks" and Chinaman go home" were quite devastating to my father" (75). This is a real firsthand account of racism. According to Hurst, "color continues to be a highly significant criterion defining the position of a group in the U.S. ethnic hierarchy" (Hurst 136). This kind of experience only increases the feeling of alienation and fear in immigrants. In the same way, it promotes inequality between groups in relation to their social status.

The American culture places great emphasis on **social status** and how they are **symbolically** represented. In other words, what you wear, the way you speak, the mannerisms you use, the town where you live, shows your position in the social scale. Some immigrants place a greater emphasis on this than others. For example, a cousin of mine came here when she was fourteen years old. She finished high school and went to college, very similar to what my sister did. The great difference is that my cousin was never encouraged to speak Spanish and actually was encouraged to completely immerse herself into the American culture. She is the prototype of what an American woman is or should be. She is a professional; married a professional man and both have excellent salaries and work full time. They have a beautiful home, two cars, two girls, two cats and a dog. She does not speak Spanish anymore and in the same way, does not encourage her daughters to speak Spanish. All of her friends are Americans and she doesn't even speak in Spanish to her mother who is an elderly woman with limited English vocabulary. My cousin sends her daughters to private school and has them signed up for three extracurricular activities after school. When her daughters are not in school or after school activities, they spend their time at home with a baby-sitter. Now, by the American standards, she is doing the right thing. Her children are going to an excellent Catholic school, they have anything they want, and they are well-rounded girls who know how to play the piano, the violin and how to dance ballet. But, are they learning respect and the importance of family values? I'm afraid they are not.

As I said earlier, we live in a society where material possessions are more important than family values. In the PBS documentary *Affluenza*, we are exposed to the truth that many know but nobody talks about. We are a materialistic society where shopping centers have become the center of people's lives. We believe that material possessions are going to make us feel better about who we are, when in reality, all these temples of consumerism do is mask the emptiness inside us. Modern society has twice as many material possessions as it did in the 1950's and still fewer people consider themselves happy. This is a result of **capitalism** where seeking private property, wealth, and profit as ends in themselves are encouraged. In the same way, as **Weber** says, "capitalism has become a rational system, an '**iron cage**' in which people have become money-making instruments" (Farganis 91). With so much money, people have nothing else to do but spend it. Now, companies are targeting children and teenagers with their advertisements by ads and games that will teach them to be consumers. The increase in material possessions is breaking up families because mother and father have to work twice as much so that they can provide everything their family needs. Accordingly, they spend less time with their children and therefore become alienated from them. Even if the parent spends time at home, there are so many material possessions in the home that everybody is in their own room doing something different.

In my cousin's house, there are four TVs, one for each family member; there are two computers, one in the living room and the other in the older daughter's room. This brings to mind what Charles Hurst said in *Living Theory* (2000): "internet usage over time resulted in decreases in family communication and maintenance of social relationships and increases in loneliness and depression" (Hurst 53). Children spend more time in front of a computer than with their parents. In the same way, "greater use of the internet is also encouraged by a sense of security bred by the apparent anonymity of communication among a multitude of strangers" (Hurst 53). Earlier I said that one of the roles of parents was to **socialize** the child; in other words, to show and teach her or him how society is structured. If parents fail to do this at home, then who is going to do it? Many parents think that the educational system is responsible for teaching their children how to behave and what constitutes moral behavior. But as Durkheim argued, "moral behavior requires *discipline*. Such discipline makes both social order and a meaningful goal-oriented existence for the individual possible" (Hurst 85). The main goal of the school system is to teach children academic material but moral values are not a priority.

I believe that some teachers are truly concerned with accomplishing both tasks but the majority are not. Math teachers can't spend their class time talking about respect and moral values instead of teaching children how to add and subtract. In the same way, if parents fail to convey moral values to their children, teachers will have trouble "commanding respect in the classroom." It has been suggested that "a majority of parents have only some or little confidence in the educational system." (Hurst 86) I believe the problem is not entirely in the educational system. The presence of parents at home is extremely important for the development of morale. I did not first learn that I had to be polite towards my teachers at school; I was taught by my mother that I had to respect my teachers. My mother used to tell me that teachers were like parents to us and that we had to treat them accordingly.

As a Spanish teacher in a Catholic school, I find that children behave differently depending on the amount of time they spend with their parents. On the one hand, children whose parents spend time with them are regularly better behaved than children whose parents spend less time with them. It's reasonable to say that children who spend more time with their parents have a model authority figure to emulate. On the other hand, children who spend less time with their parents have difficulty obeying an adult because they lack the figure of authority at home. Usually, if parents spend little time at home, like my cousin, they make up for it by indulging their children with anything they want. For Christmas, my cousin's daughters are given ten to fifteen gifts each. They open the gifts, look at them, put them aside and then add them to their already full closets. Sometimes they don't even get to play with all their gifts in one year. In the same way, there are promised lavish prizes if they do well in school, again, teaching them that ultimately everything comes down to material goods. What happened to the idea of learning in order to be a better person? Humans are capable of rational thinking, of deciding what is good or bad, in terms of **intrinsic values** of things, not just for **extrinsic rewards**. This subject has been studied, among others, by **rational choice** theorists in sociology. We are conditioning our children to be materialistically rationalizing and calculating by giving them extrinsic rewards in order to obtain a desired behavior instead of teaching them to think and rationalize why it is important to learn. At the end of the documentary *Affluenza*, a list of preventive actions is given and one of those actions is teaching our children that money and material possessions are not going to fill their inner self with happiness. Happiness is found in **voluntary simplicity** and a better family life.

Since I was little, I observed very closely what my siblings and friends did and later decided what I like and dislike about their behavior and tried to incorporate it or avoid it accordingly. If my brother or sister did something that my parents didn't like, I tried to avoid it. In the same way, if they did something that pleased them, I tried to incorporate it into my behavior. I guess that is the advantage of being the youngest in the family. My sister has always been a role model for me and she exemplifies the qualities of a young intelligent woman. When she finished high school, she went on to college with the intention of getting her BA in management. While she was studying, she met a hard-working man, fell in love and decided to obtain her Associate's Degree instead and then married her boyfriend. Pretty soon their first-born child came and soon their second child was born. Although this country influenced my sister, she maintained strong ideologies from the Hispanic culture. The fact that she had her children at a young age and decided to be a housewife instead of a working mom is a good example of her strong Hispanic background. I admire her because she has no trouble with her identity. She sees herself as a Hispanic woman living in this country. Most of her friends are Hispanic and the way she thinks and the food she cooks reflect the way she sees herself. She is a loving mother who spends time with her children, keeps her house clean and neat and always has a warm meal ready for her husband when he comes back from work. In the American culture, she might be criticized for not fulfilling herself as a working mother. But, who says she is not working? Her housework should be considered respectable. This brings to mind an episode when a housewife was asked, what her occupation was, she answered: "Well, I am a chauffeur, a cook, a nurse, an accountant and a teacher." I believe she is right, being a housewife implies tremendous amounts of responsibility and energy. It's not correct to undermine the importance of the work of a housewife for our society and in the same way it is not fair to say that staying home does not fulfill women. I know that my sister is the happiest woman staying home because she can spend time with her children, she can see them grow and she does not feel guilty because she is with her children when they need her the most.

In the movie *Erin Brockovich*, Erin feels good because she has a job and is supporting her family. In her mind, she is doing it for the well being of her children. But, she finds herself emotionally distraught when her boyfriend tells her that her baby girl spoke her first word and she missed it. I think that what made her feel worst was the fact that her little girl's first word was "ball" instead of "mom." It's a very difficult task to juggle work and family especially for a single mother. When Erin's boy was arguing with her as to when she was going to take him to a sporting practice, she answered that she didn't know because she didn't have time. His remark was that in his friend's home, his mom took him to practice. Erin's answer was that his friend had both parents at home; so deciding who was going to take him to practice was not a big deal. Erin was working and managing her family at the same time so it was more difficult for her. Being a single parent is very difficult and I think it carries the same problems that parents have when both work. When Erin is able to earn a salary, she goes out with her children to buy them toys. In a way I think she was making up for the time away from them.

All my life, my family and a close circle of friends have protected me. I have been pampered as the youngest daughter and the youngest sister. I was never expected to be responsible except for school-work. I think that in a way, I was living in a **Matrix,** a world where we think we are in control but we are not. I especially like the scene in the film *The Matrix* where Neo is seen being fed intravenously. He is sleeping, his eyes have never been open, his muscles never been used. He is waking up for the first time. This is how I felt a year and a half ago when my husband and I decided to marry. It was the first time I had to think about getting a job, the first time I was in charge of managing a household, and the first time I had to get up when the alarm went off and not when my mom came into my room to wake me up. And curiously, it was the first time I questioned my role as a woman. During the first few week of marriage, I felt awkward cooking and cleaning the house. I thought to myself, "I have never done this, why am I doing it now?" In part I was doing it because I felt like that was expected of me because I am Hispanic. But, my experience of growing up in the U.S. had led me to believe that I was American and that I didn't have to cook like my sister did, but that it was something to be shared with my husband. I had seen my cousin and her husband, and they both share the responsibility of making breakfast and supper. This is when I realized that my role as a woman was still not completely specified. If I felt that I was a Hispanic woman I shouldn't question why I was cooking. I don't see my sister questioning herself as to why she stayed home and why she cooks. In the same way, I don't see my cousin questioning why she goes to work and why she leaves her daughters with a stranger.

When I'm with the Hispanic community many people ask me, "When are you having a baby? You have been married for a year and a half by now?" But when I'm in the American community, I'm encouraged to stay in school as long as possible because I'm young and it's not time to have children yet. In the same way, my American friends encourage me to teach my husband how to cook because he has to help. But when I talk to my mother, she tells me to prepare delicious food for my husband, to take care of him and to keep my house nice and clean. **Dorothy Smith** says "the very organization of the world that has been assigned to us as the primary locus of our being, shaping our projects and desires, is determined by and subordinate to the relations of society founded in a capitalist mode of production" (Farganis 380). I believe she is right about how women's consciousness under capitalism is often **bifurcated** due to the works done at home and work. In my case, this bifurcation is exacerbated by the pull of the different cultural traditions as well. I think I have been assigned two organizations of the world or two societies that have shaped who I am, that influence what I do and what I want. I have been influenced by two different societies and cultures and each pulls me in a different way. The fact that I'm still going to school and that I'm postponing motherhood is an indicator of the strong influence by the American culture. On the other hand, getting married at the age of twenty says a lot about the influence of my Hispanic heritage. It is very difficult for my American friends to understand why I got married so young. In this society, this is the time when young women are supposed to be having fun and going out. It's not a time when young women have to be responsible. When my husband told his friends about my age, everybody told him not to get married. They didn't know me but they knew that at twenty most women are not willing to seriously commit in a relationship. In this case, I think that my Hispanic background has helped me not to fall in the **stereotype** of the twenty-year-old woman. Now that his friends and coworkers know me, they realize that I'm not a party girl but a mature woman.

I also have an ethnic dilemma. When someone asks me the question, where are you from? My answer is, I am from Guatemala. But am I really from Guatemala? Does it matter that I have received most of my education and ideology in this country? What makes us to be from this country or the other? Is it that we were born there or that we grew up in that country? I don't have all the answers for those questions. But I do believe that as an immigrant woman I have the option of fully integrating myself to this society or of maintaining my cultural background. This is a central problem for many immigrants who come to this country as young children. I know I'm from Guatemala, but when I talk to my family members in Guatemala, I find that I don't use the same vocabulary they use, I don't have the same accent they have and many of our points of view differ. But then, the same thing happens when I talk to my American friends.

Instead of seeing this as a problem, I have decided to see this as an advantage. By having two cultural backgrounds, I have the opportunity of having a broader sense of the world, two different perspectives. I don't want to give up my cultural background like my cousin did; on the other hand, I don't want to feel alienated by not integrating myself into this culture. The best solution to my dilemma is to accept that I am influenced by two cultures and to try to keep the positive aspects of each culture and integrate them into my life as well as learn from the negative aspects of each culture.

REFERENCES

Dutcher, Jennifer S. (2003) "A precarious Balance: views of a working Mother walking the tightrope." Human Architecture: Journal of the sociology of self-knowledge. Volume II, Number I, Spring.

Heim, P. (2002) "Alien Nation." Human Architecture: Journal of the Sociology of Self-knowledge. Volume I, Number I, Spring.

Hurst, Charles E. (2000). *Living Theory: The Application of Classical Social Theory to Contemporary Life,* Boston: Allyn and Bacon.

Farganis, James. *Readings in sociological Theory: the classical tradition to post-modernism.* 4th edition. McGraw Hill College Division. 1999.

Wallace Ruth, and Alison Wolf. *Contemporary Sociological Theory: Expanding the Classical Tradition.* New Jersey: Prentice Hall, 1999

Wong, William. (2002) "My Asian American Experience" Human Architecture: Journal of the Sociology of Self-Knowledge. Volume I, Number I, Spring.

Films:

"The Matrix." (1999). Warner Brothers.

"Affluenza." (1997). KCTS-Seattle and Oregon Public Broadcasting.

"Billy Elliot." (2000). Universal Pictures.

"Erin Brockovich." (2000). Universal Pictures.

Who are "I"?:
A Sociology of My Traditional, Modern, and Postmodern Selves

Marie Neuner

UMass Boston

It is not something of which I was always afflicted, but only recently, in the last five years, did I begin to question it. It has become more and more challenging for me since I had always believed that I knew myself, my passions, my desires, and my beliefs without reservation, doubt, or hesitation. But despite the years past and my increased education, I have begun to realize that I know little about myself and its composition. Using a **phenomenological** approach, I will treat my inability to strictly adhere to one set of beliefs as a problematic in order to understand why it puzzles me and why I have an urge for change, even if the change proves to be unnecessary. Through this investigation I hope to explore my **self concept** in both personal and global contexts.

In this quest I have begun to view myself in a seemingly uncharacteristic way, a way that invites the notion of inner multiplicity. I have begun to identify myself by accepting and investigating my multiple selves. These newly discovered and emergent selves have complicated my simplistic notions of the self resulting from prior socialization, somewhat confusing my **self-identity**. Is the true "self" a cut and dry construction that displays one personality over the other, founded on solid beliefs, or can the "self" be the sum result of all the various internalized roles, displaying inconsistency? Is admitting to think and feel one way at a given moment but to also think and feel differently about the same issue at another given moment a sign of hypocrisy or of balanced sincerity? I ask these questions, questions that echo the many conflicted thoughts I battle with daily, in order to understand myself more deeply in relation to society and the world.

The critical assessment of the type of woman I want to be and the fashion in which I want to carry out my life and raise my children are issues that I am presented with daily. The questions are chronic, oftentimes disruptive, and begging to be examined and maybe even resolved. Do I want to be a mother and homemaker or a professional woman? Do I want to be the monogamous and loyal wife or the single lover of many? Do I want the simple life in exchange for the complex? Am I conservative or liberal? These questions are easily answered by many, but not by all, and certainly not by me, at least not yet. So, to what can I attribute this discrepancy? Is it a result of my modern upbringing? A traditional quest for balance and harmony in my everyday affairs? Is modern society overwhelming tradition, including in my inner life?

Having grown up in the distinguished Irish-Catholic section of Boston, my family and personal history is steeped in community and custom. My struggle to discover my true self among the many contradictory drives in my life arises from the battle between the traditional and the modern. My parents are happily married and have been so for thirty years. As a child, I attended Catholic school, made my First Holy Communion and received my Confirmation into the Catholic Church as a teenager. I played Catholic Youth Organization (C.Y.O) sports for many years, hung out at local community centers before graduating to the corners, and I never missed a St. Patrick's Day parade. At the same time, however, I did deviate from the norms of my community in many other areas. I have often done things differently than most people of my age in South Boston: for instance, I did not go to a Catholic high school, but chose to go to a public examination school and had a diverse group of friends with varying ethnic and religious backgrounds. I never took Irish-step dancing and never dated anyone from the town; I listened to different (i.e. "**deviant**") genres of music. I enjoyed learning, debate and discussion. I questioned Catholicism and, overall, I was more liberal socially than those in my community. I was never an outcast, however. In fact, I was popular. This popularity kept me in the middle: I was not forced by either side to migrate to one extreme or another.

I was socialized into my community through ritual and custom. Because both of my parents had always been more open-minded than the average person of the town (my mother slightly more than my father), I was fortunate enough to understand that I had choices in regards to my behavior, and I began to analyze and observe the world around me. In my observations of my community, friends, and family life, I realized that because of my moderate nature I could not commit to any solid philosophical position about my life; they always seemed too extreme. Is it because of my less consistent life experiences and thoughts that I am less certain about the woman I am, or the type of woman I want be? I am certainly less certain than my parochial hometown friends who practiced and continue to practice more regularity in their daily routines, teachings, and beliefs, and I am also less certain than my superliberal friends at work and school. So which approach to understanding my life and myself is more useful, the singular or the plural model?

Let me do a brief comparative interpersonal study. Sandy and I are best friends and have been so for at least ten or twelve years. We used to be inseparable, but that changed as we grew older. Sometimes I feel as if she never grew up, as if her growth halted or mine excelled, or both. She is a twenty year old single mother who moves from job to job, living from paycheck to paycheck. She is street smart and tough, a great mom, and unafraid to fight for her honor and that of her loved one. She cares very little for extravagance or flair, but lives day to day and is amazingly content with doing so. At first glance, having a three-year-old daughter at twenty seems outrageous and unconventional, but to Sandy it is customary: she does not believe in abortion. Sandy operates her life through favors-cycles of giving and taking. If it were not for the help she received, financial among others (babysitting, errands, networking, etc.), Sandy could not function in her society. Under modest circumstances, I am more than happy to offer this help, help that has come to be viewed as obligatory in our community.

George Herbert Mead's notion of **symbolic meaning** can help outline this example of an everyday issue that communicates my confused identity. When Sandy calls, the phone rings, and the simple act of it ringing which may mean nothing to another is an extremely telling **"gesture"** to me. Sandy relies on others too greatly for support—ninety percent of the time when the phone rings it is her calling. This gesture has acquired an additional symboling meaning for me. When the phone rings now, I dread answering it because I know that I must come to her aid or defense by somehow providing, giving, or ensuring something. The mere act of the phone ringing, not even the act of Sandy asking for the favor, but simply the phone ringing, ignites a negative response in me. This negative response leaves me feeling confused. On the one hand, I want to be there unconditionally for Sandy with the ability to provide her with whatever possible, but, on the other hand, I selfishly want to spend the time or money I would donate to her on myself. The ambivalent interpersonal allegiance has thus split me into two: for me Sandy does not only exist as an external entity since I have subconsciously internalized her and allowed for her to exist symbolically within me. I am torn between a self that wants to help her and a self that wants to escape her. The conflict arises as a result of the social interaction between these two different selves.

According to Mead, an individual engages in social interaction with him/herself (**self-interaction**) through the practice of "**taking the role of the other**" (Wallace and Wolf, 200). By doing this, he begins to develop and come to know particular selves that are needed to carry out certain roles in particular situations. According to Mead, there are two phases of the self: an "I" phase and a "Me" phase. The **"I" phase** is subjective and displays innovation and creativity resulting from less constrictive social interactions. It is unorganized, spontaneous, and represents the part of the self that is impulsive. The **"Me" phase** of the self is an affected object. It is shaped by social forces and has a more organized and concrete set of ideas based on the assumed attitudes of others in society. The "Me" phase of the self is more easily influenced by others' ideas and assumes certain viewpoints based on the perspectives and habits of others. So, following Mead's notion, my "Me" selves are conflicted too, each having both traditional and modern beliefs reflecting the conflict existing in the society at large. In the example above, my caring and avoiding "Me" selves associated with Sandy and unconventionality are expressions of my traditional and modern (individualistic) selves. So is this split common, necessary, detrimental? If detrimental, is there an "I" in me that can help bridge this gap?

Mead attributes the development of these multiple selves to social self-interaction and taking the role of the other. Through this interaction we are able to undertake certain roles and see how we view ourselves in them. If we are aware of this process, we can ultimately decide if we feel comfortable in those specific roles and either accept or reject them. A basic example of this idea can be noticed in our everyday "mood swings." When someone has a dramatic shift in mood or disposition, it can be seen as an emergent self attempting to oppress the preexisting self. My swinging from caring self to avoiding self, somewhat representative of traditional and modern values in society, is a good illustration of this mood swing.

In the film *Twelve Angry Men* Henry Fonda's character puts himself in the shoes of the elderly witness to the defendant's alleged murder of his father, in order to test the old man's account of the situation. He maps out the distance, walks with a limp, and discovers that it would have taken the old man at least 40 seconds to walk from the bedroom to the downstairs front door, which is inconsistent with his testimony of roughly 15 seconds. Other characters continue to take the role of the other by "supposin'" they were the one on trial. **Self-interaction** is important in this film because it displays how each character begins to understand himself more deeply after having viewed himself as an other. It is inferred and can be assumed that the jurors who were more convinced of the defendant's guilt but who later changed their votes had to battle with their own many multiple selves.

I too am able to better understand myself in regards to my community by reminding myself of my prior self-interactions and taking the roles of others. I would undertake various roles like "the bully," "the tough chick," "the unquestioningly loyal friend," and "the racist," all prominent traditional features of my community that did not come naturally to me because my home environment did not produce or perpetuate them. By reflecting on such self-interactions I am able to conclusively know that I was not the bully, I was not the tough chick, I was not the racist, and I was not always going to be blindly loyal to a friend if I disagreed with the specific circumstances or her motivations. Seeing myself in an unfavorable light was difficult, but helped me define those things that I am not.

As a child though, it was sometimes difficult to stand up to opposition, and though I would never join in anything of which I did not believe, I would condone it for fear of reprisal or opposition. Though I was unaware, the process Charles Cooley called the **looking-glass self** may have contributed to the perpetuation of my behavior. I did come to view myself based on the imagined perceptions of others: I believed I had to act in one or another way towards Sandys of the world in order to be accepted in this or another community. According to Berger and Luckmann, "the self is a reflected entity, reflecting the attitudes first taken by significant others toward it" (Charon, 35). My **primary socialization** contributed to my strong social bond and, when my unconventional self acted peculiarly in response to other social pressures, it forced me to ask, "Do they think I'm different? Strange? Disloyal?"

Patricke Heine (1971) explains that, sociologically speaking, identity crisis has much to do with social setting, explaining that "modern society presents us with many possibilities of role and identification… that the core of the problem is related to successful internalization…[that] in the presence of choice, there is an incapacity to choose, in the presence of decision, indecisiveness" (Heine, 140). Erving Goffman's **dramaturgical theory** incorporates the idea of social setting as a theater by asking us to view our everyday social interactions with others as if we were actors on stage. He suggests that we project those images of ourselves that we want to be seen and remembered by others. As a child I gradually learned to absorb a sense of the **generalized other** through **primary** and **secondary socializations**; but, despite having also a sense of my own identity without the need of another person to act as reflecting board, I sometimes felt the need to project a safe image of myself that would not reveal my strangeness or contrasting viewpoints that were in conflict with the traditional **norms** of the society that I had been raised in. Conversely, in situations where my unconventional self would have been the norm, I felt the need to keep hidden my conventional self. This process of hiding particular selves is well illustrated in "The Drinking Matrix: A Symbolic Self Interaction" (2003), when Neo Morpheus describes how "we… try to block out and alter our selves to deal with some sort of pain" (Morpheus, 13). The urge to dramaturgically keep my opinions and opposing beliefs hidden was not always easy to do, but oftentimes necessary in order to eliminate any potential pain that might arise as the result of being labeled a 'deviant' or a conformist.

Rational Choice theorist James Coleman explains how families play a major role in socializing children and establishing the norms of society. His concept of **social capital** focuses on aspects of society that allow individuals to achieve certain things more easily or more effectively. Strong familial bonds can be a type of social capital and Coleman, like Durkheim, worries that the long-term ability of society to maintain cohesion and enforce social norms is in jeopardy, especially with the decline of the family as the primary agent of socialization (Wallace and Wolf, 361). **Exchange Theory** proposes that individuals enter into relationships based on the perceived benefit to them. Sandy approaches me because she perceives the possibility of gaining some

extrinsic benefit from our interaction. My traditional "Sandy" self would like to help her, perhaps simply for **intrinsic benefits** in return. However, my unconventional non-Sandy self, seeing no extrinsic rewards in return, shuns Sandy. The conflicted family life that Sandy was socialized into did not allow her the opportunity that I was afforded to find or create an unconventional "I" self, the self that broke boundaries and did things differently. Sandy was physically, verbally and emotionally abused by her mother prior to her parents' divorce. The partnerships that she has since established, including her partnership with me, work to her benefit because she is now continually supported. The inner conflict of my traditional and modern selves is an expression of the clash between traditional and modern modes of exchange, of "rational" action. The inner conflict I have in regards to the external Sandy is perhaps itself a result of the conflict between traditional and modern lifestyles and their respective "**dysfunctions**" in society.

I had often viewed this conflict in myself as a weakness. It seemed that indecision was the only reality I could depend on. My conflicted identity was a pressing issue on the forefront of my everyday affairs and often still is. It can be observed in my quest to choose a political party, my decision to remain single or in a committed relationship, and it is alive in the battle between duty and pleasure. Does **labeling theory** explain why I feel compelled to make a decision—i.e., to avoid being labeled by one community or other as being different? Yes, it is more likely that labeling theory is the reason why it has become impossible to make that decision. Nobody wants to be viewed as deviant by their peers. Thus, if my traditional and conservative friends sensed any deviance on my part from their strict beliefs they would label me as deviant. But, if I allowed myself to conform by applying a particular self to fit the particular situation, I would not be labeled as such.

Despite the detriment to personal well-being that dramaturgy as a theory in action can cause, by doing this throughout childhood, adolescence, and even today, I was and am not held to certain convictions or dogmatic beliefs. My views of myself and society thereby become fluid and always changing.

The PBS documentary *Affluenza* warns American consumers that they themselves are being consumed by the unhealthy cycle of earning and spending that our modern *capitalist* society creates. It asks consumers to consider an alternate lifestyle by practicing voluntary simplicity and reverting back to more traditional and customary living arrangements and behaviors through the desertion of the unhealthy, modern, and complex lifestyle. The documentary illustrates how some American families, realizing the harmful effects of the rigid consumer-lifestyle, have begun to live together in small familial communities, sharing food, water, chores and pastimes. *Modernity* is viewed as a threat to society and tradition, pushing more and more Americans away from each other and into seclusion.

The documentary addresses the American family and stresses one of the most pressing issues in regards to the battle among tradition, modernity, and post-modernity. I dream to one day have a large, loving family, but I often wonder if that can be achieved in a society that values individualism over community, *Gesellschaft* over *Gemeinschaft*. I have a large extended family, but only two brothers. What if they decide not to marry or have children? Where are my children's cousins? Where is their sense of family, community, and love that I was so fortunate to grow up with? Will their socialization into society be markedly different from my own?

Why is *pluralism* and heterogeneity subconsciously avoided in American society despite the conscious respect for the "melting pot"? Is sitting on the fence a sign of weakness? Are you perceived to be a stronger and more powerful individual if you conform and stick to one set of beliefs without faltering? Catholicism is a religion guided by *metanarratives*, universal truths or habituated structures of thinking: "I believe in one God, the Father Almighty, Creator of heaven and earth, and in Jesus Christ, His only Son, our Lord" (The Apostle's Creed). I have been influenced heavily by this *tradition* where 'apparent' unfailing and divine truths have been revealed to humankind. But aside from my religious upbringing, my daily life is full of these presumed truths about society, from epistemological ideas about what constitutes knowledge, to popular medicine, to ideals of beauty and fashion, and politics. In "Repairing The Soul: Matching Inner Beauty with Outer Beauty" (2002), Kristy Canfield explains how the *social construction of reality*, the taken-for-granted realities that are constructed by television, media, and peer groups among others, made it possible for her to believe that she was inferior to others because of her speech impairment, enabling her low self esteem to flourish (Canfield, 25). By feeling compelled to choose one "self" and one identity over others, am I oppressing myself by perpetuating society's oppressive ideas about universal truths? When we believe in these metanarratives are we imprisoning ourselves in a *carceral society* that Foucault described?

According to Paulo Freire, to be fully human is to live "in an incessantly liberatory process of intersubjective dialogical praxis, of united critical reflection and applied action" (Tamdgidi, 5). Since I can be regarded as oppressed by certain structures of society that place emphasis on labels, categories, and 'sides,' it seems as if my traditional and modern selves are battling each other to imposed themselves on one another, thus, in certain situations, both selves becoming oppressed and oppressive in the I/Me cycles of everyday life. *Reification* suggests that society often forgets its own ability to author and re-author itself because it has come to view certain societal structures as firm and fixed. Because I now understand that I can be creative and that I have choices in regards to my beliefs or disbeliefs, my old sense of conflict is transforming into a new sense of equilibrium. I no longer feel compelled to choose a singular drive. Given the dialogical interaction I have had with my selves and others and my critical reflection of it, the only practical action I can take is to accept the multiplicity of my self-concept. To be compelled to choose either tradition or modernity is oppressive and non-liberating, and understanding that I do not have to choose allows me to feel more free.

The same idea of oppression is further illustrated in the movie *The Matrix* when the machines destroy society by breeding human beings into slavery in order to nourish the development of their own civilization. The matrix world eliminated altogether human beings' ability to function to their full capacity. In the matrix world humans were unable to think critically about their enslavement and take practical steps to liberate themselves from oppression, mentally and physically. Like Neo I need to awaken to my oppression by metanarratives of tradition and modernity, engage in dialogue with others and myself, and seek critically and practically to do something about it—tough I realize that full liberation requires similar actions by all in society. According to Freire, "the oppressed realize, or should begin to realize, that they can only liberate themselves by liberating the whole humanity" (Tamdgidi, 7).

The *postmodern* attitude allows tensions to exist among multiple modes of knowing and liberates one from the pressures that mount when forced to make a choice between two apparent truths. Thus, in order to remove impediments against imaginative exercises of social interaction, we must practice more "open systems" in regards to individual thought and action (Farganis, 443). ***Relativism*** is an essential component to the postmodern theory. As stated by Jean-Francois Lyotard, "Postmodern knowledge... refines our sensitivity to differences and reinforces our ability to tolerate the incommensurable" (Farganis, 435). Because postmodernists see reality as a social construct, there are no universal truths to adhere to, and human beings are free to investigate, explore, and invent without the authoritarian limitations of ***Bureaucratic*** society.

A perfect current example of the freedom provided by a postmodern approach in a global context can be illustrated through a historical overview of the computer operating system, Linux. Linux was created by Linus Torvalds in 1991 when the problematic Minix, a UNIX operating system (OS), was denied modification for improvement by its creator, Allen Tanenbaum. Though the concept of "free software" had been advocated by MIT's Richard Stallman since the early 1970's, Linux created a revolution. When Torvalds created the Linux "kernel," or original main component of an OS, he posted it on a message board on the Internet and asked other computer programmers to contribute to what is now the largest global collaborative project in history. There are thousands of different distributions or versions of Linux that cater to an array of particular user needs, making it more versatile, reliable, stable, and cost effective. The open source revolution has those at the oppressive, closed-source, mega-corporation Microsoft worried about its future. Linux, the not-for-profit business endeavor, has created a new era in computing, because "the Linux user are not just a passive subject reacting to what the OS lets you do but an active 'developer' [who] can mold the OS to what you want" (Linux Online). Lyotard discusses a similar idea in his "The Post-Modern Condition: A Report on Knowledge" when he describes science as a model of an 'open system,' stating that when there is a division in the scientific community between decision makers and executors a major obstacle is in fact impeding the development of knowledge (Farganis, 443).

In the film *Billy Elliot*, Billy was able to free himself from oppressive patterns in his **class** and ***gender socialization*** and expectations by rejecting the norms of his culture and embracing difference and modification. He was socialized to believe that boys must traditionally play games such as boxing. Because Billy wanted to dance ballet many people also assumed that he was homosexual. Billy disproved and resisted such social ***stereotypes***. His rejection of the oppressive and traditional role of boxer enabled him to experience freedom in choosing his career. Postmodernism also plays a part in the film *Erin Brockovich*. Erin needed to balance her family life with her career. The dialectical convergence of these two generally opposite lifestyles, the family representing tradition and the career representing modernity, crossed boundaries and faded into one another. The balanced lifestyle is an increasingly desired characteristic in postmodern society. Erin's challenge in the film, or in her real life, was to find a way to balance the two rather than be forced to choose one over the other.

For me, seeking the postmodern means seeking freedom from the urge to make impossible decisions between dualized pathways, freedom to think and act according to diverse selves in diverse social settings. Postmodernism deconstructs society's constructed realities, not to prove them impossible, but to prove that anything possible. Though some deconstructive interpretations of postmodernity suggest that the theory is a denouncement of both tradition and modernity in favor of neither, I believe in a **constructive postmodernist** approach that is open to all that has come before it. I agree with the view that "this type of postmodernism is not simply antimodern, since it is not calling for a return to the premodern, nor is it rejecting rational, enlightened thought; it arises as a response to the threats posed for humanity—and, indeed for the survival of our world—in the face of modernism's materialistic epistemology and its negation of the spiritual and ecological impulses of [the] human being" (Thoday 2004). Freedom from social oppression in politics, from bureaucracy, from stereotypes, from norms, and from assumed truths can revitalize society. Constructive postmodernity allows us to reclaim our power as creative beings of praxis that can facilitate *social change* and experience true freedom in both personal and global contexts.

References:

Canfield, Kristy. (2002). "Repairing the Soul: Matching Inner beauty with Outer Beauty." *Human Architecture: Journal of the Sociology of Self-Knowledge*, I, 2, 20-26.

Charon, Joel M, ed. (1999). *The Meaning of Sociology: A Reader.* Sixth Edition. New Jersey: Prentice Hall.

Farganis, James. (2004). *Readings in Social Theory: The Classic Tradition to Post-Modernism.* Fourth Edition. Boston: McGraw Hill Inc.

Heine, Patricke Johns. (1971). *Personality in Social Theory.* Chicago: Aldine Publishing Company.

Locher, David. (1999). "Unacknowledged Roots and Blatant Imitation: Postmodernism and the Dada Movement." *Electronic Journal of Sociology.*

Morpheus, Neo. (2003). "The Drinking Matrix: A Symbolic Interaction." *Human Architecture: Journal of the Sociology of Self-Knowledge*, II, 1, 12-18.

Tamdgidi, Mohammad H. "Freire Meets Gurdjieff and Rumi: Towards the Pedagogy of the Oppressed and Oppressing Selves." University of Massachusetts, Boston, April 7, 2004.

Thoday, Kim. "Constructive Postmodernism." *John Mark Ministries.* May 4, 2004.

"Getting Started with Linux: Lesson One." (2004). Linux Online, Inc. May 2, 2004. <http://www.linux.org /lessons/beginner/index.html>

May 9, 2004. <http://www.sociology.org/content/vol004.001/locher.html>

<http://www.pastornet.net.au/jmm/articles/11621.htm>

Films:

"The Matrix." (1999). Warner Brothers.

"Affluenza." (1997). KCTS-Seattle and Oregon Public Broadcasting.

"Billy Elliot." (2000). Universal Pictures.

"Erin Brockovich." (2000). Universal Pictures.

My Life's Tapestry:
Casting Theoretical Lights on the Social Threads That Tie Me Down

D. M. Rafferty

UMass Boston

I view my life as a large and ever changing tapestry. I am cut from a bolt of very strong, durable, and coarse working class material. Being born female certainly factored into the pattern of this design. However, woven deeply in my foundation are also threads of limitation resulting from the classist and sexist attitudes that still persist in today's society. Socio-economic **class** and **gender** roles constitute the two most influencing social **stratifications** that have shaped the outlines of my life. Reviewing personal experiences in light of the classical, contemporary, and postmodernist theories in sociology will hopefully reveal new hues and textures in the ever changing tapestry that is my life.

My mother dropped out of high school during her senior year to help financially support her siblings. Her mother had run off and left my mother, her younger sisters and brothers with their aging paternal grandmother. Working as a clerk in a department store my mother helped raise her sisters and brothers.

My father was her first boyfriend. They were married on my mother's eighteenth birthday and a month before my father's eighteenth birthday. My father, also in his senior year, quit school. Working to support his new bride became a priority. My brother was born seven months later. I was the second child of June and Joe Rafferty born thirteen months and eight days after my brother.

My parents assumed the traditional social roles of husband and wife. My mother was to maintain a clean and orderly household, assume full responsibility for the children, and provide for all my father's needs. My father was to work and financially support his family. Unknowingly true to the **theory of Functionalism,** my parents believed that their interdependent roles provided the best avenue for achieving shared goals and desires.

Owning a home in the "burbs" was their ultimate dream. Sending my brother to college was also a goal. It was believed that higher education was for the males because they would have to provide for a family of their own someday. The goals that were set for me were far different. I was to graduate from high school, get married, and have children—hopefully in that order. And I was supposed to be happy and fulfilled with that **functional role**.

Moving to the suburbs meant providing a better life and better choices for their children. To my father it also meant moving out of the working-class lot to a more acceptable middle-class life-style. My father was well aware of the increasingly polarized **class structure** that we lived under. He claimed to be fueled by justifiable working-class anger. He often spoke of the inequitable services that our social institutions doled out. Affordable housing, quality education and decent health-care should be the right of every citizen and not benefits that only some can afford.

My father was an activist. He campaigned for political candidates that he believed would make a difference. He recognized social ills and strived to correct them. I listened to my father and took on some of his perspectives. His truth became the beginning point for my personal **stock of knowledge** at hand. I began to form my opinions based on what my father said. My perspectives of society and life in general were viewed through a poor working-class lens. To this day my life experiences have only reinforced some of these beliefs.

Unfortunately my parents' goals were never realized. When my father was thirty-three years old he had an aneurysm burst at the base of his skull. His brain was submerged in a pool of blood. The necessary life saving surgery left him partially paralyzed and with brain damage. For years he was in and out of hospitals, mental institutes, and various training programs. As the dutiful wife my mother now had to arrange her schedule to include daily hospital visits. Visiting hours were 2-4 and 7-9 in the afternoon. It was by their gender-hued "**rational choice**" that I was determined to be the one excused from school early to enable my mother to meet the strict visiting policy of the hospital. Watching my younger siblings and preparing supper became my responsibilities. When my mother returned from the afternoon visit, supper was on the table by 4:45 p.m.; at 5:30 p.m. the table was being cleared. My mother would spend about an hour with the younger children while I cleaned up the kitchen. Then she was off for the evening visits with my father. My domestic duties would end when I put the children to bed. This pattern of **anticipatory socialization** was preparing me for my future roles as housewife and mother. At that time my brother moved in with my aunt so he could continue to dedicate his time to his studies. He was in his junior year at an exam school preparing for college.

When the insurance ran out and all social services were exhausted my father was sent home. And there he remained. He stopped going out. He stopped washing. He stopped getting dressed. He stopped eating properly. He sat around all day and night in his dirty underwear and robe, smoking cigarettes, drinking coffee, and watching T.V. He became verbally abusive to anyone within earshot and physically abusive toward my mother and younger siblings. I became my family's protector. I made my father fear me.

Being raised in Roxbury, a working-class ghetto in the city of Boston, prepared me for this **role**. I was fourteen years old and a ninth grade student at a Boston public junior high school. I had street smarts and was considered quite wise for my age. I knew life wasn't easy and sometimes you had to fight for your rights.

After living on the "house savings" for two years my family was forced to go on welfare. At that time it was called "Aid to Financially Dependent Children" (AFDC). Although most of our neighbors were also "living on the system" my mother felt degraded. She never thought this could happen to her. She was thirty-three years old, a high school drop out, and the mother of four. Depression set in. The women in my neighborhood were very supportive of one another.

The **blasé** attitude in the metropolitan lifestyle that Simmel speaks of (Farganis, 132) somehow did not exist in the mid-sixties on the streets of Roxbury where I grew up. Due to the obvious lack of money my neighbors created a rather tight community. The "**reciprocal relations, or exchange, within social associations**" (Farganis, 263) was a daily phenomena. My mother's girlfriends watched my younger siblings so my mother could run some errands. Running errands was a valid excuse to get out of the house for a while. In exchange my mother would pick up things like milk or bread that one of the neighbors may have needed. They drank tea and listened to one another. The **intrinsic rewards** resulting from such exchanges of solidarity added texture to my life's tapestry.

The Federal Government had a food

program. On the fifteenth of each month most families in my neighborhood would walk down to a storefront at Roxbury Crossing. There they would collect staples such as butter, peanut butter, cheese, corn meal, oat meal and canned meat. You could not pick and choose. You had to take it all or you would receive nothing. The food was passed out by a couple of white men in shirts and ties. There was a noticeable difference between us. They became our **generalized others** for they represented "the system," the government. They also represented white middle-class America, a sector of the population that saw us as less than them. They spoke to each other about wanting to beat the traffic out of the city. They were concerned about their cars that were parked unattended in the back lot. They barked orders at my neighbors, the children and my mother as we lined up to receive our rations. The way they spoke to us and treated us led some of my neighbors to feel ashamed.

My mother would hold my hand a little tighter and assure my siblings and I that there was no need to feel badly. "Your father and both of your grandfathers worked for years and paid into the system. This program is here for people who have fallen on hard times. We need some help and the social welfare is here to aid us," my mother would say. We refused to accept the social attitudes of the generalized others. But we all **internalized** them nevertheless.

When Max Weber speaks of the **capitalist** and **bureaucratic** forces that "oppress and dominate individuals in modern society" (in Hurst 39) I immediately think of the food program and those state workers. Durkheim's vision of a more enlightened society where there was a common humanity (Hurst 28), the belief that we are all part of something interconnected and greater than ourselves was certainly lacking in the **collective conscience** of these social workers.

My grandfather used to say, "How you view an issue all depends on where you sit." It seemed the dominant view in Roxbury proclaimed that if you had two parents living at home, your father had a job and you attended a parochial school you were definitely a better person than one who was raised by a single mother, or on welfare and attended a public school. These factors were major contributors to how one was seen. They determined your **social worth**.

Attending public schools, it was not uncommon to run out of paper before the school year was even half-way through. New books were not the norm. Sharing old, tattered books with your classmates was very common. In my elementary school if you lost the two pencils you were given at the beginning of the school year you were destined to finish the year writing in crayon. Of course points were lost when your penmanship was illegible.

During my junior high school graduation the principle began his address by announcing that, "this would probably be the last graduation for more than half of you." This attitude and the limited amount of extended **social capital** damaged many young people's psyche. However it strengthened my ribbon of resolve.

Recognizing **unequal opportunities** in education at an early age gives me a deeper understanding of the **iron cage** that Max Weber spoke of (Farganis 91). The bureaucracy continues to support public education with real estate taxes. Although this has proven to be grossly unfair it continues. We are trapped in this cage despite our intelligence and creativity. Ironically, it is the educational system that hinders our individual advancement. While charter schools, parochial schools, montessory schools and other privately funded schools prosper, our urban public schools continue to disintegrate. This certainly leads to conflict among the masses. This conflict should be dealt with in the political arena. For this is a perfect example of what Jean Jacques

Rousseau calls "**moral or political inequality**" when he discusses the "two kinds of inequality among the human species" (Farganis 2). Yet having the same types of politician (rich, white men) as our candidates of choice I'm not certain peaceful change is possible. Perhaps Marx's **social revolution** is yet to come.

In her essay, "The Struggles and Predicaments of Low Income Families and Children in Poverty" (2002) Jennifer VanFleet shares her perspective of the low income families in her hometown. She speaks of a family that lives in an old ice cream stand in the middle of town and how they scrounge through other peoples' garbage looking for things that could serve them. She states that "some people like this don't want to help themselves or are happy living the way they are." (39) This young woman from a middle-class family is attending college to become a social worker and help people like this. Reading her essay I was very sensitive to her perspective of the "low-income families and children in poverty" that she hoped someday to help. It appeared to me that she was viewing them as a **stereotyped** generalized other, devoid of first hand knowledge and understanding about why people live as they do. However this is very common. It is definitely a perspective that must be changed in order to bring about significant changes in the social services industry that she someday hopes to serve. Realizing that we are all members of the same society is a good first step toward achieving a more **equitable society**. We live in a country that maintains an hourly wage that keeps people below the **poverty line** when they work forty or more hours a week. Poor working class people who are unable to secure better paying jobs for a multitude of reasons take what they can get or not. This is their choice. This is their "iron cage," a non-living **minimum wage policy** legislated by the Federal Government. And today's iron cage also has a "glass ceiling," a silent understanding commonly held among top executives at large corporations that limit the advancement of women beyond a certain level.

As a young, divorced mother of two I spent a brief period of time accepting Transitional Aid (TA). That was the current name for AFDC. During that stint I had several social workers that were very well intentioned. However they were not prepared for the lack of support the government provides for poor people. They were not prepared for the anger and defeat that are common emotions for families that have suffered through generations of poverty. They were not prepared for the deep rooted depression that many poor people suffer. **Phenomenologically** speaking, as the client of several young, white, idealistic case workers I witnessed on a daily basis their burn out. In a matter of months they became totally disillusioned and discouraged because their college degrees did not prepare them for the reality of the injustices committed within the **social constructs** of the welfare system.

Henry Fonda starring in *Twelve Angry Men*, a movie made in 1957, was the only juror who had a reasonable doubt concerning the guilt of the defendant, a young, poor, non-white boy from the slums who had been charged with the stabbing death of his father. In his quiet manner Fonda managed to change the minds of the other eleven jurors. All he did was continue to recall the evidence and the facts of the case. **Prejudices** and preconceived notions were addressed and questioned until finally all the twelve men concluded that the possibility of innocence did in fact exist. The inability to form an **objective** opinion hindered the jurors. Initially they were operating from a purely **subjective** base. One man viewed all people from "that part of town" as "those people" while another man had a bad relationship with his son and projected those negative feelings on all young men around the age of his son. Perhaps if more people took the time to critically re-evaluate the **"shared values"** and beliefs that were handed down to them society could more quickly evolve toward another period of enlightenment.

"Inadequate Programs Assisting Mothers in Poverty" written by Jessica Udice (2002) begins to question the programs that our government established to supposedly help women and children out of poverty. She speaks about the work program that is to aid in the transition of stay-at-home moms to working-moms. There is little to no support in the way of child care, affordable after school programs or even transportation vouchers to get the children home from school or the mothers to work. The anger that some people feel towards welfare mothers and their children is touched upon in this essay. The feelings of shame, guilt, despair and low self-esteem that welfare mothers experience are also addressed. Udice ends her paper with some worthwhile ideas about alternative programs that could and should be better supported.

When Rousseau wrote about the social inequalities and class privilege that should have changed when science became the "critical instrument in the pursuit of truth" (Farganis 2) did he realize how deeply rooted the aristocracy was in the constructs of social reality that he criticized? Here we are in the twenty-first century still being governed predominately by white, upper-class men practicing patriarchal beliefs and establishing a capitalist, profit-driven, value system.

When Morpheus claims in the movie *The Matrix* that, "This is the construct, Neo, residual self imagining. Free your mind! Unplug!", I believe there is an element of truth in that statement. Questioning what you see is the theme of this film. If **self** is a "social product" as Mead claims it is (Farganis 144) how can the truth be determined about our "self" living in a society that constantly gestures falsely. What societal constructs support equality for the masses? America is considered the land of equal opportunity, but our native tongue is double speak. We must "unplug" to get in touch with our true "self."

Then we have the film *Billy Elliot*, in which a young boy who knows what he wants to be is ready to do almost anything to make that dream his reality. He is a coal miner's son who wants to become a ballet dancer. This is definitely not the **norm**. In this two hour film the young, motherless boy is able to overcome all sorts of prejudices from town folks as well as his father and brother. Due to sheer determination, perseverance and belief in himself Billy achieves his ultimate dream. Movies are enjoyable because they are an escape from our everyday reality.

In "A Precarious Balance: Views of a Working Mother Walking the Tightrope" (2003), Jennifer S. Dutcher shares with us her ever changing views as a woman who became a mother, a student, an employee and a wife. Dutcher shares that maintaining traditional roles has worked for her and her husband. Gender-based roles determine who cooks, cleans and provides most of the child care. She admits that most of the domestic work is her responsibility. She also speaks of the **bifurcation of consciousness** that she experiences daily. When she is at the office her mind is sometimes busy with other functions that need to be tended to at home. This working consciousness as described by Dorothy Smith (Farganis 375) is very common among women. Dutcher ends her essay recognizing some changes that could be made on her domestic front that would make her life easier but all in all she is happy and successful in all her roles. I believe self-reflection and constant re-evaluating are necessary steps for self actualization.

Erin Brockovich is a movie about a self actualized woman. Here is an extraordinary story about a woman who started out unemployed, penniless, and stressed out. She is a single, working-class mother of three desperately seeking employment and feeling more like a loser with every rejected job offer. Hollywood portrayed Brockovich as a provocative dresser with a quick temper and a foul mouth. She uses creative license to plant herself as an employee in a lawyer's office as a last ditch attempt to find meaningful work. The lawyer breaks down and gives her the job and so the story begins. The main theme of this movie is how an average person can overcome multiple odds, make a difference and become rich and famous. Brockovich becomes the driving force that finally brings down a large gas company that was slowly poisoning hundreds of families. With a multi-million dollar settlement everyone lives happily ever after.

Subliminally the movie reinforces the gendered notion that women take better care of others than we do of ourselves. During the entire movie all the star ate was fast food. She worked long hours and didn't get enough sleep. Her relationships with her children and boyfriend suffered miserably. In one scene her son is angry at her for working so much. She patiently tells him how she's helping all these sick people. The little boy doesn't care and is still mad because all he knows is that his mother isn't around as much as she used to be. He's not interested in her other roles. He just wants his mother. The "mother" realizes this but feels there is nothing she can do. It is this **gendered social structure** that causes the bifurcation of consciousness that most mothers are familiar with. Until society starts taking the raising of children seriously and our government starts providing more affordable, good quality day-care, better educational opportunities, and a more supportive social welfare system women will continue to suffer socially and psychologically.

"Bureaucracy is the means of transforming social action into rationally organized action. Therefore, as an instrument of rationally organizing authority relations, bureaucracy was and is a power instrument of the first order for one who controls the bureaucratic apparatus." states Max Weber in a piece titled "The Objective and Subjective Bases of Bureaucratic Perpetuity" (Farganis 105). But as far as class and gender are concerned, we seem to be still continuing to follow our forefather's **charismatic** and/or **traditional authority**. We are still being governed and controlled by the patricians. I believe education, and not **rational-bureaucratic authority**, is the first step to improving the human condition.

Inequities that presently exist are there for reasons that were best expressed by Wallace and Wolf (1999:82) when detailing the three propositions that lay at the foundation of Marx's **class conflict theory**. The first is that people of the same economic position will support one another. The second states that economic classes are the most important groups as their history has shaped the history of human society. And last is that these groups are mutually antagonistic. I believe our government perpetuates these class conditions. By experience I have learned to distinguish between classes by the benefits bestowed. In my neighborhood there was a belief that you could tell from a person's teeth where he stood in terms of class. If he had straight, nice white teeth he must have money because dentists cost money. The only work my neighborhood dentist did was fill or pull. Medical attention was costly, health insurance was a benefit most of my working neighbors did not have. So it had to be something extreme to generate a visit to the dentist or doctor's office. Health care, in other words, was a class issue. It pulled at my threads of injustice.

Patriarchy and class systems separate people and divide society. Believing that there is not enough wealth to go around creates an atmosphere of fear. That fear is passed down to us through various media. And that fear fuels capitalism. "The more things we possess the happier we'll be" is a common way of thinking. So we buy and buy and buy but we are not any happier. We are only deeper in debt. The film *Affluenza* illustrated this very well. It was interesting to see the anti-commercials that a group of activists had created which graphically portrayed how our greed was detrimental to our planet. They talked about how much trash and garbage our nation creates and the uncreative ways we use to dispose of it. Yet none of the major television stations would run the anti-commercials because their message did not support capitalism.

As I am learning more about social theory and all the concepts that we covered this semester I am pleased to be able to bring language to action. Having recognized and applied the six major perspectives of sociological theory, I believe that social change can best be made by one's own example. Working to create alternatives to the patriarchal and class systems that governs us is a worthy cause. I believe our power begins in the personal realm. As I have grown, I have changed. Raising consciousness has broadened my perspectives. I choose my issues carefully and decide where I will use my time and energy. Social theory helps me make those decisions. "Things don't change, we do" is a well known platitude that also helps me make worthy decisions. With education people can modify their behavior and that is an action that certainly produces change. It is our responsibility to make quality education affordable for the people if we are to reach our full potential as human beings. Our elected officials should fully support higher education and lobby for the necessary funding to support a class "A" education system. Social theory needs to be a necessary part of that education because it helps us, by exercising our **sociological imaginations**, to understand the tapestries of our selves and broader society in relationship to one another—"if we can name it we can change it."

The tapestry of my life has been enriched and strengthened with the new language and understanding of social theory that I have gained.

REFERENCES

Dutcher, Jennifer. (2003). "A Precarious Balance: Views of a Working Mother Walking the Tightrope," *Human Architecture: Journal of the Sociology of Self-Knowledge*, Vol. II, No. 1, Spring. Endicott, NY: OKCIR.

Farganis, James. (2000). *Readings in Social Theory: The Classic Tradition to Post-Modernism*. Third Edition. Boston: McGraw Hill.

Hurst, Charles E. (2000). *Living Theory: The Application of Classical Social Theory to Contemporary Life*, Boston: Allyn and Bacon.

Udice, Jessica (2002). "Inadequate Programs Assisting Mothers in Poverty," *Human Architecture: Journal of the Sociology of Self-Knowledge*, Vol. I, No. 1, Spring. Endicott, NY: OKCIR.

VanFleet, Jennifer. (2002). "The Struggles and Predicaments of Low Income Families and Children in Poverty," *Human Architecture: Journal of the Sociology of Self-Knowledge*, Vol. I, No. 1, Spring. Endicott, NY: OKCIR.

Wallace, R and Wolf, A. (1999). *Contemporary Sociological Theory: Expanding the Classical Tradition*. Fifth Edition. New Jersey: Prentice Hall.

Films:

"The Matrix." (1999). Warner Brothers.
"Twelve Angry Men." (1957). MGM.
"Affluenza." (1997). KCTS-Seattle and Oregon Public Broadcasting.
"Billy Elliot." (2000). Universal Pictures.
"Erin Brockovich." (2000). Universal Pictures.

From Alienation to Exploration:
Breaking Free From the Iron Cages of My Life

Annie Roper

UMass Boston

The social experience of **alienation** has affected most of my life. I grew alienated from my core self when I attended Catholic schools and I've been working on changing that ever since. Those rules were hard to live by and they took their toll on my life, leaving me with social scars. I went from living what amounted to a child's **utopian** life to one like prison, where I attended school and met **bureaucracy,** discipline and repression. My imagination was stifled, my creativity crushed, and my expectations became nil.

Alienated and demoralized, I became a factory worker. I smoked pot, worked and drank. I abandoned free thinking for years, repressing memories and drinking and drugging to keep away pain and fear. My social worldview narrowed to tunnel vision—with only a bottle in sight before me. It is only now that I am facing my demons in this paper. I'm allowing my **sociological imagination** a free rein: I'm finally putting my personal troubles into broader perspective in reference to family, society and my place in the world.

My early years were happy and free, basically unrestrained by societal restrictions. We had the benefit of a summer home where I happily played and swam daily with my siblings and many cousins. We jumped into the water when the tide came in and didn't leave the water until the tide went out. We ran barefoot and in bathing suits. We had no hot running water: we hosed off the salt under the outside hose and our parents heated water in the kettle for our Saturday night weekly shampoos. We were a captive audience on Sunday mornings. We had to put on shoes (!) and wear dresses for Catholic Sunday Mass. We sat chafed and bored for the hour or so and then it was back to our freedom.

The patriarchy of the Catholic Church kept the laws for our adult relatives, but we knew who ruled us—our grandmother was our matriarch. The women in our lives were the **dominant authorities** but my grandmother's **gender role** resembled more of a **patriarchy** than a **matriarchy**. She ruled the roost. Everyone knew her as Ma and her authority was well respected. She kept a watchful eye on us all, seeming to know just what every child was up to. Hers was a gentle benevolence: we respected more than feared her. This was the life I knew.

Then came kindergarten. My family was Catholic, bringing us up that way too. One year, when summer had come to an end and we were back in the city, I was sent to kindergarten in a parochial school run by Lithuanian nuns. I believe that I just drifted along with absolutely no idea that my life was about to change drastically. I was just sent there, I didn't get much preparation: I just got a uniform, a white blouse, and a navy blue skirt with matching navy blue knee socks, and navy blue lace up shoes. I went from basically living in a bathing suit with no shoes to being encased in a uniform, my feet being choked in orthopedic style shoes. I went from belonging to one group, family, to instant **domination** by the

authoritarian figures, the larger than life nuns. The worlds in my life changed from one **socially constructed** through my interactions with family, to one constructed by the nuns and the church: my new **subjective reality** was fraught with terror and confusion. My social reality was turned up side down. As Berger and Luckmann put it when defining alienation, I experienced "A loss of meaning: ... a disintegration of the socially constructed knowledge system" (Berger and Luckmann, in Wallace and Wolf, 277).

I vaguely remember some things like enforced nap times, naps on blankets on the floor and saltine crackers for snack time. I mostly remember being shut up in the coat closet for talking. The coat closet was a press where the wooden doors pulled down from the ceiling. I stood in there for I don't know how long with the smell of wool in my nose and surrounded by coats. I stood in that "iron cage" cloakroom experiencing **double consciousness**, a concept which I learned recently from the readings of W.E.B. DuBois; I had to now think of myself in terms of a duality. I knew I was not bad, I really had no idea what had just transpired yet someone in authority was telling me that I was so bad that I needed to be shut away from the other children, shut away from society. I had to separate my child self and the self dictated by society, wondering which one was true. This new society was fraught with confusion: my world had turned upside down. My real "I" was lost in that cloakroom. This was my first lesson in discipline from the nuns and it set the pace for the next eleven years.

The nuns introduced a new order to me; despite being women themselves, they showed none of the love I had previously received from the women in my family. I was trapped in a world where the "I" had no shelter in which to run. Dorothy Smith says it well, "We [as women] began to discover that we lived in a world put together in ways in which we had very little say." (Smith, in Wallace and Wolf, 285). The dominant patriarchal order of the Catholic Church as embodied in the nuns was the antithesis of **feminism.** We were made to study religious **dogma;** the catechism by rote, to not dare question any religious tenets or question authority. they acted like "shortsighted petty bureaucrats." (Weber, in Ritzer and Goodman, 213). **Domination,** a form of authority as described by **Max Weber**, consists of, "The probability that certain specific commands (or all commands) will be obeyed by a specific group of persons" (ibid., 213). The nuns ruled us, and indeed our parents, through both **traditional and charismatic authority**. Traditional authority is that "based on an established belief in the sanctity of immemorial traditions and the legitimacy of those exercising authority under them" (ibid., 213). This, coupled with **charismatic authority** or "authority legitimized by charisma [which] rests on the devotion of followers to the exceptional sanctity, exemplary character, heroism, or special powers of leaders, as well as on the **normative order** sanctioned by them." (ibid., 213) was what our parents, our authority figures, believed. We were, in effect, given over to the authority of the Catholic Church. "The nuns are always right," is what we heard at home: "If the nun says you did wrong, then you did."

Phenomenologically speaking, my whole structure of reality and authority was turned upside-down; the transition from home to school was a terrifying **shock** in my **reality par excellence**. Gone forever was the feeling of safety in that my parents and my grandmother could protect me from everything. I had to believe in the nuns completely in order to survive. In my elementary years I swallowed the Catholic **ideology** whole—hook, line, and sinker. I believed in it to such a degree that I remember wanting to die when I was about seven years old. I wished to die so I could go straight to heaven before I committed one of the many sins that would send me immediately to hell.

My parents knew nothing of my feelings. They believed that they had done their duty and handed us over to the Catholic Church for the rest of our moral education. The ideology of my parents was based on the notion that religion made and kept a person good. I couldn't turn to them with whatever the nuns were doing to me. They, like the priests and nuns, had faith in God and left any intellectual contradictions alone. They believed that faith was all that was necessary. It gave them comfort: that was enough. **Karl Marx** was right, "Religion is the sigh of the oppressed creature, the heart of a heartless world, just as it is the spirit of conditions. It is the opium of the people" (Ritzer and Goodman 66). It was for my parents, anyway. Catholic religion, to them, was good, holy and sanctified by God. There was no opiate for this individual, though. I was confused and in pain and had no one to turn to for relief. I did not find my opiates until my later years, and then it sure as hell wasn't religion.

The **dualism** of the nun's behavior was stunning. Their use of the catechism flew in the face of all the wrong and mean things that the nuns did to us at school. There we were told, "What happens in this classroom stays in this classroom." I left kindergarten each day with the fear that I could be locked in the cloakroom at any moment. There was no one to whom I could turn for help. I never told my parents or my grandmother of the absolute shame of being locked into that cloakroom. The combined influence of the Catholic nun's behavior and my parent's behavior, who only saw the nuns as living saints, kept alive my alienated "**selves**" for a very long time.

The next summer I ran gleefully again with my siblings and my cousins, putting the past school year behind me, as only a child could. I never gave a thought to the following school year: I knew I would be going to a different school and I thought that when I got to that school, things would be different, and better. I still hated to see the end of summer and the beginning of another school year. I entered first grade and a different school, named The Gate of Heaven, but I was surrounded by more nuns. They were to become the demagogues who ruled my life. I was filled with anxiety when I saw them. My daily defense was to daydream of my summer home, my cousins and the ocean that I loved so much. This only kept me in constant trouble.

I was a creative child, I liked to draw and paint. That first day of first grade, the nun handed each of us a lined piece of paper and told us to print our names. I turned the paper sideways because I liked the lines vertical, and I did as I was told. When the nun saw my work, she yelled at me very loudly, handed me a new piece of paper and told me to do it again. So I did. I had no idea what I had done wrong. She saw the second paper and became furious: her face got red and looked like it was going to burst out of her wimple. She screamed at me and told me to take my paper to the principal and show her what I did. Crushed and still bewildered as to what I'd done wrong, I took the long walk down the hall to the principal's office. "Sister told me to show you what I did," I said, giving her my best smile. I was terrified but I was smiling. I was learning at a very young age how to kowtow to the persons in power. Looking back now, I see that this was an early experience in Goffman's **dramaturgical theory** in action. I certainly was acting one way and feeling another, splitting the inner **back stage** and the public **front stage**. Seeing my big smile, the principal looked at my paper and said, "very good" and sent me on my way. When I returned to class the nun asked me what the principal had said. I related, "She said 'very good.'" I thought the nun was going to literally explode. I can't recall any more after that; I blanked out. I was too frightened to hear her. Later, my older sister explained to me that you were not supposed to write on a paper with the lines vertical. I never told my parents, I had already learned my lesson well from the nuns: You don't tell what goes on in here.

After the lined paper incident, that nun hated me. My first grade experiences were miserable, setting up the rest of my parochial school years. I blanked them out, never remembering the names of any of my nuns, except to hear their names from my sisters and brother when their times came. We all shared that fear and loathing for the nuns. The nuns typified and **stereotyped** us. I had a sister one year older than I who had to do battle with the nuns first. They remembered your family name and treated you as they did the one before. I felt really bad for my younger sisters and brother: we were all **co-conspirators**. None of us told our parents about the cruelty of the nuns. Indeed, my brother only recently told me that one nun dangled him by the ankles, bouncing his head on the floor. It was the first time he talked about it. Such was the shame they instilled on us. My siblings, like me, would cry and beg not to go to school. We became sick a lot.

I suppose that we also stereotyped the nuns. All of them were not bad: I had a nice one once. Unfortunately, their uniforms were a horrible **symbolic** representation of their punitive actions, so they all looked alike to us. I really believe that once you were shoved down severely by one, you shut down and saw all the others as the same. I know I was deathly afraid to show myself, my real "**I**," to any nun for fear of more shattering of my self into alienated fragments. With them, I was only "**me's**" to use a distinction highlighted and explored by George Mead. The very symbol of the black and white habit, the nun's uniform instilled in me a very real fear. Fear translated into physical illnesses, real or wished for.

I had a ritual on Sunday night, falling into what Talcott Parsons calls the **sick role** pattern. I would very dramatically take my role as the sick one, the only role that I learned to play that actually worked to keep me away from the nuns. I utilized what amounted to Erving Goffman's dramaturgical approach, becoming a very active self, capable of changing my own social drama. Back-stage, I would work up my fears of the next day, until I would feel pretty sick with apprehension. The front stage performance was easy. Complaining of not feeling well, my mother, the other star of my play, would break out her **prop**, the thermometer. We both kept to our assigned roles as both actors and audience. She would play nurse and I, the "sickie." I would sit with the thermometer in my mouth willing my temperature to go up so that I wouldn't have to go to school on Monday. I would drink hot cocoa and try to jack up my temperature with it, sitting next to the radiator in the dire hopes that the heat would raise my temperature level. My mother played her role very well and she was a most appreciative audience. I think my mother would relent sometimes because of the fervor in which I used trying to stay home. We would become co-conspirators. That would only work sometimes; she either got wise or sick of me. My sick role had to become more dramatic to work. In a later grade, a girl taught me a simple trick. "Chew some saltine crackers then spit them into the toilet," she told me, "It really looks like throw-up." It worked for me, though I actually did become really sick a lot. I was the one who would bring home the measles, mumps, scarlet fever, whooping cough, etc. The bug or whatever would pass from me to my siblings around the house and then I would get it again.

I hated school so much I blanked out half of my school years. Every year I would beg to not be sent to Catholic school, but to no avail. "Catholic school is good for you," our parents would say. The nuns intruded on all aspects of our lives. We couldn't even play freely. The nuns would warn us to stay away from public school children, saying they were bad children, who would go to hell. There seemed to be no way out.

According to G. I. Gurdjieff's theory of "three-brained" human beings, the development of the fully completed "I" hinges on the development of the other three parts of the self; the physical, the emotional, and the intellectual centers. Gurdjieff states, "The fundamental evil among contemporary people is that, owing to the rooted and widespread abnormal methods of education of the rising generation, this fourth personality, which should be present in everybody on reaching responsible age, is entirely lacking in them" (Gurdjieff, 1092-1093). I could not reconcile my own intellectual perceptions with my emotional ones. I quote a juror in the film *Twelve Angry Men*, "Facts, you can twist them anyway you want to." I saw this twisting of my self-identity throughout my education and I couldn't integrate my symbolic self. As Gurdjieff explains, we are constituted of three parts, struggling to achieve the harmonious four part person, the completed "I." He likens this disjointed self to a carriage in which the "coachman" is the intellectual self, the "horse" the emotional self, the "box" the physical self, and the "passenger" the master self representing the complete "I." My "coachman" kept taking free breaks from school, my "horse" plodded in every distracted direction, my "box" was soaked in drinking, and my "passenger" was simply not there. The master self had checked out of the body already—the **symbolic self-interaction** was simply not happening.

I finally escaped from the hell of Catholic School and in my eleventh year of school, went to South Boston High School. That was the freedom that broke me. For the first time in my life I was changing classes. There were boys in my class (my first two years of high school had been segregated by sex), and I felt both acutely shy yet free. I fell in with the misfits like myself, and began to learn all the wrong things. I had years to catch up on. South Boston High School was like the film, *The Blackboard Jungle*. It was a wild school. The students sometimes ruled the classrooms. Kids cut classes and hung out in the halls and the locker rooms. There wasn't any direction given to students, especially the girls. The vocational counselor was the football coach, so if you weren't a football player he advised either shop for the boys or typing for the girls. This was before feminism and the women's liberation movement came into vogue and ensured the stock of my everyday **commonsense knowledge**. I was told that you needed secretarial courses to succeed in life. The idea was that you would fall into and reproduce accepted social **typifications**. You were expected to work briefly as a secretary until you married and had children.

The students I fell in with were just like me; we had no futures awaiting us and we found better outlets with which to vent our collective alienation. I was afraid of the sudden freedom, confused about my feelings and feeling really lost. I learned to drink in school. As Neo Morpheus (a penname) stated in his article, "The Drinking Matrix: a Symbolic Self Interaction," "I now feel that the unhealthy urges are weights holding me down from getting to know the real 'I' within." (Morpheus, 12). My new school actually had unofficial holiday drinking days the day before each holiday. The boys would drink up on Dorchester Heights, which was a park behind the school, and the girls, segregated, would drink in the locker room. On those days, the primary thing learned was how to cut class to go and drink some more. The teachers specialized in crowd control and practiced "not in my back yard" principles in those days. They turned a blind eye to the goings on. So did my parents. I would come home from school, go upstairs and read until dinner. We kids ate separately from the adults; it was a matter of space. There were six children and four adults living at home. We had an **extended family**: my grandmother and my mother's best friend, who had polio, also resided with us. After dinner I would slide on upstairs, do my homework, and then fall into bed.

This was my life for the last two years of high school. I lived for the summers and hated the (school) winters. By now I was in a state of **anomie**, in the midst of fast-changing social environment characterized by lack of regulating influences. I had drifted into a bad crowd. They became my extended family: They felt more like family to me than did my own. We were all lost souls, jaded and **blasé**. I had found the friends that resembled and reinforced my own **looking glass self**; they were as alienated as I. Bored with the trappings of our **bourgeoisified** industrial blue-collar families, we suffered from **affluenza**. We were not happy with all the toys, the symbols of urban success. We had all learned the coping mechanisms of drinking and using drugs, some more than others. There were a lot of us outcasts and **deviants** and we found comfort and strength in each other.

I moved away from home as soon as I turned eighteen, getting an apartment with my older sister and cousin. I never did go to college: it seemed pointless. What did I want to be when I grew up? Who cared? I became, not a secretary, but an envelope stuffer at a stamp company. I worked my way up to stamp appraiser, but was then laid off. I collected unemployment benefits. Well, that was the life! I collected my unemployment checks, got to read books all day and partied at night. We all partied at night after work. Friends came over and we drank and smoked pot half the night, only to get up the next day and do it all over again.

I worked for the federal government by then, working for the Department of Labor and then the Coast Guard. These **bureaucracies**, especially the Coast Guard, were enmeshed in paperwork. The "Coasties" had to have all their documents in order, before I could help them. This is a classic example of Robert Merton's **dysfunctional consequences** in bureaucracies. "When adherence to bureaucratic rules becomes an end in itself, a situation Merton calls 'ritualism.'"(Ritzer and Goodman 49). My boss would sweep in and search through the pile of forms, those of the men and women yet to be processed. She would then pull out her friends or the officer's forms and put them on the top of the list, to be done first. "All men are created equal, but some are more equal than others." (*Animal Farm*. George Orwell). The hypocrisy sickened me. I saw the false class of people being put ahead of the real "Coasties" and I, as a lowly peon, had no say or power to effect change or to make things right. My friends and I were all suffering from the same alienations. We labeled ourselves as hippies and our carefree dramaturgies kept us smugly entertained. I loved the trappings of our lives; our hippie clothes; our props were water pipes, and we would consume anything that would alter our conscious states. I drifted from boyfriend to boyfriend, never quite being able to form the deep love and connection that I so needed. The **symbolic interactions** of our group as hippies ironically never allowed us the freedom to explore ourselves as individuals or as a couple. The **group** was our social reality. Everything else, like work and love took up the back stage. We were clueless and stoned. Back then, we thought we had everything, and knew everything. I realize now that I had a **false consciousness.** As hippies, we thought we were no longer a part of the mainstream **bourgeoisie,** but we were. What we thought was counterculture, in retrospect, was just a middle class phase of growing up in society in the 80's.

I left the Coast Guard to go and work for the Post Office. I found out that there were more money and no responsibility working for the P.O. I felt another burst of freedom working there. Compared to the rigidity of the Coast Guard, I felt like I was back at Southie High. It seemed easy at first—then the insidiousness of the bureaucracy crept in. There was an upper echelon in work; it was you versus the bosses. We were stepped on and ground down every night; it was a lot like Catholic school, but even more **hierarchical,** stranger, and with more crazy rules. Talk about a dramaturgy; they literally had an "acting supervisor." The "acting" supervisor had to answer to the supervisor, who had to answer to the manager, who had to answer to the district manager, who had to answer to the postmaster. The acting supervisor's job was to oversee us as we manually "threw" mail into metal slots at a work station. The boss would sit and stare at us all night as we threw the mail, calling breaks with a bell. It became oppressive very quickly. You could be "written up" for any number of infractions, such as remaining in the bathroom too long.

How do the theories of Marx, Simmel, Durkheim and Weber shed light on my life back then? I not only could see, but I very deeply felt alienation and the exploitation of myself, at the hands of the **capitalist boss,** or its **state bureaucracy**. As a postal worker, I was constrained and constricted, stuck in a manual job and experiencing the ever-increasing industrialization with its rapid technological changes. I lived the "the iron cage" experience daily. The Post Office was the mother of all bureaucracies. I "**rationalized**" my situation as the most economically beneficent, but the job gave me no room for personal development, restricted my personality and reducing it to that of an **automaton,** draining my personality and imagination. I was not alone. It was an "us" versus "them" mentality. These fellow workers became my **agencies of socialization** and we did become cohesive to a degree. We were all powerless, unable to express an idea or show a personality. The **division of labor** ruled that out. The bosses kowtowed to the bureaucracy. We all hated work; we were unanimous and stood together in that respect. The workers of this world were united here. According to Georges Simmel, "Opposition gives us inner satisfaction, distraction, relief." (Ritzer and Goodman 131).

"We are part of someone's constructed world." (Morpheus, in *The Matrix*). I worked nights and drank days with my fellow workers. We worked from 10:30 p.m. until 7:00 a.m. When we got out of work at 7:00 a.m., we went directly to the Am Vets Post. We would go to the bar where there would be about one hundred fellow postal workers, all drinking and partying. There, we drank and partied from seven a.m. till one p.m., went home, slept and did the same thing all over again the next night. The only freedom was what we could take for ourselves. It consisted of getting messed up after work every morning. We became our own "**gated community,**" sitting around bars; we knew that we were an organization unto ourselves. We had our own social order, our own distinct lifestyle. Outside of work we formed our own **social identity**.

Once at work, we, the workers, eventually became like machines. As in the film *The Matrix*, we "evolved." Only we actually devolved into the drudges who worked for the giant bureaucracy. Once upon a time, the postal worker was a heroic lone man on horseback delivering mail: we were now human **automatons**, forced to feed the massive machines, which voraciously sucked up the mail and our energies. I, as the machine, became increasingly alienated. I chose the "red pill" of that matrix and got out, though from a nightmare, not a dream. I do not agree with Emile Durkheim that the individual is free to develop his talents and imagination through the **specialization of labor**. At least not in my case.

I do see that the loss and isolation caused by industrialized life (anomie) can and sometimes does lead to people "going postal." Going postal is a common enough

phenomenon in the **stratified society** of the Post Office. Some people, already alienated from social life, find their last vestiges of self-dignity and self-worth shredded to pieces by the management. Their lives go downhill until hopeless; they go postal. They become either homicidal or suicidal or both. It happened to a postal custodian in Boston not too long ago. He shot his wife, stole an airplane and strafed the postal facility with bullets from the airplane. Of course, the management did not tell the workers inside the building what was going on outside. They would have lost production time. Such is the institutionalized madness of the post office. It infects the workers. The release of getting drunk was a survival technique brought on by the daily insanity of the post office. My life went on like this for a while. I worked and drank until the bottle owned me and I became nothing more than a **slave** to my addictions.

In class we recently saw two films, *Erin Brockovich* and *Billy Eliot*. These two characters, one real and one fiction, are both postmodernists in my view. The true character, Erin Brockovich, had a really strong personality and her own ideas in dressing and other behavior. She made her social reality work for her by creating her own job, turning situations to fit her personality instead of vice versa. Her input in her lawyer's company changed and improved many people's lives, including her own. She saw no reason to abide by established rules and "meta-narratives" (as critiqued by the postmodernist Jean Francois Lyotard) of "proper behavior," broke patterns of behavior and argued for change. The fictional Billy Eliot also saw beyond the established patterns of life in a small Welsh town. He found inner strength and changed his social reality. He went from having a future as an out of work miner's son to becoming a ballet dancer. Both questioned and challenged their social existences and their supposed roles in life. I identified with these people, as they, like I, were square pegs in round holes. They had to find their own ways to fit into their social worlds, finding strength in their own uniqueness. I formerly thought that the only way for me to fit into my social world was to stay with the underclass, the so-called "free-riders." I believed that we had our own world and there, I had found my place. I went to a bar where, like the bar in the television show Cheers, "everybody knows your name." Like Erin Brockovich and Billy Eliot, I had to evolve.

One fine Fall afternoon, my friend and I were driving along and we were hit head-on in a horrible car accident. The world as I knew it came crashing to an abrupt halt. My friend suffered many injuries, including a massive concussion.. I fractured my sternum and broke five ribs, also damaging my neck and shoulder. I ended up bedridden and on painkillers. The pain medication helped me physically, but I needed to drink in order to cope mentally. This realization about my life was stunning: it jarred me to the core. I also had all the time in the world to think, realizing very clearly for the first time in years that this was not the life I was supposed to be living. I was out of work and all the social rules that had held my life together in a **structured world** were gone in the blink of an eye.

I didn't know what to do with myself. I knew that "I" was in big trouble. My façade crumbled. As Megan Murray wrote in her paper, "Treading Water: Self Reflections on Generalized Anxiety Disorder," "I acted confidently and in control at all times, never allowing my true emotions to emerge. I felt that my identity was missing. I was never confident of myself and who I was." (Murray 51). Now I had all the time in the world to figure out who I was, where I had been, and where I was going. I was going nowhere and I wasn't anyone. This 'reality check' showed me the person that I was—a deeply unhappy person. I was alone with no one to guide me, including myself. M.

Goltry quotes George Herbert Mead in her journal article, "Theoretical Reflections on Peer Judgments," "Our actions are always engaged with the actions of others, whose response to what we do send us signals as to their approval or disapproval" (Goltry 159). I was bouncing my actions off my loved ones, people whom I had worn out. They were no longer interacting with me. The only approval I met with was to be found in barrooms, approval by people who really didn't care about me at all. I was through. And I knew it. Goltry focuses on society as a major influence in our self-development. We need society to form our opinions of ourselves, but we can choose which part of society that should be, including ourselves. I had been without society to bounce my need for approval on. I learned to find approval in myself. I made a **rational decision** that day.

I went to my doctor and told him that I had to quit drinking. I knew that this was long overdue, and as Gurdjieff would recommend, it was time to reconnect my intellectual driver, with my emotional horse and carriage body. I went in for treatment, both physical and emotional. The results were that one-day I emerged clean and sober, feeling like a spring chick. I had cleaned up the body but also needed to replenish a strong mind and the energy that I once had. I needed to get back to basics and rekindle my sense of creativity. I knew that if I wasted any more of my life then I would be committing emotional suicide. I decided to go to college, something that had been a dream of mine before I had drifted away from life with drinking and drugging. My mother had graduated from Boston State College when she was fifty four years old. It was time for me to follow her lead. Deciding that it was time for me to find my life's path, I enrolled into UMass Boston and felt hopeful for the first time in a long while. I no longer felt alone and hopeless. I was in charge of myself—or the first time in years.

Now that I've been sober for a few years, my quest for self is beginning in earnest. I am changing myself and others. I still don't know where I'm going, but I have a much better sense of who I am. I still have a basic distrust of relationships, but I'm working on that. School causes a constant shift in my feelings, from euphoria at a discovery or a job well done, to the sudden and deep anxiety that I will fail. It's overwhelming at times and I have to keep reminding myself that it is just a moment and that moment will pass. My inner voice can sometimes be extremely negative and I have to be constantly aware of that fact. I work hard to keep depression from keeping me down and sometimes have to really fight to keep going. I think that I have moved on from being alienated to being a connected knower. While I know that my inner voice is pretty much on target, I know I have to plumb deeper to use my **critical thinking** and to further develop my integrated "**I**."

Growing is both a joy and a frightening adventure. I just wish that my mother was alive to see me today. I know that she had the same struggles in developing her personal life and that she had succeeded in finding herself. I take her strength as mine and pray to her that somehow she is with me on my journey. I still fear my feelings and writing a paper like this helps me face and express those fears. Marge Piercy has a poem entitled, "Unlearning To Not Speak." In it she states, "She must learn again to speak. Starting with I." This is I: I have found my own way to live. I have to be true to myself. In order to truly grow, I must keep myself in perspective with my own world, with myself, and my sojourn as my priority. I've sprung myself from all the iron cages that had once imprisoned me. I'm flying now. And I can't wait to find out where I will land.

References

Farganis, James. (2000). *Readings in Social Theory: The Classic Tradition to Post-Modernism*. Third Edition. Boston: McGraw Hill.

Goltry, M. (2003). "Theoretical Reflections on Peer Judgments," *Human Architecture: Journal of the Sociology of Self-Knowledge*, Vol. II, No. 1, 2003. Endicott, NY: OKCIR.

Gurdjieff, G.I. (1950). "From the Author," in *All and Everything: Beelzebub's Tales to His Grandson.*, First Edition. Endicott: Harcourt, Brace and Company. pp. 1089-1135.

Morpheus, Neo. (2003). "The Drinking Matrix: A Symbolic Self Interaction," *Human Architecture: Journal of the Sociology of Self-Knowledge*, Vol. II, No. 1, Spring. Endicott, NY: OKCIR.

Murray, Megan. (2003). "Treading Water: Self-Reflections on Generalized Anxiety" Disorder," *Human Architecture: Journal of the Sociology of Self-Knowledge,* Vol. II, No. 1, Spring. Endicott, NY: OKCIR.

Orwell, George. (1945). *Animal Farm: A Fairy Story.* London: Secker and Warbur.

Piercy, Marge. "Unlearning to Not Speak" (http://courses.lib.odu.edu/engl/jbing/Piercypoem.html)

Ritzer, George and Douglas J. Goodman. (2004). *Classical Sociological Theory Fourth Edition.* New York: McGraw Hill Co. Inc.

Ritzer, George and Douglas J. Goodman. (2004). *Sociological Theory Sixth Edition*. New York: McGraw Hill Co. Inc. .

Wallace, R and Wolf, A. (1999). *Contemporary Sociological Theory: Expanding the Classical Tradition*. Fifth Edition. New Jersey: Prentice Hall.

Films:

"The Matrix." (1999). Warner Brothers.

"Twelve Angry Men." (1957). MGM.

"Affluenza." (1997). KCTS-Seattle and Oregon Public Broadcasting.

"Billy Elliot." (2000). Universal Pictures.

"Blackboard Jungle." (1955/1996). Turner Home Video.

"Erin Brockovich." (2000). Universal Pictures.

Body Image:
A Clouded Reality

M.D.

UMass Boston

When I think back to when I was a child, I remember not worrying or caring about major issues that now, as an adult, I can't help but worry about. Although I worry, I don't always do what I should to prevent the things I worry about from happening. Further details on this will be presented, as I try to gather what I have learned over the years and apply them to understanding the theories behind my actions.

During my adolescent years, I, as many have, dealt with cancer in many instances. Losing my father at a young age to cancer, and having similar experiences with other close family members, I couldn't grasp the concept of why people got so sick and why they had to suffer. I was so scared that I too would be diagnosed with cancer, and was afraid that every time I became ill or just didn't feel right, I was sure I had cancer. Sounds a bit depressing, I know. It's not that it controlled my life, but the thought was always in the back of my head, haunting me. As I matured, I realized more and more that just because I didn't feel well didn't mean I was going to die. Not only was cancer an issue, but sickness in general. I remember as an adolescent watching the movie *Steel Magnolias* in which a woman has diabetes and ends up dying due to complications with the disease. I just didn't understand why she died; she seemed so young with so much life left. I swore I would keep my body as healthy as possible, to avoid any chance of ever developing cancer or any other sickness. Here is where my problem begins.

We live in a **materialistic society**. We spend a ridiculous amount of money on clothes, makeup, jewelry, etc. On top of being materialistic, we are obsessed with how we look. We care how other people view us, how we view ourselves, and how we compare to the people we see in magazines, on television, and in movies. In Charles Hurst's book *Living Theory* (2000) which we have been studying, there is a section I found interesting, entitled "The Superficial Self." One sentence sums up what I am about to discuss. It states "Many Americans are willing to go to great lengths to manipulate, reshape, sculpt, and downright torture their bodies in order to present the ideal body to others" (Hurst 100). **Body Image** is a huge part of our society; it can control people's lives and force them to do things to their bodies they wouldn't normally do. Body image can be defined as how individuals view themselves in terms of weight, shape, and size. A few years ago, without even realizing what had happened, I developed an eating disorder. At the time, I wasn't aware of what I was doing to myself, how much weight I had actually lost, and especially what it was doing to my friends and family. What I knew was that I was getting compliments from people saying "you look so good, did you lose weight?" It added fuel to the fire. With every compliment, I kept going. Hurst's discussion of body image is one I can relate to all too well.

Charles Horton Cooley's concept, the **looking-glass self,** explains exactly what happened when I interacted with people. The looking-glass self is the self you imagine and feel yourself to be through your imaginations of how you appear to others and how they judge you. It can therefore be broken down into three elements: the imagination of how we appear to others; the imagination of their judgment of our appearance; and the self-feeling obtained as a result, such as pride in our appearance, or being ashamed of how we appear. Every time I came in contact with someone, I went over in my head how I thought they saw me. "Do they think I'm fat?" "Are they looking at my body?" are all thoughts that ran through my mind. I constantly thought people were talking about me, good or bad, and I couldn't go anywhere without believing people were staring at and judging me. I was constantly being told it was just my imagination, but I was convinced otherwise.

Many sociological theories can shed light on what causes eating disorders, and what role society plays in them. A **theory** is a tested/testable description or explanation of **social reality**, and with social reality comes the realization of what exactly our society entails. My theory is that people in capitalist society, especially women, feel constant pressure to look perfect at all times. Open a magazine, turn on the television, and tell me what you see. It's highly unlikely that a model in a magazine will be a size 14 trying to sell jeans. It's not "sexy" or "attractive." Meanwhile, the average sized woman in our society today is a size 12. Shouldn't they be targeting the average woman instead of throwing abnormally skinny girls in our faces? In the film *Affluenza*, we see just how commercialized our society is. We are drawn to the images we see on television, and we then assume that what we see on television is what we should be. Commercials for diet pills, facial creams, and workout videos flood the airwaves with images of how to create the "ideal" body. But who decides what the "ideal" body type is? Certainly not the advertising companies putting these commercials on television; we're brainwashed to believe that the people on television are perfect.

The reasons we place such high expectations on ourselves as to how we should look is because of the way we view celebrities. They are social creations whose lives seem so interesting and exciting, yet seem so distant and different from the average persons. The appeal to their lifestyles may be "the combination of familiarity and extraordinariness that gives that celebrity its ideological power" (Hurst 110). We tend to envy their lives without realizing that the lives we lead are just as great if not better than the ones in which they lead. We rely on them for fashion, entertainment, and gossip; we live vicariously through them.

As time wore on, my priorities began to diminish. I felt that attaining my "perfect" body was more important than school, work, and family. The gym was my second home, and being around my family only made me aggravated and annoyed. I was driven by a **false consciousness** of my gender and human existence; I was forgetting what was really important in life and was turning my back on the things that used to make me happy. At that time, being thin made me happy. What I didn't realize was how miserable everyone around me was becoming because of my selfishness and false consciousness.

When I was dealing with my eating disorder, I seemed to be practicing a **self-fulfilling prophecy**. A self-fulfilling prophecy is a prediction someone has regarding an issue and by acting it out helps realize that prediction. There were many things in my life I couldn't control, i.e., losing loved ones, and the one thing I could control was what I ate and how much I ate—yet, I disregarded how it was hurting me. I finally did gain "control" over my life, thinking that only I could control the outcome. I proved to myself that my life was "in control," and I also proved that I could fit society's standards of what makes a woman beautiful—her body. I was extremely thin and in control (or so I thought). I had successfully fulfilled my prophecy in my eyes.

Emile Durkheim broke down culture into two spheres; the **sacred,** which deals with the extraordinary and higher elements of life such as reason, morality, science, conceptualizations, altruism, holiness, and the soul. The other sphere is the **profane**, which includes sensations, body, materials, egoism, and the concrete everyday life (Hurst 148). Durkheim believes that these two spheres are constantly engaged in a conflict with each other. I believe this to be very true, especially in the case of eating disorders. The mind is telling you "this isn't good for your soul, you need to stop being obsessive about weight," but the body is telling the mind "you're fat, you need to lose weight." Durkheim did not consider the body as part of the sacred level of the two spheres; however, in today's society the body has gained much more importance as it signifies beauty. Durkheim similarly explains that individuals have **two sides to their nature**. We all possess an egoistic side as well as a social side. The first is embedded in biology; the second derived from society. As these two sides remain in conflict with each other, they continue to intensify. We need the social to restrain our selfishness.

In applying the different sociological theories, we can first attend to the **phenomenological** perspective. Being that I once suffered from an eating disorder, and the phenomenological perspective focuses on the point of view of the person involved rather than from other's point of view, we can use this perspective to help in better understanding eating disorders from a more hands-on approach. The everyday life a person lives in can affect how they view themselves, their body, and their minds. **Dorothy Smith's Feminist Standpoint Theory**, grounded in the phenomenological perspective, sheds light on how women are viewed in society. She uses the example of the cosmetic displays in shopping malls and how they "document the underlying pattern, or the underlying social order" (Wallace and Wolf, 288) shaping women's lives. She explains how the use of pastels and the expression of softness gives the impression that the feminine woman is "yielding, pliant, and compliant" (Wallace and Wolf, 288). Even the smallest thing such as a display in the mall can give the impression of what women are expected to be. Just because pastels may exemplify a certain femininity, it doesn't mean that all women should now dress in pastels. How is a woman who wears pastels any less feminine than a woman who wears black, blue, or brown? The same goes for body image. Just because skinny women are plastered all over the place, doesn't mean that a woman who is heavy-set is less feminine than the size two model on the billboard.

In the phenomenological perspective the **commonsense** refers to the **take-for-granted** aspects of everyday our knowledges about the world and ourselves. We all possess commonsense, taking for granted the world of reality which we actually create through are *own* thoughts and actions. However, commonsense is itself conflictual. One commonsense tells us that body image and how we look aren't as important as other things going on in the world. But we also create another reality and commonsense knowledge that says "what you look like matters immensely, because society will accept you more if you look how they want you to look." You're pulled at both ends. You know in your mind what's more important, but society is pulling you the other way telling you something completely different.

Symbolic interaction plays a significant role in persuading people to act or look a certain way. For example, I am a dancer, and have been for many years. I was never overweight, and always had the same body type as most of my friends. As I matured, and began dancing in a company, I took more notice of my body and found myself constantly looking at myself in the mirror. My dance friends did this all the time; my other friends didn't. When you interact in dance class, you are watching each other, your bodies, your movements, and your placement. It's not that people are doing it to judge you, it's just how a dance class works. That's why people dance—to have people watch your movements. It's sometimes hard to deal with the fact that, while you're dancing, the only interaction you have with the audience or with the people watching you in your dance class is your body. Your body symbolically represents you and speaks for you to the audience. When you're around people who are constantly concerned with their bodies, you can't help but look at your body and think "OK, what's wrong with *my* body?" The groups which we associate with help influence our views on what we look like. Chances are if there is an individual dressed in all black with piercings everywhere, he or she is going to associate themselves with people who dress similarly. It is highly doubtful they would associate with a group that dressed in khakis, plaid shirts, and sweaters tied around their shoulders. My group of dance friends were all very conscious of their bodies at all times, which in turn caused me to suddenly become very aware of every "fault" my body had.

In watching the film *Billy Elliot*, the stereotypes placed on dancers are obvious and outlandish. Because he is male, and he wants to dance, he is judged as being homosexual, and is laughed at by his peers, and looked down on by his father. The same sort of stereotypes are placed on female dancers, only their stereotypes are placed on their bodies. If you are a dancer, you are expected to be thin. If you want dance to be your career, you *have* to be thin. There have been multiple cases of women in ballet companies such as the Boston Ballet who were told they weren't skinny enough, and ended up dying because they got too thin. The way in which society places stereotypes on people, as we saw in *Billy Elliot*, can either make or break you. Billy chose to rise above them and reach his goal. Unfortunately, for a woman, those goals can be deadly.

Social status and economic **class** can be a factor in dealing with body image and what the ideal person within these classes should look like. It is suggested that people often tag upper-class individuals with the notion that they should be tall and slim, whereas working-class individuals are deemed heavy and clumsy. Sure, with plenty of money to waste, it's easy to mold your body into what you want it to be. A lot of working-class individuals, however, will empty their bank accounts for one cosmetic surgery, just to live up to the expectations set forth upon them. Many individuals who alter their bodies tend to be suffering from what **Karl Marx** called the **fetishism of commodities**. A commodity, according to Marx, "is, in the first place, an object outside us, a thing that by its properties satisfies human wants of some sort or another" (Hurst 107). What makes it a fetish is how the "outside object" controls us, our desires, goals, and aspirations. Body parts, especially ones altered by surgery, have become fetishes. They are viewed as independent objects but are really "manifestations of a set of social relationships in society" (Hurst 107).

Max Weber's outlook on the trend towards increasing **rationalization** in society is one that is taken into account when discussing body image. He looks at rationalization as a process whereby social relations are organized in such a way as to make the most effective decision to increase efficiency, wealth, power, etc. Weber believes we live in an **iron cage** characterized by increasing rationalization and bureaucratization of social relations. No one *wants* to live with an eating disorder. We feel that in order to live up to society's expectations, we *have* to do whatever it takes to mold and shape our body to fit in with society. We all take on certain **roles** in terms of how we act and look within society. To many, women are expected to take on the role of being the caretaker, of always having to look pretty and put-together. We are expected to know about make-up, hair products/styles, and fashion. A **role conflict** begins when a woman doesn't fit the expected role she is "supposed" to play. A woman who is a size fourteen, or a woman who dresses in baggy clothes with no makeup is deemed unattractive and unable to fit the roles set forth upon them.

In one of the articles I read in *Human Architecture: Journal of the Sociology of Self-Knowledge*, Emily Margulies wrote about her experiences with smoking. She said she knew it was bad for her, and at first, she started smoking once in a while, then gradually began smoking all the time. She knew she was killing herself by smoking, but it was an addiction. She thought she looked "cool" by smoking, and felt as though she fit in more. This is exactly how an eating disorder works. It becomes a habit, a way of life. You do it to fit in even though you know it's bad for you. Society tells you this is cool, so you think, "what's the harm?" There was also another article in the same issue of the journal dealing with the same problem of addiction, but here with regards to the drinking habit. If you were to ask someone why they drank, they could say a number of things. "I like how it makes me feel," "because my friends do," and "because it helps me escape" are a few common responses. An eating disorder, mainly bulimia, is like alcoholism. It's addicting, first and foremost, but it can also make you feel great. After you eat, you know you can just get rid of it afterwards. As weird as this may sound, it was a great feeling to rid your stomach of food; it was like a drug. For those few minutes, nothing else in the world mattered. It's the same as being drunk—you don't think about the problems you may have or the pain you may feel—it all goes away. The downside is, like alcoholism, you are never really completely cured; relapses are not uncommon.

When we watched the movie *The Matrix* there was one particular scene where they are standing on a sidewalk with people dressed exactly the same walking by them. Standing out is one woman in a red dress. This scene grabbed my attention for a few reasons. Within our society, we are constantly trying to be like everyone else. Think about it. If we see someone wearing something that we like, chances are we would go to the store in which that item was sold at and purchase it. Soon that style becomes the new "fad," and everyone is walking around wearing basically the same thing. Individuals within our society have lost their sense of **individuality;** they don't do what makes them happy or what they feel is right; they do what they think will make society happy or what society feels is right. If someone isn't dressed with the latest fashion, we deem them "weird" and look at them as if they're from another planet. It's the same thing with weight. When seeing an overweight person, many quickly shun them away, without getting to know who the person really is. We only see what's on the outside. That's how our society has become. There were or still are other societies where large women are viewed as beautiful and healthy. Today, we see size two models strutting down a runway modeling clothes that *we're* all supposed to wear? Is this real?

Functionalism and **conflict theory** provide macrosociological perspectives on our on body images today. Both are concerned with overall characteristics of social structure and see human behavior as being predictable. In contrast to functionalism which suggests that values motivate human social action, conflict theory suggests that interests motivate human social action. Conflict theorists are more concerned about explanation than functionalists. They are mostly concerned with providing explanations of how certain events are created by the actions and interests of different groups (classes, status, or power groups) within society as a result of changes in technology, resources, and ideas.

In regards to body image, I would have to take the side of the conflict theorists, because I believe that human beings are motivated by self or group interests. In this society we do things to please ourselves first, then worry about the others around us. Now maybe I'm looking at this pessimistically, but I would tend to disagree with the functionalist idea that humans are motivated by values. Society today lacks value. We are a "quick-fix" society; we'll do what makes us happy at the moment, not taking into account the effects it will have on society or, in a more micro sense, the people surrounding us in our lives. Eating disorders are a perfect example. It's a quick fix, it satisfies the interest of the individual with the eating disorder, and it pushes values to the back burner, for if we took values into account, we would be fully aware of just how bad eating disorders are.

Speaking of conflict theory, we should further look at stratifications based on **gender.** Women are paid less, are considered inferior to men, and have expectations placed on them that far exceed that of a men. I think a main reason why women tend to put so much time and effort into worrying about their bodies is because they think that it's something that men can't control. In their view, men can control the economy or the nation, but they can't control what size a woman is. The fact is men do exert influence on a woman's view of her body, but this does not mean that she *has* to change it for them.

In the film *Erin Brockovich*, we see a woman struggling against all odds and fighting for what she believes in. With all the advances in our society and the degree of progress we've made in technology and science, you would think that the stereotype of women would somehow advance as well. We are expected to look a certain way and act a certain way. If we dress scantily clad, as Erin did, we aren't taken seriously. So we dress down, and are then considered a "tomboy." In our textbook, *Contemporary Sociological Theory,* Wallace and Wolf state that women are in fact expected to maintain a stricter personal front, whether it be the clothes they wear, the way their hair is styled, or the makeup they are wearing. The sociologist Erving Goffman is quoted as saying "for a woman to appear in public with her costume disarrayed can be taken as a sign of accessibility and looseness of morals" (Wallace and Wolf, 230). The stereotypes placed on women are ridiculous and immature. Not only do we have to prove ourselves as being feminine and beautiful, but we have to prove on a daily basis that we are capable of handling any task that a man can. It's exhausting.

As time wore on and I continued with my eating disorder, I began to realize how miserable I felt about myself. The weight was coming off, but the depression was packing on the pounds. I felt alone, confused, scared, and most of all, angry. I didn't understand why I had to be going through such an awful thing. I was killing my body, and I swore I would never do that. I was taking an Abnormal Psychology class at the time, and one of the topics was none other than eating disorders. I started crying in class and walked out. I finally began to realize why I was doing this to myself. I wasn't doing it because I wanted to; I was doing it because I thought if I did, I would be accepted by society even more than I already had been before the eating disorder began.

According to the sociologist George H. Mead we wouldn't have a **sense of self** without society. I believe this to be true and false at the same time. We need things like social interaction and language to help us grow into a human being who knows how to communicate with the world around them. Without language, we wouldn't have a sense of self. We need to communicate with people on a daily basis, whether it is at work, at home, or at school; everyone we come in contact with helps us in some way to grow as a person. However, society does have negative effects on individuals as well. My eating disorder did come about for reasons other than society. I withheld a lot of emotions over the years I had never realized existed. Society, however, can be a mean force that pulls you down and holds you there until you can't take it anymore. An eating disorder is something that I will never forget, and will always run the risk of developing it again. It's a challenge and a struggle to get over such a s socially conditioned disease. We can't escape it, we can't run from it, and we certainly can't get rid of it.

To link my fear of sickness and my eating disorder, you have to look at the psychological as well as the social aspect of it. Its as if there is a another self living in your body, telling you what to eat, what not to eat, how you look, and how you feel. You can't think for yourself. For a long time I was damaging my body. There are people all over the world, of all different ages, all different shapes and size, who develop horrible diseases everyday and have no control over the outcome. I was selfishly killing my body when I should have been appreciating the fact that I had a healthy body before all this began. Society tells you skinny is beautiful, yet when people find out someone has an eating disorder, they automatically **stigmatize** that person as pathetic or an attention-seeker. Where is the fairness? If people would stop and appreciate themselves for the real persons they are, and our society wasn't so highly based on looks, we could eliminate many of the issues surrounding body image. There are more important things to worry about in life than what size your jeans are or how much you weigh.

In life, we all take part in **dramaturgy**. According to Erving Goffman, we all play different roles in our everyday lives, as an actor would in a play. When I look at my eating disorder and how it affected me in regards to society, I notice that I took on a front-stage/back-stage attitude. The **front-stage** is what everyone you come in contact with sees, i.e., what the audience sees when they watch a play. The **backstage** is what happens in the background, like when undergoing a costume change or someone rehearsing lines, involving emotions and behavior that are not meant to be seen by others. In my front-stage persona I was confident, skinny, and beautiful. In my backstage persona, however, I was scared, confused, alone, and miserable. As Goffman describes the backstage region, we can "drop our front, forego speaking lines, and step out of character" (Wallace and Wolf, 231). Basically, we can be ourselves when we are backstage. We put on different acts as to what we think society expects of us. I was skinny, so I in turn *must* be happy. Not the case at all. We rarely get a chance to be our real selves. We are constantly putting on a front, acting a certain way, looking a certain way. A majority of the population, more likely than not, do not even know who they really are.

We seem to have two images of ourselves, one for the outside and one for the inside, sort of the like the backstage/frontstage personas. According to Thomas Cash quoted, "Beauty is no guarantee of a favorable body image, nor is homeliness a decree for a negative body image" (Hurst 102). We know that during the process of socialization, we learn to see ourselves as other people see us and learn to look at ourselves on the basis of their attitudes toward us. The body is the most visible aspect of ourselves, especially for women in society today. In other words, how a woman presents herself physically reflects on her own self-image.

With eating disorders, it's like a double-edged sword. On the one hand, you feel you are being more accepted by becoming thinner; on the other hand, people tend to react to eating disorders as if it were something to be ashamed of. There is a sense of **discrimination** toward people suffering from an eating disorder; they are judged on their sickness and labels are placed upon them. They accuse individuals with eating disorders as attention-seekers, or judge them as if they were cursed with the plague. It seems that everyone today, in one way or another, is trying to reform their body. Exercise, dieting, and surgery are the three main ways in which we try to alter our bodies into the "ideal" body type. Weight Watcher's meetings and aerobics classes are a chance for people with similar goals to get together. I have a friend who is a part of the Weight Watcher's program, and it seems as though the people within the group are very supportive and want to help each other reach their goals in a healthy manner.

Objectivation seems to have some truth to our society. We "apprehend everyday life as an ordered, prearranged reality that imposes itself upon but is seemingly independent of human beings" (Wallace and Wolf, 279). In regards to our society today, we don't live life as if it were a blessing, as if it was a reality created by us for our good. We look at it as just there, with things in it to fill up our time, our money, and our emotions. We have detached ourselves emotionally from the things in life that make us happy.

I think body image has become a **social dilemma** in our society. Eating disorders are too common among women, and I put 100% of the blame on society. But how did our society become so clouded that we actually believe that someone who looks as though they haven't eaten in months is beautiful? In the past, women like Marilyn Monroe were considered beautiful, and being full-figured was praised. I would give anything to live in a society where that was the case, as I'm sure many women today do. We know what eating disorders do to the body, so why do we continue to torture our bodies? We as a society need to take a step back and look at what we have become: A materialistic, image-obsessed society that praises beauty more than it praises knowledge, love, and life. We are made up of individuals all with a false consciousness of what we really want.

I think our society has a clouded image of what is beautiful. Women all over the world are killing themselves to conform their bodies to society's standards. Instead of praising women for being healthy, we criticize them and place pressure on them to be like what they see on television, in films, or on the runways. Eating disorders are growing problems which many seem to brush aside, assuming those afflicted by the problem will take care of themselves. The only way to change the growing rate of eating disorders is to change the way our society functions as a whole.

REFERENCES

Margulies, Emily. (2003). "Why I Smoke: Sociology of A Deadly Habit," *Human Architecture: Journal of the Sociology of Self-Knowledge*, Vol. II, No. 1, Spring. Endicott, NY: OKCIR.

Farganis, James. (2000). *Readings in Social Theory: The Classic Tradition to Post-Modernism*. Third Edition. Boston: McGraw Hill.

Hurst, Charles E. (2000). *Living Theory: The Application of Classical Social Theory to Contemporary Life*, Boston: Allyn and Bacon.

Wallace, R and Wolf, A. (1999). *Contemporary Sociological Theory: Expanding the Classical Tradition*. Fifth Edition. New Jersey: Prentice Hall.

Films:

"The Matrix." (1999). Warner Brothers.
"Affluenza." (1997). KCTS-Seattle and Oregon Public Broadcasting.
"Billy Elliot." (2000). Universal Pictures.
"Erin Brockovich." (2000). Universal Pictures.

Obsessed with Impression Management:
A Critical Sociology of Body Image in Capitalist Society

Michelle B. Jacobs

UMass Boston

I can not tell you how many times in my life I have said "if only I were thin." I honestly feel that life would be much easier for me if I were thin. The key word is "easier." I think that thin and beautiful people reap the majority of the benefits in this society and I, of course, am not one of them.

I have felt this way for as long as I can remember and I really believe it to be true. My weight is something that has always been an issue for me. I can not really understand why I don't lose weight. I know I can do it, like a person who knows she can ace a test if only she studies for it. That is how I feel. I know I can do it. I know it is all in my mind and seems to be just an issue of will power but I can't seem to go down to the weight I desire. Why?

Sometimes I think that it is genetics, but then I look at my sisters. Sometimes I think that it is the demand society puts on me to lose weight so I feel that I have to—that the only reasons I even feel like I need to lose weight is because that is what has been thrown at me in the mass media all of my life. From television, to magazines, to my home life, weight has been a constant underlying factor in my life and it just never goes away.

From the age of five years old and on I have had a weight problem. One of my main memories of my childhood is my grandmother placing food strategically out of my reach at the dinner table so that I would not overeat. My entire childhood and life thus far has been based on looks. This is true for both the girls and the boys in my family. This is something that is very important to everyone and they pride themselves on our being a good-looking family. Not to brag, but I do have a very good-looking family and none of them is overweight except for me.

It all started with my grandmother. Her mother had to be institutionalized in a mental institute and her father just could not take care of three children on his own. He put them into an orphanage. This is where my grandmother stayed until she was eighteen years old. From that point on she was on her own and she believes that her looks got her what she needed in life and if she did not have them she would not have been able to survive.

That frame of mind has traveled down the generations in my family—from my mother and aunt and now on to my cousins, sisters, and myself. **Sociobiology** explores how the body and physical experiences are of central importance to the individual and social life, while the **Sociology of the Body** explores how our attitudes towards our bodies are socially constructed (Wallace and Wolf, 369). My whole life can be explored using these notions. I am not only an outcast in society because of my weight, but I am the only one like this in my family as well. My whole life has been an emphasis on the body and physical experiences. I can clearly remember walking out of the door at twelve years old and my mother saying to me "put some lipstick on for goodness's sake, you're going out." In most families, someone that age would not be allowed to wear makeup, but I was taught at a very early age that if you go out of the house, you should have makeup on your face.

This brings me to **Phenomenology**. This is a sociological perspective that begins with the individual and his/her own conscious experience and tries to avoid the prior assumptions and prejudices. It really asks us to question our way of looking at and being in the world. This perspective asks us to assume the role of a stranger by "putting ourselves in other peoples shoes" (Wallace and Wolf, 276). There are three major concepts of phenomenology and all these aspects support the notion that reality is socially constructed. The first is **externalization**. This is where individuals, by their own activity, create their social worlds. The second is **objectivation**. This is the process by which the person apprehends life as an order ed or prearranged reality. The third is **internalization**. This implies that this same social world will, through the processes of socialization, acquire the status of reality within the consciousness of the individual.

These concepts really apply to my problem. You will almost never see my grandmother or mother in public without any makeup on; they *externalized* this pattern of behavior while we as children grew up. It has simply turned into an *objectivated* common sense norm for women in my family to put makeup on and make sure we look good before leaving the house and going out in public. All my life I have *internalized* the notion that it is important to look good and be thin; this has become a part me and I wouldn't feel comfortable any other way.

These three aspects of phenomenology are Berger and Luckmann's three key concepts of the **Social Construction of Reality**. This is basically the notion that social life is created. Once constructed, social reality then in turn influences how we view ourselves. It has to do with habituation and doing something over and over again until you subjectively internalize the constructed reality. This is what I have done or should I say what my family has done to me. I stress and I stress over how to achieve the ideal body or image. If I read in a magazine that a hairstyle is out, you will never see my hair like that again. If the latest makeup fad is heavy on the eyes and light on the lips, that is how my makeup will be. I feel like I have socially and personally created my own reality within the one that has been created for me by my family.

The concept of social construction of reality makes me think of the movie *The Matrix*. In this movie, it is brought to the attention of the character Neo that the reality that he is living in is not actually the reality at all. It is all just a constructed computer program. This is how I feel. Do I feel that I am fat because society has constructed my body image to portray a fat person? Is it because today's magazines and television programming promote advertisements encouraging women to meet impossible personal standards? The capitalist society plays a crucial role in people's lives and how they view their bodies and whether or not they have a good body image of themselves. This is also shown through today's society in terms of consumerism. The movie *Affluenza* explores the materialistic society we live in and how it effects us. The way products are marketed for the public give people the notion that they need to look and be a certain way in order to fit into society. We need to have a certain type of body so that we can buy what we see in the magazines and on television, so that we can fit in the consumer society that we live in. I am not really sure but I think that if I was living in a different culture or a different time period I would not be considered fat and I would not look at myself as fat.

This reminds me of the piece "Theoretical Reflections on Peer Judgments" *(2003)*, by M. Goltry. The author writes about how in high school she was not following the socially constructed norms of what women were meant to look like. She was not what society would consider "beautiful." She had glasses and was overweight and was not society's ideal-looking woman. That is how I feel about myself. I feel that my body is going against the norm even though my mind does not want to. So in order to deal with this problem, as Goltry tried to do when faced with negative peer judgments, I find that I should maintain **group solidarity**. I feel the need to follow the groups or the social norms to reap the social benefits. I feel that **Labeling** plays a big part in this. If I choose to have friends that are labeled as very thin and boyfriends that only have slim bodies (which I often do), I feel that by association with the group I will also be labelled thin and slim. If I hang out with only thin people then perhaps I will look thinner and more appealing as well. But the contrary may be true as far as my **looking glass self** image is concerned. If the people I choose to interact with are very much set on society's standards then I will most likely have a worse self image of myself than if I were to surround myself with very positive, socially open people who do not care about meeting impossible standards regarding weight and looks. In "Why I Smoke: Sociology if a Deadly Habit" (2003) the author, Emily Margulies, tries to explain how she developed her smoking habit as a result of participating in a group life that reinforced her habit. My group life that surrounds me consists of two sisters, both under five foot four and weighing less than one hundred twenty pounds each. My groups of friends are also approximately this size. This is the group that I surround myself with and this is what I compare myself with everyday.

Charles Cooley's notion of the looking glass self applies perfectly to me. It states that the "self that you understand is a result of the information reflected back at you in the judgment of others with whom you interact" (Wallace and Wolf, 195). More precisely, Cooley identifies three steps of the process: "the imagination of our appearance to the other person; the imagination of his judgment of that appearance; and some sort of self-healing, such as pride or mortification" (Wallace and Wolf, 195). I do tend to judge myself based on how I interpret the reaction of the others around me. I know whether I look good or bad based on my imagination of the reaction I get from people when I go out. From the movie "Twelve Angry Men" I have learned that people are very quick to come to a decision but are not as quick to change that opinion. Jury members were judging the person on trial before they even put the whole story together. Luckily the man had someone on his side to point out the holes in the story and the things they missed to see. They now had something to reflect on instead of just their first impression. Most people do not have a person on their side to disprove and resist public prejudice. I often have only my appearance to make the first impression on a person. I do not have someone standing with me explaining to people that I am a great person with a great personality and someone they should get to know. The accused man in the movie did have someone to fight for him. Someone to show the other side of the story and make people realize that things are not always the way you see them.

I am obsessed with **Impression Management**. We want to act or do things in a certain way in order to give people a certain impression about us. Maybe that is why I chose to hang out with a majority of thin people. That is the impression I want people to get. I want them to see that even though I am on the bigger side, I am still just like the thin people everyone is used to seeing—that I am just as good.

Due to **gender socialization**, I think that it is harder for a woman to be socialized into the norms of society than it is for a man. I mean, look at the movies we see. A man does not have to be good looking to make it and have everything he wants—take Danny Devito as an example. But the number of women who are bigger or really just not that attractive is much smaller in show business. I think **Exchange Theory** explains much of this pattern in show business. Exchange theory suggests that human behavior is based on perceived punishments and rewards expected in performing an act. This, to me, is how the social system that we live in works. For example, if you go to a bar and look good, guys will buy you a drink—that is a reward because you do not have to spend your own money. There have even been studies done that two people with equal qualification will apply for the same job and the good looking one will get the job—that is a reward. That is what it seems our society is based on, looks. Consider what Dorothy E. Smith states in her **feminist standpoint theory**, which explores everyday and everynight worlds of individuals situated in subordinate positions, particularly of women. If women are put in lower positions because of their gender anyway, they may as well feel that looking good can help her upward mobility. She needs her looks to get the rewards society has to offer. It is just like my grandmother, believing that she needed her looks to get by in life and then passing this idea down to her family.

At one point in his essay "Defying the Sweatshop, Sociologically Speaking" (2002), Steve Sacco wonders if his views towards taking a stand on sweatshop labor in contrast to his peers could possibly be a result of biological factors. He finds it implausible, and I I feel the same. I do not feel that my issues have to do with biology at all. Instead, like Sacco, I feel like it all stems from the social factors that I have been surrounded with since birth. I seem to always want to impress the **generalized other**. I try to represent myself in the way that will get the most desired response from society.

Unfortunately, I think that my family really caused trouble in the way of **socialization**. I have been taught or socialized since a young child to look good and make a good impression on the people around me. Sometimes, I really do not want to care. Sometimes, I just want to lay back and like me for who I am and not have to worry about the impression I am making on other people around me. There is not a mirror or a window that I walk by that I do not look in. There is not a day that goes by that I look at another woman and think to myself, "I wish I had a body like hers."

Rational Choice theories state that people will base their individual actions on what they think will be the most effective way to achieve their goals. I just feel that society (which includes ourselves) has made it such that we have to be one step ahead of the next person. We have to have better hair, eyes, nose, and body in order to survive in this society that we have created for ourselves. Looks mean a lot of things to people and until there is some radical social change, a lot of young women are going to feel just as inadequate and unappealing as I do at times. I wish my family had emphasized something other than looks and body type. I wish my family had pushed education or kindness instead of this. Then again, maybe they are just as much victims of the social reality that we live in as I am.

Why are we victims of the social reality that we live in? Why do we strive so hard to find social acceptance in trivial things such as looks? Why does something like looks weigh so heavily in our lives? These questions relate to a much bigger social problem. We have created a society obsessed with looks and appearance. We have done this through media outlets such as magazines and television, all of which reflect the interests of big corporations and the type of hold the corporate world has on the individual and society as a whole.

As I stated earlier in this essay, social exchange is often seen as involving taking actions to reap rewards and/or benefits. All that we are bombarded with are pictures in advertising that tells us how we should look, dress, and act. This has created a society of women who strive to achieve a body type that may be impossible in order to receive these rewards. This is because we see these beautiful women in magazines and want to live the life that they seem to live. We also want to get rewarded with the life of luxury because of our looks. Unfortunately, this is not as easy as it sounds. "Female models are becoming thinner at a time when women are becoming heavier, and the gap between the ideal body shape and the reality is wider than ever. There is a need for more realistic body shapes to be shown on television and in fashion magazines" (Maclean's, 2000:2). So why are we striving for this level of impossibility? It is because we live in a society driven by profit motif, our images (among others) exploited by those who control the relevant productive resources.

Think about it. The companies that want us to buy their clothing advertise in all of the magazines and on the television shows that are most commonly watched or read. They each help each other without giving an inkling of thought to the consumer and how what they are advertising is effecting their lives. The ads that run for a store like the Express show young pretty women who are thin and look happy and in the prime of their lives. This leads people to go out and buy the clothing that is shown. But what happens if someone can not fit into that type of clothing. Then they are going to go out and buy some diet pills at a store like GNC that is even advertised in the same issue of *Cosmopolitan* that just made the girl want that new skirt. All of the companies are intertwined someway or another and it is all about profit, not consumers well being.

The movie *The Big One* by Michael Moore illustrates how corporations and corporate decisions shape and influence our society. The corporations are what really matter, not the workers who keep the plants alive by producing the goods, or the consumers whose needs are created by same or other corporations to buy those products. Only the big corporations are what matter. This is why all of the advertising is geared to making you want the unachievable because it keeps us striving and buying until we finally reap the social benefits. But the only ones who reap the benefits are the big corporations who do not really care if we reach these goals. They do not care if they give young girls eating disorders as long as the products are being sold.

Conflict theories see power and struggle for power as being central to social life. Max Weber and Karl Marx both "…viewed different groups competing for different social rewards, they agreed that society was fundamentally unstable, and that the operative force behind change was the conflict which inevitably arose between various social groups in competition for social changes" (Farganis 219). It is all about a society controlled by companies, a society in which people's worth is based on their **socioeconomic status**. These magazine ads that we see tell us that in order to be the best we have to dress up and be like those portrayed in the ads. These magazine and television ads are just depicting an image and yet social happiness and acceptance is based almost entirely around them.

In *Billy Elliot* the little boy, Billy, wants to take dance classes instead of the boxing classes his father urges him to take. This is not acceptable for the family of this young boy. This is because he would be socialized into a different role than what people in his community are used to. Society has put pressures on him to be, look, and act in a certain way. That is what magazine and big corporations tell us to do. They say that we should look and be a certain way and if we do not, then we are not up to society's standards. So how does this affect the people of different **social classes**?

Those of **lower class** standing may not

have the means to buy the things that they see in magazines and on television. This could mean that they have an even lower self-esteem because they can not portray themselves in the socially acceptable way that is suggested in the ads. Those in the **middle class** may have the means to achieve a certain ideal that is portrayed in the media but their means are even more aggressively targeted by the corporations who seek to make a profit our of their impression management needs. Those in the **upper class** can certainly afford to be like the girls portrayed in the magazines. They can afford to buy the clothing, makeup, and diet pills to make them socially acceptable and they do not have to worry about the economic recourse. As a matter of fact, the images that are portrayed in the magazines are actually often the **ideas of the ruling class**. These are the dominant ideas that are present in society. So does this mean that the upper class women have a better body image because they themselves have created this image? I would argue that the mainstream concepts and realities that women face in society today are often hard to achieve, even for those in the upper class. In fact, women in the upper class are even more aggressively sought as advertising targets.

"The growth of feminism is an important reason for sociologists' growing interest in the body" (Wallace and Wolf, pg. 380). Gender is an important issue when talking about ideal body image in a capitalist society. Women are the highest portions of consumers in this country and the advertisements are really geared toward them. The way the media fluctuates decade after decade with changes in body ideals, plastic surgery seems to be a no-brainer of a solution to the potential problems women face. Breast augmentation and liposuction advertisements grace the pages of magazines. They encourage young girls that "thin is in" and that in order to be happy they must look like the girls that grace the pages of the magazines. This just fuels the consumer society and destroys people's images of themselves.

There are some stores that cater to the not socially ideal looking individual. These stores' goals are to tell the public that "beauty is more than fitting into a size four pant" (Maclean's, 2002:2). This is not however the mainstream reality. On the whole, the portrayals of body image in the consumer society really are not true or realistic. "It is more likely for someone to fully recover from cancer than it is for an obese person to lose a significant amount of weight and maintain it for five years" (Saltzberg & Chrisler 150). If this is the case, it is really unbelievable that the magazines would gear so much of their advertising around body image and achieving a certain look.

Emile Durkheim inspired **Functionalism**. He supported and viewed society as an entity in and of itself. "Society is external to us in that we feel its pressures to conform, but it is also internal to us in that it forms the collective moral conscience" (Farganis 55). Basically, collective human acts are what create social norms and this is reflected in everything from morals and behavior to looks and body ideals. But we were not all born with the thought that we have to be thin so we can fit into the society that we live in. Some people constructed this external "**social facts**," which have already been externalized and objectivated in society and we then internalize them to make them a part of us.

Durkheim distinguishes two basic forms of social organization, **mechanical solidarity** and **organic solidarity**. People with basically similar social roles characterize mechanical solidarity. These people have a tendency to share many things and have a common culture. They have little specialization or division of labor. These people who share a common culture and share many of the same things will strive to achieve the image that is portrayed in the media of women. It is a common cultural look and this may help gain them acceptance. The organic solidarity is a little bit different. It refers more to the modern society. There is a difference in the division of labor and an abundance of specialization, making people not conform to the norms as much. The people in organic solidarity with one another are also dependent on one another, though allowed to be more individual when it comes to how they want to look instead of portraying what is shown to society. This perhaps explains why the obsession with individual looks and impression management is so widespread in a modern society.

Once these obsessive behaviors become **social facts**, existing independently from a given individual act, they provoke conformity to the social norms. "If I do not submit to the conventions of society, if in my dress I do not conform to the customs observed in my country and in my class, the ridicule I provoke, the social isolation in which I am kept, produce, although in an attenuated form, the same effects as a punishment in the strict sense of the word" (Farganis 59-60). This is the fear of most people in modern life. If they do not conform to the body ideals set by society then they are going to be punished by society. They will not be able to achieve all that they can regardless of the talents that they hold. They have learned that we live in a society based on looks just as my family made me realize a long time ago.

Robert Merton's concepts of **manifest** and **latent functions** are also relevant to the issue of socially approved body image. Manifest functions, according Merton (Wallace and Wolf, 52-53), are the consequences that people easily observe and expect when performing an act. The manifest functions of beauty is to supposedly please our senses. The good looks is assumed to play such a manifest function in society. The latent functions are those that are not intended or recognized. The costly ability to maintain and achieve good looks certainly plays the latent functions of adding to corporate profits and disenfranchising those who cannot afford the means. In this society we expect that the better-looking woman is going to get the job over the fat and ugly one. That she will reap the social benefits while the girl who is not socially approved will not receive the benefits. I don't think that society actually planned on penalizing those who did not look socially ideal. I think that this is just what things have evolved to in society and that this is just one of the outcomes of it.

The issues with impression management that we have in society today are perpetuated through the media and how it portrays body image. Just as my family affected me, society and media are influenced by the consumer/capitalist society. It is made so that we all have a certain role to play and a certain way to look and if we do not fit into that then we do not get as far in the social world as one who may be ideal in the looks department. They reap the social rewards that society has to offer. Big corporations feed on this and make the public even more needy of the ideal body image by throwing it in their faces everyday on the television and the magazines.

Writer Allen Ginsberg once said; "Whoever controls the media—the images—controls the culture" (Maclean's 1). This is a very true statement. Society is based on looks and the capitalist society that we live in does not promote realistic beauty ideals or cater to the average woman. We all have issues with our bodies whether it comes from being bombarded with these wafer thin images portrayed in magazines or from the family we were raised in. At both micro and macro social levels, obsession with body image is a social dilemma we will all face in our lifetime.

REFERENCES

"Body Dissatisfaction in the Media." *Nutrition Research Newsletter* 19.5 (May 2000): pg15.

Farganis, J. (2004). *Readings in Social Theory: The Classic Tradition to Post-Modernism.* Forth Edition. Boston: McGraw Hill.

"Magazine Ideals Wrong." *The Journal of American Medical Association* 286.4 (July 2001): pg409.

Saltzberg, Elayne A. & Chrisler, Joan C. "Beauty is The Beast." In *Reconstruction Gender, Estelle Disch: A Multicultural Anthology,* 2nd Edition (California: Mayfield Publishing Co., 1997), 146-156.

Wallace, R & Wolf, A. (1999). *Contemporary Sociological Theory: Expanding the Classical Tradition.* Fifth Edition. New Jersey: Prentice Hall.

Underwood, Nora. "Body Envy: Thin is in—and people are messing with Mother Mature as never before." *Maclean's* (August 2000): pg36.

Films

"Affluenza." (1997). Bullfrog Films.

"The Big One." (1998). Miramax Home Entertainment.

"Billy Elliot." (2000). Universal Pictures.

"Erin Brockovich." (2000). Universal Pictures.

"The Matrix." (1999). Warner Bros.

"Twelve Angry Men" (1957

The Roots of Procrastination:
A Sociological Inquiry into Why I Wait Until Tomorrow

Jennifer M. Kosmas

UMass Boston

Ever since high school, I have struggled with handing in papers late, withdrawing from classes, and failing classes due to incomplete work. I have always wondered why? When my academic work first became negatively affected, I thought it was due to my diagnosed depression. I would take time off to "recover" and then when I felt "ready" for school again I would enroll. And yet my cycle of failure persists to this day. This has brought forth much frustration and aggravation throughout much of the latter part of my life, especially because I particularly enjoy learning and taking classes. I realize this compulsive habit may be due to my lack of self-confidence.

We began this semester by watching the film *The Matrix*, which pertains to **George Herbert Mead's** theory of **symbolic interactionism** and **the self**, as it is only through self-knowledge that one can best determine one's own actions. In **Herbert Blumer's** view, the individual has the capacity to critically reflect on what s/he learned in the past, and through **self-interaction** make his/her own interpretation and decisions regarding what course of action to follow, even if at odds with what broader society prescribes. The notion is especially important to Mead because he believes that the "human act is formed through self-interaction" (Wallace and Wolf, 201). The Matrix is an artificial reality that the individual perceives as being actual reality; therefore, when Neo learns that his mind is actually a part of the Matrix, through training and exercise learns to experience the Matrix as defines it for himself. In this situation, Neo is self-interacting, but his self-interaction can generate the virtual reality of the Matrix. But to arrive at that power, he had to relearn his past. During the movie Neo is shown a sign that reads, "Know Thyself." This is to show that we must try to understand ourselves and acknowledge our own incarcerations in the society we find ourselves so that we may set ourselves free from social prisons that may be partly a result of our own actions and the virtual realities we have create for ourselves through our harmful self-interactions. If we can become aware of our own social constructions, then we can also break out of the self-destructive habits by knowing ourselves. For instance, in knowing that low self-esteem causes my problems with procrastination, I know I can reinterpret my behavior based on my past knowledge and by using and applying this new knowledge obtain a different outcome. If I explore and can understand the reasons for which I procrastinate, then I will be able to change my self-destructive behavior. It is all whether one wants to know the truth or not. Would you take the red pill or the blue pill?

I joke about my procrastination with others, but when I look at the feelings I experience when I try to complete certain tasks, such as when I sit down to write a paper, some of them include: agony, anxiety, depression, mental block, embarrassment, lack of self-esteem, loneliness, and guilt for not having made more of an effort to finish to my full potential. Of course it would be easier to just do things on time; I create even more stress for myself by not doing so. But I do not procrastinate in all areas of my life, only those with which the feelings described above are associated. That is why I believe that my lack of self-confidence is a viable explanation for my recurring hindrance.

The distinction between my making jokes with others and the emotions I face when I am by myself can be described using Erving Goffman's theory of **dramaturgy** in everyday life, or the ways in which we present ourselves theatrically, as if on a stage. All of us seem to play roles of **actors** on an increasingly global stage. "Goffman looks at the ways individuals in their everyday lives present themselves and their activities to others; in particular, he focuses on **impression management**, the ways in which the individual guides and controls the impressions others form of him or her" (Wallace and Wolf, 230). When I seem calm and collected and joke about my problem with procrastination, I am merely trying to manage the impressions I am giving to others on the **front stage**, so that the audience that is observing me does not really know the feelings I experience in the **back region**, where I experience my anxieties and negative feelings about myself. What I would not want to show in the front region are the feelings of embarrassment I experience for both those that know me well and those that don't—since my procrastination often leads to a lasting reputation that is not indicative of my true capabilities.

When I contemplate as to *why* I may have such negative feelings about myself in the first place, however, I need to examine the interaction that I had with my parents growing up. In her essay, "Honor thy Father and Mother," Nancy Chapin states that "parents are transmitters of attitudes that the child adopts in forming a self image" (Chapin, 47). Undoubtedly with good intentions, (mainly) my father had unreasonable expectations of me throughout my life. He expressed this disparagingly, which always left me feeling inadequate. I began to see myself as if no matter what I did, nothing would be good enough, and I too, now, have high expectations of myself that I feel I cannot fulfill. While today I know that these feelings are unfounded, his attitude still had detrimental effects on my overall self-esteem. Berger and Luckmann's **phenomenological** view stresses that "**face-to-face** interaction is where the real action is" (Wallace and Wolf, 278). Face-to-face interaction allows me to internalize "knowledge about myself from others ... as in a 'mirror response'" (Berger and Luckmann summary, class handout). Seeing the disappointment and disapproving looks on my father's face when I brought home an A- instead of an A, or the distress I received throughout my high school softball career are just a few examples. When I **internalize** what appears to be **objectivated** rules of school evaluation set in the family as **externalized** by my father, I end up with certain perceptions of myself which often turn into **self-fulfilling prophecies**. If I keep telling myself that I will not succeed at certain tasks, then I am setting myself up for my own failure. Berger and Luckmann's "**social construction of reality** theory argues that whenever individuals engage in internalization, they are conforming to the expectations of existing social institutions" (Wallace and Wolf, 282). By internalizing my perceptions of myself through my father's objectivation in what is my **primary group** of **socialization**, I am not only conforming to my father's expectations of me to do well in school and sports, but I am also conforming to **social norms** which have been set in society for individuals' in terms of excelling in school and sports.

The kind of interactions I had with my father growing up also illustrates Charles Horton Cooley's important concept in the symbolic interactionist sociological perspective: **the looking glass self**. Cooley defines this concept as being constituted of the following three elements: "the imagination of our appearance to the other person; the imagination of his judgment of that appearance; and some sort of self-feeling, such as pride or mortification" (Wallace and Wolf, 195). These "mirror" imaginations, which were reflected back to me through my perception of my father's reactions, were more often than not negative. As Mead states, "Our behavior is seen as reflexive because we are able to understand and react to what others think and say about our behavior" (Farganis, 159). Mead also goes further to distinguish between two divisions or phases of the self—the "**I**" and the "**me**." The "me" is what you are given by the outside world, or society—it is how others perceive you. The "I" responds to the "me," and is how you interpret and respond to the "me." My "I" responds to my "me"s negatively because I am constantly being given negative messages about myself through how I interpret and internalize my father's reactions towards me. This sets the stage for the self-interactions that I have with myself—"the internal conversations one has with oneself are an essential part of the Meadian perspective because they are the means by which human beings take into account and organize themselves for action" (Wallace and Wolf, 200). Mead's "most significant insight," in fact, "was his view of human behavior as reflexive, by which he meant that you and I think before we act in many of our important activities" (Farganis, 159). When I am preparing to sit down and write a paper, for example, the interaction that I have with myself leads me to imagine the negative reaction I would be receiving from my father, which in turn, through my negative self-interaction, leads to procrastinating tendencies. I then become unmotivated to write my paper in fear that whatever the outcome I will feel as if I did poorly, and as if doing my best would never be good enough anyway. Sometimes I may not be even thinking this out in my head, but previous negative "self-feelings" have left their marks in my mind, influencing my behavior subconsciously.

Mead stresses the importance of **symbolic meaning**, or, how we create and use symbols and attribute subjective meanings to them in our social interactions. As individuals, we communicate to each other through the use of symbols such as **gestures**, which are physical indications of a predictable action and can stimulate a reaction. In a single gesture, we can communicate to another and give meaning to a situation without the use of words. Through the use of symbols we are able to come to our own conclusions, make decisions and act upon them, which give individuals control over their own lives as well as the potential for intervention. The gestures I received from my father included such things as making sure that I saw him shaking his head in disgust and walking away during the middle of a softball game while I may have not been having my best day at pitching. He expressed his ways of discouragement through symbols which I had learned were negative reflections— "gestures thus internalized are significant symbols because they have the same meaning for all individual members of a given society or social group, i.e., they respectively arouse the same attitudes in the individuals making them that they arouse in the individuals responding to them" (Wallace and Wolf, 203). I can only assume that this was my father's way of trying to help me do better, but when I needed positive support the most, he usually did things which always left me feeling badly about myself because I had learned that his gestures were meant to be negative.

Mead's concept of symbolic meaning and gestures go hand-in-hand with Harold Garfinkel's theory of **ethnomethodology**. Gestures are used to portray meaning as a form of communication, assuming that the gestures have the same meaning to all individuals involved. Scholars who use ethnomethodology pay particular attention to and study the taken for granted elements of every day life. Some gestures may seem like common sense to certain individuals, but if they do not carry the same meaning for all the individual involved then the symbolic meaning of what is being conveyed—and, more importantly, the communication itself—is lost or misinterpreted. I possibly could have been taking for granted what my father was trying to impress upon me, and that this was his way of showing his love and encouragement to me because he wanted me to be the best at school and softball. Maybe this was the way in which his family brought him up, and he was passing that on to me because those were the ways he learned and knew for raising children.

The film *12 Angry Men* can be useful when we look at Mead and Herbert Blumer's theories. The twelve men in the courtroom have all been exposed to the same situation, and yet each comes to their own conclusions about the case. The information in the courtroom is processed by each individual differently as each of their personal experiences brought along their own biases. These biases, stereotypes, and/or different experiences led to the inability to relate to people, in this case the convict, on a personal level. Henry Fonda's character is different because he has a constant awareness of what is going on around him, and is able to "put himself in the shoes" of another individual. Fonda's ability to resist the group's pressure through his initial vote against the guilty verdict pressured everyone to "take on the role of the other" and come to a rational conclusion about the case.

Up until this point, I have been trying to explain my issues with procrastination through **microsociological** perspectives, or those that are concerned mainly with one-on-one encounters. But there are some *macrosociological* perspectives which can certainly get to the root of my behaviors as well, or those which can be explained through larger-scale interpretations of how society affects us individually. George Homans, a *social exchange* theorist who still focuses on the micro social interactions, explains "social behavior as an exchange of activity ... between at least two persons." (Wallace and Wolf, 307). He goes on to set up five propositions, three of which I find particularly helpful in explaining my troubles with procrastination:

> (1) the *success proposition* states that for all actions taken by persons, the more often a particular action of a person is rewarded, the more likely the person is to perform that action; (2) the *stimulus proposition* states that a person is more likely to perform an action in which there was the occurrence of stimuli present where a person's action has been rewarded; and (3) the *aggression-approval proposition* states that when a person's action does not receive the reward he expected, or receives punishment he did not expect, he will be angry; he becomes more likely to perform aggressive behavior, and results of such behavior become more valuable to him (the frustration-aggression hypothesis). (Wallace and Wolf, 306-307)

Basically stated, people will repeat rewarding actions and avoid actions for which they are punished. In my case, I was looking more for emotional rewards and positive reinforcement, but repeatedly was not given one. **Randall Collins** has suggested that **rational choice** theory should take the approach of "emotions rather than material rewards as the primary force driving human actions. What he labels 'emotional energy' can be seen as a continuum, from confidence, enthusiasm, and happiness through to depression and gloom"

(Wallace and Wolf, 365). If we relate this to the interactions which I had with my father, it can be seen that my father's reactions to my performance in both school and sports always led me to feel as if I were being penalized and reprimanded even when I tried my best. Therefore, it would make sense that one would not want to repeat actions that are punishable. I was not rewarded emotionally for my performance as a student or a pitcher; instead I was repeatedly disciplined, leading to the lowering of my self-esteem.

I can relate a lot to the main character, Billy, in the film *Billy Elliott,* as I am all too familiar with the experience of an authoritarian father. My father became very involved early on and throughout my high school softball passion, and soon enough wanted me to succeed and nothing other than the best was good enough. As a pitcher, I practiced everyday, and I could not get involved in any other activities. I wanted to participate in drama but was not allowed to, since my father did not think this activity would not be as valuable to me as sports. This assigned value was a direct reflection of how society viewed, in this case, playing a sport versus being a drama kid. "Homans uses the assumption that people value approval to explain how conformity is created and maintained in informal groups" (Wallace and Wolf, 315). It became all about competition and making an impression on other people. Peter Blau, a major social exchange theorist, also "emphasizes the importance in social exchange of 'impression management,' or how people present themselves to others. (Wallace and Wolf, 329). When Billy was found to be taking ballet classes instead of going to boxing classes, his father insisted on his going to boxing and never to ballet classes again—even though Billy had a natural talent for ballet. His father reacted as such partly because of the stereotypes associated with boys participating in ballet, and also because of the ways in which others would view him; he was initially embarrassed by his son's dancing. We can see how macrosocial factors such as class and gender stereotypes affected Billy's growing up. When Billy's father intervened, Billy began losing his concentration, and became frustrated and angry—even briefly giving up his dreams of ballet. To this day I have these same feelings. Although I quit softball before I started college, I have struggled with completing schoolwork for years because I fear persistent failure. Unlike Billy's father, my father never realized how his behavior was oppressive, despite his good intentions. Robert Merton's distinction between **manifest and latent functions** may somewhat apply here, as the manifest function of my father's efforts in helping me served the latent function (or, in this case, **dysfunction**) of inhibiting my school work.

I found interesting studies which linked authoritarian parenting to the personality development of daughters in general, and particularly the predisposition to procrastination in female adolescents. The characteristics of the types of parents which lead to low self-esteem, depression, and procrastination in daughters were very similar to those of my own. For example, fathers which tended to be hostile and were judged as authoritarian had daughters who claimed low self-esteem (Ferrari & Olivette, 963). The research indicates that parental authority has an impact on their child's academic performance. "A growing body of literature suggests that chronic decisional procrastination may be a maladaptive personality tendency ... A cognitive antecedent of performance delay, decisional procrastination, or indecision, is said to be a coping pattern used to deal with decision-making situations perceived as stressful" (Ferrari & Olivette, 963). It is also noted that while procrastination can be related to low self-esteem, it is not associated with lack of intelligence. In a study, "46 procrastinators compared with 52 nonprocrastinators claimed lower self-esteem, greater public self-consciousness and social anxiety, and a stronger tendency toward self-handicapping" (Ferrari, 455). I was similarly not invited to be part of decision-making; to this day I have difficulties with effective decision-making.

I have been realizing recently that over time I have learned to use avoidance as almost a coping mechanism. As with procrastination, which is really just a way of avoiding the present, I avoid confrontation of any kind because I no longer want to experience negative self-feelings that I associate with the interaction that I had with my father. It is expected that "further research will provide evidence for persistent procrastination as a personality disorder that includes anxiety, avoidance, and a fear of evaluation of ability." (Ferrari, 455)

I see my family's behavior and attitudes as a direct result of society's views and values. I would consider my family to be fairly well off and very much involved in our capitalist economy. I, on the other hand, have found useful Marx's ideas and critique of capitalism. Marx believed that "individuals cannot reach their full potential as human beings because they are restricted by the relationships in which they are enmeshed" (Hurst, 12). This then leads to *alienation* from others and one's own potentials. This is very much a result of dominant *ideologies*, or beliefs which reflect the interests of dominant classes and groups in society. Marx also believed that "people behave the way they do because of the nature of their involvement in economic relationships" (Hurst, 12). Capitalism is the driving force of our everyday lives, as the obsessive search for the "American Dream," defined in terms of materialistic goals and values, has become more and more a goal for individuals and society as a whole. In each of the other films viewed in class—*Affluenza* and *The Big One*—we are able to see numerous examples of just how the materialistic culture affects us as a whole and as individuals. People now are spending beyond their means so that they are perceived as middle-class, or better off than they really are. I am very much against consumerism, whereas I have noticed my own family to be very much involved in impressing others with the wealth that they accumulate. I believe that this drives people further and further apart, and will be devastating for individuals and society in the end. I do not have the same ideals as my family in this regard—and am therefore viewed as "**deviant**" in a way—because I do not strive to consume and therefore project the idea that I am or seek to be wealthy. They probably worry that I will be viewed negatively by society—or perhaps they do not want to be viewed negatively themselves.

Talcott Parsons's **functionalist theory** emphasizes the process of socialization, "where societal values are internalized by a society's members" (Wallace and Wolf, 27). Parsons's views on *pattern variables*, or "variables which represent a problem or dilemma that must be solved by the actor before the action can take place" (Wallace and Wolf, 32), can also be applied to my own issues. The first pattern variable is between *ascription* and *achievement*, or quality versus performance. Modern society is supposed to help people base their actions on achievement rather than ascribed qualities they are born with. This means that I am supposed to be judged by others (such as my family) more by what I am supposed to "achieve" in life, than who I am. Another pattern variable that applies here is *affectivity* versus *affective neutrality*, which requires from individuals in modern life to maintain emotional detachment and neutrality in the conduct of their social tasks. basically on whether or not an individual will expect emotional gratification in the relationship. Lastly, the *collectivity-self* pattern variable directs us in modern life to seek self-interests in contrast to collective and communal bond characterizing traditional social life. A "functioning" capitalism then tends to favor self-interested, over-rationalizing, over-achievers in modern life, disregarding who they are, what they feel, and their social bonds. These all are macrosocial factors that can influence individuals' actions, such as those of my father or myself, depending on whether and how we internalize and accept them through the process of our socializations.

We do not have to accept such social influences, however, even if we are labeled as deviant as a result. Robert Merton's theory of deviance treats anomie as "a discontinuity between cultural goals and the legitimate means available for reaching them" (Wallace and Wolf, 56). He arrives at five approaches to goals, means and adaptations which help to explain the different types of *deviance*. "Merton chose to use a plus sign (+) to indicate acceptance of the goal of monetary success or the means to the goal, and he used a minus sign (-) to indicate the rejection (or unavailability) of the goal or means to it" (Wallace and Wolf, 56). The results of each of the available options leads to five *modes of adaptation*: (1) *conformity*; (2) *innovation*; (3) *ritualism*; (4) *retreatism*; and (5) *rebellion*, all of which are actually treated as forms of deviance by Merton. This can be applied to Erin in the film *Erin Brockovich*, because she was viewed as a "deviant" by those with whom she worked because of the clothes she chose to wear; yet, she resisted the social pressures to change and went on to be successful in her endeavors.

Although it was never the case, I was and still am seen as "rebellious," "deviant," or as someone who does things just to hurt my family. This is because I, as an individual, do not necessarily accept the things that I was taught and brought up with. I come from a conservative family, which is not open and accepting to new ideas, whereas I am very liberal, and an activist for causes that I feel passionately about. It was around the time when I was getting old enough to have my own ideas, opinions, and developing my own individuality that my father really began cracking down on me and we grew more and more distant. I have always felt as if my voice was never heard or, if heard, was rejected. I quickly became afraid to share my values and opinions with others because of the fear of being judged and not taken seriously. This is because my morals and beliefs were different than those of my family. I felt as if my opinions were never validated and that my individuality and independence was discouraged. I developed ideas of my own and acted not in accordance with the societal norms that my father tried to pass on to his children. As Kristy Canfield states in her essay, "Repairing the Soul: Matching Inner with Outer Beauty" (2002), "'The grass is greener on the other side' until one takes the initiative to search within one's self for improvement. Oppression is a social construct of this society but ultimately our social standing depends on our will to rise above others' actions and words" (20). As a result of feeling "oppressed" by my family, I may have turned to procrastination as a way of controlling something in my own life—I can choose to fail instead of being assigned failure.

But the right answer to my dilemma should be to resist and set myself free from the social pressures exerted by my family, and thus act according to my own conscience. "Liberation is not simply a possibility, but a necessity for humanity. It is the unity of these capacities of critical reflection and practical action in the organism ... that actualizes a fully human potential; any one-sidedness either way would bring about only 'verbalism' on one hand, or 'activism' on the other—both equally regarded by Freire as being deviations from the path of humanization" (Tamdgidi, 4). Looking at my behavior of procrastination in this new way has shown me a solution. I am now beginning to understand the reason why I feel so negatively about myself. I need to look in a new way at myself in the context of my family and society, and thereby change the course of my previous actions. This paper has already been a new journey of understanding myself. I never conceived of the reasons why I procrastinated. Knowing this, I am able to see a solution in the end, where I am able to change my own behavior to meet my own needs.

References

Farganis, James. (2004). *Readings in Social Theory: The Classic Tradition to Post-Modernism*. Fourth Edition. Boston: McGraw Hill Inc.

Ferrari, Joseph, R. *Compulsive procrastination: some self-reported characteristics. Psychological Reports*, April 1991 v 68 n2 p455(4).

Ferrari, Joseph, R.; Olivette, Michael, J. *Perceptions of parental control and the development of indecision among late adolescent females. Adolescence*, Winter 1993, v28, n112 p963(8).

Farganis, J. (2000). *Readings in Social Theory: The Classic Tradition to Post-Modernism*. Third edition. McGraw Hill College Divison.

Tamdgidi, H. Mohammad. (2004). *Freire Meets Gurdjieff and Rumi: Towards the Pedagogy of the Oppressed and Oppressing Selves*. Department of Sociology: Umass Boston.

Wallace, R and Wolf, A. (1999). *Contemporary Sociological Theory: Expanding the Classical Tradition*. Fifth Edition. New Jersey: Prentice hall.

Films:

"Affluenza". (1997). Bullfrog Films

"Billy Elliot". (2000). Universal Pictures.

"The Big One". (1999). Miramax Home Entertainment.

"The Matrix". (1999). Warner Brothers.

"Twelve Angry Men". (1957). MGM.

Honesty, Trust, and Love—In That Order:
A Sociology of My Emotional Kaleidoscope

Lynne K. Marlette

UMass Boston

Should I take anti-depressants? I've been thinking about this question on and off for the last few years. And, for the last six months, this has been one of many questions that I have asked myself. Although I am better equipped emotionally and mentally than I have ever felt, lately I have been endlessly asking questions about values such as honesty, trust, and love—so much so that I end up completely depressed.

Why anti-depressants and not talk therapy or just letting everything work itself out? Clearly, if I wanted the easy path, I would have been a prescribed patient long ago. Laziness may be one of the many reasons for my delay in pursuing a prescription, for even the latter involves going and talking to a doctor, and driving to CVS for a prescription. However, another reason may be my fear of anti-depressants as a band-aid. There are well documented side-effects of psychotropic drugs and I've seen first hand these effects on a close friend.

It has been a long six months of what seem like endless hours thinking about my past filled with negative emotions and memories, linking them to my present in pursuit of finding answers. I would have argued exactly six months and a day ago that my many years in therapy had allowed me to make peace with my childhood, but here I am today without that peace. I don't feel desperate, nor do I feel as alone as I once did, but sometimes I feel overwhelmed with thoughts and emotions—making my brain feel as if it's on a psychological vice, giving me moments of mental clarity and "feeling" happy. It's my hope that through the exploration of my understanding of how honesty, trust and love are defined and used in my life, I can answer the question, "should I take anti-depressants"?

I am reminded here of an experience I had as a child, looking through a kaleidoscope. I remember seeing the colors and being in awe of how the slightest touch, or twist could drastically change the outcome and visual presentation of the infinite combinations of shapes and colors. I often wondered if anyone else who was looking at it at the same time as I would have experienced or seen exactly what I saw. I now think of that experience as being indicative of the question whether there are universal standards of perception. This experience with the kaleidoscope solidified in me the feeling of being alone, which was already deeply rooted in my subconscious mind and conscious awareness.

Although others may argue that there are universal truths associated with all of the three values mentioned above, I feel I need my own exploration of their meaning since in my kaleidoscopic view they are subjective in nature. It is not such an easy task to analyze my thoughts regarding the three values clearly without exploring all the elements of my life that have shaped who I am—which makes my head swim in confusion. But, amidst this confusion, I've managed to come to some conclusions about myself and at the core of this change of heart is a friend who unknowingly

---

Notice: Copyright of *Human Architecture: Journal of the Sociology of Self-Knowledge* is the property of Ahead Publishing House (imprint: Okcir Press) and its content may not be copied or emailed to multiple sites or posted to a listserv without the copyright holder's express written permission. However, users may print, download, or email articles for individual use.

changed my perception of who I am.

When watching the movie **Erin Brockovich** in class, I often sympathized with what Erin might have felt facing challenges in life but making the decision to fight and make her life better. She let her instincts guide her—not really knowing but having the inner faith needed to sustain the energy to find possible answers. When she discovered the obvious discrepancies in a box containing real estate information with medical records of people living near the Pacific Gas & Electric Company plant, guided by her own motivations (disregarding company policies), Erin investigated for a week away from the office. Not surprisingly, she went back to the office, shocked to find out that she had been fired from her job. Others' misperceptions of her work ethic and prejudgments about her choice of "inappropriate" office clothing exerted a lot of pressure on her to accept a wrong picture of who she was—but her confident attitude prevented that from happening. I felt akin to Erin, but I also wonder about how many times, with my bottom chin trembling, I have accepted without a word wrong perceptions others have held of me, my head steaming in hurt and contentiousness but not doing anything about it.

A casual outsider might consider Erin to be a strong woman facing the Pacific Gas & Electric Company, but I think she like me is a vulnerable and sensitive person who, when pushed too far, when desperate enough, becomes a soldier. Erin did get to that point; she was feeding her kids fast food, herself eating out of a can dodging cockroaches while balancing her baby on one hip. I definitely don't have that kind of physical strain, but the last six months of mental agony has also pushed me to my limit, wondering if there is no other choice than to fight against what is making me so sad.

I have spent a lot of time rehashing old memories and sharing some of them as background information may be useful in providing a context to the my exploration of meanings of honesty, trust, and love in this paper. Before the age of eight, I was a homeless girl living on the streets of Seoul, Korea, until somehow miraculously I landed in an orphanage and was in turn adopted a few months later. My reality then was shaped by the space of the streets in which I lived, and that space was one that was filled with darkness, mistrust, loneliness, and of course, loveless-ness.

Honesty

Berger and Luckmann argue that our everyday lives are shaped through communications with others. During my early years, my **face to face interactions** were limited only to those between me and my brother. We **socially constructed** our reality together based on what we observed around us and others' behaviors, which were very limited in scope. I remember putting conscious effort into trying to understand the world in which we lived, but obviously since there was so little communication with other people, my reality back then was warped and shaped by a child's brain. Since I only interacted with my brother, how true were my observations of my surroundings, if I had so few interactions to compare them with? And how accurate are my perceptions now of what I experienced as a child? In therapy I learned that memories have a way of changing every time they're spoken out loud depending on such things as the day, the mood, prior night's dreams, and mental imagination.

The universal truths that were presented to me about honesty, trust, and love were poorly shaped back then. At that time, if I was honest, I would not have survived. If I respected others, I would not have eaten. Aside from the innate love I had for my brother, I did not feel love for anyone or anything, including myself. The **macro** world, outside of my **micro** world did not exist for me because when you don't have any other purpose in life other than to find food, the larger macro world is just an indistinguishable, uninteresting blob. Plus, it was easier to deal with life not admitting the possibility that a colorful and delicious meal existed in the world outside. Why commit false feelings to what were impossible realities?

Berger and Luckmann's notion of "**here and now**" consciousness in everyday life is so relevant to my understanding of my reality back then. In my mind, however, I often tried to escape the here and now reality I lived in. My immediate reality back then was filled with anger, hunger, and confusion about a world that I didn't have a choice in. Even then, I didn't live in the moment. I often tried to take me away from the reality of the moment, imagining other possible realities. All I did was to recreate the conscious moment(s) of my here and now by tricking my brain to imagine the state right before sleep, when you can see shadows of darkness in the blackness caused by your eyes being closed. No goals, no ideas, no dreams, no visions, no wishes, just escape from the present moment.

Just as I didn't choose to be born homeless, I didn't choose to be adopted. This is another reality which I have struggled to understand. How utterly absurd and miraculous is it to be adopted into an upper-class white family with seven other siblings, living in a 99.9% white suburb after living the first eight years of your life homeless—to be raised now in the midst of love and support? It's safe to say that my **self-identity**, which was skewed from the beginning, only got more confused after being adopted. Mead suggests that "**I**" and "**Me**" are in constant dialogue with one another in society. This was so true in my life. Right away, after being adopted, I knew that I was only as good as how I was perceived by others to be doing well in school, excelling in sports and appearing happy. This is best portrayed by **Erving Goffman** when explaining how self is presented in everyday life through management of others' **perceptions** and **impressions** of oneself:

> In short, since the reality that the individual is concerned with is unperceivable at the moment, appearances must be relied upon in its stead. And, paradoxically, the more the individual is concerned with the reality that is not available to perception, the more must he concentrate his attention on appearances. (Goffman, in Farganis 365)

I tried very hard to influence how others saw me, what Goffman refers to as **impression management.** My perceptions of myself did not jive with reality since I was always conscious of the feeling that my persona was not really me at all. So, if I was only shaping my outer persona to fit the perceptions of others, what exists in reality other than just appearances?

Mead also states that we are in a constant **reflective** interaction with the world, emphasizing that we can adjust and modify how we react to the world in the future. Since adoption, I've had the time and space to be honest with myself and to react to the world around me in a manner that I was consciously aware of. Yet I have continued not being honest with myself even to this day. I know this is one of the main reasons for my confusion and depression at times. I experience self-hatred when dealing with this subject, only because I think that if I had been honest from the beginning, I wouldn't have had to constantly re-evaluate my perceptions of my reality, and desire always to re-examine my past in order to correct mistakes.

This reminds me of the book, *The Strange Life of Ivan Osokin*, by P.D. Ouspenskii. The protagonist, Ivan disappointingly admits one day that he has not turned out to be the man he envisioned. He finds himself broke, without love, and desperate for a better future. Then he meets a magician who can grant his wish to go back ten years to live again his life (without losing all his present knowledge about himself) so that he can change the outcome. Ivan in his excitement doesn't pay much attention to the words of the magician who forewarns him that life is such a strong force that in some cases carries individuals through life without their active participation in it. Ivan was granted his wish and sent back to relive ten years. Even being granted full access of remembering his future actions, he relives the ten years to the detail exactly the same, and out of his pain, he ends up killing himself.

I can't help think that I would share Ivan's fate if I had the chance to relive my past. I'll forgo the chance to go back in time for the chance of making new and wiser perceptions of my past. Just knowing that I have been dishonest with myself has changed my self-perception and not so obviously others' perception of me. One clear example is my recent evolution from denial into acceptance of my **ethnicity** as being a part of my **identity**. All I wanted was to see myself as I imagined how others saw me, as a validation for all the work I did to keep appearances, but deep down knowing a lot of my behavior was fake. I never knew how others saw me, and the more I tried to see and control others' perceptions, the more I felt dishonest. I can't think of anything more dishonest in identity construction than purposefully denying the relevance of ethnicity to who you are.

This brings me to the present. The friend I mentioned earlier who has unknowingly changed my perception of who I am did so just by being who he is; a man from a different ethnic background than I who lives out his life to the best of his ability by identifying, learning, re-learning, adjusting, seeking, probing, and without fear actively participating in his life. **Exchange theory** tells us of the importance of culturally variant **expectations** and **norms** in social interaction. I bring these up also to emphasize that all cultures are deeply rooted in these concepts. It was my expectation that I could not feel romantic feelings for my friend because of my negative perception of myself as being part of an ethnic couple and how that would be perceived by other people. I hated that I was different, and I didn't want to remind myself of that difference by being with another ethnic person, making me constantly insecure. Why was I so insecure and who or what instilled in me these expectations of others as well as my own negative perceptions? If the author Charles E. Henderson (1983) is right in talking about dysfunctions stemming from subconscious imprinting, it's easy to understand how the idea of insecurity attached to negative feelings about ethnicity can leave a permanent **imprint** on our subconscious minds. Henderson writes:

> Whether caused by one event or several, whether occurring early in life or later, the subconscious ideas formed by such significant experiences are highly resistant to decay. We ordinarily think of things growing weaker with age, but this is not usually the case with subconscious ideas and beliefs. They can retain their potency throughout one's lifetime if not either spontaneously or purposely changed. (Henderson 74)

Knowing this, I really shouldn't beat myself up for having subconscious imprints still impacting my life today; instead I should almost expect it. The last line of the passage above is what interests me in my quest to redefine my meanings of honesty, trust and love. Early on in the semester, you said something that struck and convinced me to stay in your class. It was the idea that we are a product of **habits** and you suggested that we have the ability to change our thoughts and behavior if we understand this. This is directly related to what Henderson suggests is possible as a precursor to purposefully changing the imprints leading to unwanted behavior. I think the ironic thing about habits is that you don't realize they are habits until they're so much a part of who you are that it's hard to distinguish when it started and how it became a habit in the first place. Habits also exist in thoughts that keep repeating in one's own mind. These are the habits that cause people to be drawn to or repelled by one another—habits which we all share and what prompt us into social networks in smaller or larger social contexts. These are habits which allow us to say, "okay, he's like me," or "she's like me," which make us feel we are okay. This conclusion does not work for me because the habit of denying my own identity for the sake of others' acceptance doesn't leave me with the feeling that I'm okay. In addition, being confronted with my habit of being dishonest about my identity on one hand and feeling love for my "ethnic" friend on the other hand, I need to choose to actively seek out a change in my life for otherwise I would have to live with the way I feel about myself today.

TRUST

Now I switch to the idea of trust. It has always been hard to trust myself never mind others. This is because of fear imprinted through insecurities experienced in my physical, emotional, social, and mental realities in the past—manifested in distrusting the world around me and in turn, myself. What comes first, dishonesty about who I am, or distrusting who I am? To me, it's the perfect tail chase. If I distrust first, I can understand the need to be dishonest as there would be no point to being honest. On the other hand, if I was dishonest first, of course I am distrustful because I know myself that I cannot be trusted, so why would I think otherwise of anyone else?

Symbolic interaction emphasizes the reciprocally shaped nature of "definition and interpretation" (Farganis 349) of interactions among individuals and groups in society. This leads me to believe that I have as much influence in shaping my personal characteristics as any of the strangers do on me throughout the course of my life. **Herbert Blumer** states

> '**joint action**' captures this view of social life as a process rather than structure, and projects a view of society as a complex web of collaborative actions in which participants are constantly reflecting, negotiating, and fitting their actions to others in order to achieve common objectives. (Farganis 349)

I interpret the common objective to be the desire to find communities and similar others that we can associate with in order to feel significant and accepted. I'm certainly not discounting my habits of dishonesty or distrust, or trying to avoid self-criticism by blaming others, but if the common objective is to feel accepted (and this is done through mutually shared habits as I suggested earlier), then really, I am no better or worse off than anyone else I know or don't know. Then I ask the question, does everyone lie to themselves to fit and feel normal? I really think this might be the case, and I'm willing to acknowledge it at this time, perhaps as a justification to help me accept and understand myself.

The **capitalist** society and culture we live in today is portrayed well in the documentary film *Affluenza*, which depicts our world speeding into destruction through emphasis and rewards for **competitive individualism.** Living in such a society, how would it be possible to trust ourselves as well as others or be honest with who we are? Given such discriminating factors as

socioeconomic class, racism, sexism, etc., who is to say to that honesty and trust can be equally present across the board?

LOVE

Let me turn now to my idea of love. Having expressed my views on honesty and trust, and understanding these terms in relationship to others as well as to the world, it's cathartic for me to be able to freely express my own definition of love in the way that suits me even if it doesn't fit my parents', friends', or society's ideologies of love. Having been imprinted early in my childhood that love does not exist, I felt awkward about feeling love because a lot of what I read in the Cosmopolitan magazine, or talked about with my girlfriends, or saw in movies didn't match any of my thoughts on love—never mind that I felt no love for myself, and contrary to the popular cliché of only being able to love someone else if you love yourself, I think it's possible to love another human being without loving yourself—as I loved my brother. That's not to say that I didn't feel opposing feelings of anger and resentment towards him, but love in whatever form that I was able to feel was there.

Here is an important example from my life. How can I logically believe that in the same breath I tell to one man that I have never fell more in love with anyone than him and then sleep with another person? Rationally, anyone would argue that my love is not pure, or enough, to have sustained what I said to be true since I consciously decided to sleep with another man. And in the process of doing this, lying and deceiving at the same time, all the while being adamant and believing in the realness of my love. It was not until the office meeting that I had with you that I linked this experience and other behaviors associated with love to my adoption experience, and previous understandings and interpretations of honesty, trust, and love. This multiplicity of the "selves" that allows contrasting behaviors and oppositions in the mind to occur—not always jiving—I think that all people are susceptible to this or at the very least understand the nature of this multiplicity. We are all constantly trying to juggle many things in our lives, and while appearing to make things work well in the outside world, I think there is a lot of inner struggles that only the individual sees and feels. We all face the multiplicity of having many roles that may or may not interconnect with one another, making our "selves" more complex. I think the idiom "ignorance is bliss" may refer to the idea that it's easier to be simple-minded, and not face all the complexities going on in one's mind. I've joked when comparing myself to people I know who appear to be so happy and lead simple lives—but at the same I wonder if the choices they've made to make their lives and minds simple is actually a cowardly way of not facing the "bigger picture"? Is it so unbelievable that I could have many "selves" that may or may not be working together harmoniously, but nevertheless shaping all the facets of who I am?

I look around to many of my friends that have recently gotten married, and while I do not impose my beliefs on them directly, I do so indirectly by being who I am, suggesting that marriage is a sham. I cannot help wonder why in the face of statistical facts on the success rate of marriages; do individuals not look deep within themselves to admit latent basic or primal instincts that may affect the endurance of any marriage? Is it not obvious that everyone has the best of intentions, that this couldn't possibly be the reason for not facing the truth before marriage? If there was a clause in the vows of marriage or in our cultural mores that not only allowed but encouraged sexual freedom (whatever that may be for the individual), then I would confidently say that marriage is not a sham.

I believe as most do that honesty and trust are critical factors in love, but only achieved through being honest with the one's self or "selves" first. I know that presently I cannot stay attracted to one person while abstaining from everyone else except that one, as stipulated in the bonds of marriage. I guess it's not really a matter of whether or not I can do this; it's the question having the choice given to me. If I choose to be with only one man, that is more beautiful than being subjected to the rules of marriage and pressured to stay with one man. I believe I am capable of loving beautifully one person above any other because I too desire that close bond with one other person—but for the success of our relationship, there must be mutual respect and understanding of honesty, trust and love, first given to oneself and then to another. And what would be more beautiful to share the freedom to be our "selves" with another person, not hiding, not lying, and not being held back from any thought or desire but to share with another through understanding and support?

Schutz's phenomenological theory accepts as fact that social structures are there, and "seeks to understand the world from the point of view of the acting subject" (Farganis 303). Phenomenological theory is something that I can really sink my teeth into because it already comes so naturally to me. It's the idea that in order to learn about the phenomena that happen in our every day lives, we need to dissect every little detail of our lives. Purely from a gendered viewpoint, I believe women naturally do this—though, I don't mean to say that the conclusions or even the way women get to those conclusions are rational or logical (as many of my male friends, straight or gay, would agree). When I was in Korea, interpreting and living experiences gave me some **knowledge at hand** for my future interactions with the world. My actions and feelings at that time were **rational actions** based on my knowledge at that time which was considered normal and which was expected of me. The rational actions back then did not fit in to the new conditions when I came to the U.S., thereby forcing me to interrogate anew what was normal. But ironically, these differences in my interpretations of what was normal, and being an "acting subject" who really didn't have a clue—I now feel lucky to have feelings that are different than those of the status quo. But at the same time, I don't pretend these thoughts are original or so different than many out there now. In the movie *Billy Elliot*, Billy certainly didn't fit the status quo in his Irish mining town, yet he stuck to his instinct and managed the impossible to forge out an unexpected path in life. Even though his mother was no longer with him due to her death, faith in her love gave Billy the strength to express his true feelings and desires. I would like to experience this kind of love from someone that I can also be intimate with. In my opinion, love that goes beyond the earthy boundaries as in *Billy Elliot* can be liberating and definitely achievable and attainable.

Henderson states, "One of the most important concepts related to good health has to do with personal responsibility" (Henderson, pg. 155). This is one imprint that has long existed in me and after reading this same thought in a book, I feel proud that it has been a part of who I am. I have always felt personally responsible for my life and would never allow someone else be the driver of my body through it. Yet I believe that others allow society and other influences become the drivers of their lives. I believe that many people get married or go through life not taking personal responsibility, by postponing their understanding of the immediate impacts of actions on themselves and to others hoping that the good intentions never waver. I think the philosopher and mystic **G.I. Gurdjieff** would argue that going through life not taking personal responsibility isn't all that unexpected given the fragmented nature of self and how it operates. Gurdjieff suggests that individuals are made up of not one but three brains actually. He presents these brains using an image of a cart on wheels driven by a driver hooked up to a horse and with a passenger who represents the "I." Metaphorically, the **driver** represents the **intellectual self**, while the **horse** represents the **emotional self**, and the **cart** represents the **physical moving self** all sustained and kept watch over by the **passenger**, the "I." Like Gurdjieff, I believe that we are fragmented selves all trying to control our selves but not allowing them all to work collaboratively as one. Gurdjieff sees patterns of behaviors that correspond to any one of these metaphoric components, therefore concluding that individuals once seeing the patterns, have the power to change them with the aid of such therapies as visualizations, auto-suggestions, exercises, and physical movements. This can also be linked to my prior thought of my "selves" acting opposite one another, but co-existing within one body. This also links to Ivan's life mentioned earlier where one always knows the outcome of any given decisive action—at least the probable outcome either based on knowing oneself or all possible outcomes, thereby narrowing down a probable answer. I don't think, however, that people admit to themselves that prior knowledge exists or that patterns ever emerge. As I stated earlier, I think people let others drive their lives and this is explained by observing and understanding how fragmented we are. Not taking the personal responsibility of driving one's own lives is a pattern that is common. If so, then how shall I as the passenger go about ensuring that my horse will always take my commands, my cart will always be in good shape and the driver is always awake and listening?

Like Neo from *The Matrix* I have chosen to seek answers outside of the predetermined set of standards set by the society I know, but I have chosen to do so by seeking the truth in my self with faith in myself. One issue that I touched briefly on, but will use as a means for bringing together all my thoughts is the issue of fear. Fear is an imprinted habit that has latched onto me since the day I can remember. The obvious physical fear in my early childhood is not existent today, yet it has left a huge imprint that has affected every single aspect of my physical and mental life to this moment. Some fears are so small, buried in either my subconscious or conscious minds, that I would hardly give them a second thought. I feared writing this paper. I thought hard about discussing some other reasonable topic (but one that was much more superficial), but I was also fearful of my transparency.

Really, I don't know what it's going to take to sustain this level of letting myself and others see who I really am. And why should I be so scared anyway; I may be fearful of something that cannot be detected as "abnormal" to anyone else. It's making me depressed that I am showing others that I'm depressed, but at the same time realizing that part of understanding myself is to allow for this negative interaction process to happen. Not surprisingly writing this paper has allowed me to shed some guilt over feeling so self-absorbed for the past six months. I also thought about what the word theory meant. When I've taken theory for music, it's been the supplemental education of the other side of music rather than just audio aspect of it. Given the meaning of **theory** in sociology, as being a "tested/testable description or explanation of social reality" (Notes from class on 9/10/03) I am looking forward to seeing how my theories in this self-exploratory paper hold up.

Lastly, to get back to the question posed in the beginning, I don't know 100% if I want to or not take anti-depressants. On the one hand, I think it would allow me to take the edge off of the fear that looms everyday so I would be able to confront and deal with other outstanding issues. On the other, I fear that drugs will take the problem away so much that it becomes non-existent. This would definitely be unacceptable. As far as my concern for it being a band-aid, as long as I believe that psychotropic drugs will only be used temporarily to immediately put into action momentum to change what I need to change, I think I could use them and be satisfied with the outcome.

I think about how short life is, and how many years I've spent working and growing myself into who I am; I wonder if there is really enough time in our lifetime to know who we really are. But the point is to continually try to see and perhaps influence, through our inner and outer kaleidoscopes, the changing colors, patterns, and relationships shaping our selves and our world. It's this thought that actually gives me peace and makes me think of the proverb; "Life is a journey, not a destination."

REFERENCES

Wallace, Ruth A., and Alison Wolf. Contemporary Sociological Theory: Expanding the Classical Tradition. New Jersey: Prentice Hall, 1999.

Henderson, E Charles. You can do it with Self-Hypnosis; achieving self-improvement, personal growth, and success. Prentice-Hall Inc., Englewood Cliffs, New Jersey 1983.

Uspenskii, P.D. (2002). *The Strange life of Ivan Osokin*. Lindisfarne Books.

Films:

"The Matrix." (1999). Warner Brothers.

"Affluenza." (1997). KCTS-Seattle and Oregon Public Broadcasting.

"Billy Elliot." (2000). Universal Pictures.

"Erin Brockovich." (2000). Universal Pictures.

Questioning Motherhood:
A Sociological Awakening

Keilah Billings

UMass Boston

Having a child seems, for most people, to be a natural choice. For me, the choice translates into a simple question of desire: do I want to have a child? My answer, something I feel makes me different from many people, is no.

The idea of having a child is one that seems to go against my nature. Forming families seem to be the reigning desire for most women and men as they grow older and more mature. This need for procreation rips through especially women as a freight train through its rails. Having a child seems to be a natural process that many people feel is a major part of their lives' design. To me, the idea of having a child is more of an obstacle to what I can accomplish in my life—an end to the independence I have worked so hard to achieve. I am afraid that it would mean the end of who I am today, and I fear that being a mother would turn me into someone I do not want to be. Because of all this, I feel that making the decision to have a child would mean sacrificing my being. So when I choose not to have children, I am going against the social norms I have been taught to follow my whole life.

Whether we are consciously aware of them or not, **gender roles** are clearly defined in our society. It is socially accepted that as a woman, I should be nurturing, I should not only want children but should plan for them as much as I would for my next meal. I cannot accept this role as a predetermined fate for myself. I do not believe that this socially constructed role will work for me, and as a result I am going against not only what is biologically but also socially accepted as well.

Berger and Luckmann's concept of the **social construction of reality** primarily focuses on how the world is constructed and created, and how subjective meanings become realities in daily life. The social construction of women, as portrayed in the media and acted out by the majority in society, reinforces the stereotype that they will become mothers, whether or not that is their main desire. Most television shows portray women who are seeking a man to build a family with or who are already mothers. In my own family, the assumption that the girls would get married and bear children was an unspoken one, played out in the form of rhetorical questions. As a child, I remember saying things like "when I have kids" or "when my kids are older." Never once did I say "IF" I have kids, because it was a given. I truly did not believe there was anything else for me to do, because I was a woman. When I was little people always said to me, "When you grow up and have kids of your own …." The problem with this was that no one actually asked me *if* I wanted to have kids or told me that it was possible to grow up and not have any children. It was through this socially constructed reality that I came to believe that being a mother was inevitable. I accepted this to be the truth without ever questioning until I was much older and began to open my mind to new ideas.

My sisters and I were **socialized** to believe that raising a family was the main thing expected of women. My brothers, on the other hand, were always asked what they wanted to *do* when they grew up, posed in terms of a career. They were socialized to believe that they would find meaning for their lives in their work first, and perhaps family second. Interestingly, men are not usually asked about children. When my sisters and I were asked that question it came loaded with the expectation that a family and children would be a huge part of whatever direction our lives took. Our choices, it seemed, were limited. I then accepted what my **objectified** role as a woman was based upon the way life was planned to some degree for me, and as a result grew up to believe I was somehow less of a person if I chose a full time career as opposed to raising children.

I was one of seven children raised in a lower income household. As a result I did not receive the same advantages as those who grew up in more affluent homes. Pierre Bourdieu addresses this issue when discussing the notion of *cultural capital.* Bourdieu focused on how cultural capital is related to educational advantages. To help understand his theory I have looked at my own situation critically to see if there was a link. Since I grew up in a home with limited financial resources, my parents never truly encouraged college, and I wasn't really encouraged to become whatever I chose. There was always an unspoken expectation that I would graduate from high school and start a family shortly thereafter. My parents' economic status and low level of education prevented them from giving me a broader range of options. In reference to cultural capital, Bourdieu argues, what is essential for educational success is that one is able to be confident through all aspects of their lives including higher education, interviews, and meetings. He argues that children of higher- and middle-income families learn these skills, whereas children of lower-income families, like myself, do not have that confidence mastered. Existence or lack of such cultural capital resources and networks contributing to what Bourdieu calls *class reproduction*—to the perpetuation of class differences across generations. As a result of my economic status, it has been a difficult struggle for me to make the decision to attend college, forge a career, and also to dispel the low expectations that were ingrained during my childhood. My parents believed that they were inferior because of their economic class and therefore, perhaps unintentionally, felt the same was true for all of their children.

Erin Brockovich, as portrayed in the film about her life, was poor, raising three children alone. When she obtained the position at the lawyer's office, which she had to beg for, she was able to find a way in which she could earn a living to support herself and her children. At the same time, however, she was able to help numerous people who were sick and dying get financial help to better their lives. Erin was able to find a connection between what she needed for herself and the bigger issues in the world around her. She is a great example to me of what can be achieved even when a situation seems hopeless. I wish to find a similar place in the world, one where I can earn a living but also make a difference in the lives of those around me. If I had children, I would be less able to effectively help others in need.

Erin was forced to sacrifice time with her children in order to help others, seemingly unable to balance the demands of both. In order for her to be able to make a difference, her own family suffered, and this is one of the reasons why I feel I do not want children of my own. With all her family problems, Erin found herself in the midst of a **social conflict.** Coser argues that "external conflict is essential in establishing a group's identity." Erin saw major deceit in PG&E, a major difference between what was being told to the victims and what was actually true. I think that she saw this conflict and saw herself and her children in the place of those families she was trying to help. She believed that it could have been her and her children just as easily as it was these families. I could see in Erin's eyes that her heart was breaking from spending so little time with her children, but she also knew that if she did not help these people (and hold on to her job) then her children would pay a much higher price than just losing the time she was spending away from them. Undoubtedly, Erin accomplished in her public life while raising her children; but I am not sure, structurally, all poor women are that lucky.

Mead's theory of **the emergent self** helps explain how my decisions have been shaped throughout my life through socialization and by internalizing the values assumed to be held by a **generalized other**. For me the generalized other was mediated through my family, friends, and adult figures in my life. I have observed how each responded to having children and made decisions based on how others around me reacted. In her paper "Why I smoke: Sociology of a deadly habit" (2003), Emily Margulies discusses how her decision to smoke was made through a series of positive reinforcements while interacting with people around her, such as pretending to smoke with friends and "smoking" candy cigarettes. My view of having children was formed at a young age in very much the same way. When I reached what Mead calls the **game stage** of play, I began to play games with my sisters in which I would act how I thought they would expect me to. This stage was different than what Mead called the earlier **play stage** in which I was able to pretend I was a different character, but was unable to understand how I related to the rest of the characters in the games we played with. My sisters and I never played a game that did not include a mother and her children; we never played as businesswomen or superheroes. Much the same as Margulies never associated death or disease with a simple cigarette, I never thought it possible to become a woman without having children of my own. Now that I am older and able to truly see all my options, I am able to say with certainty that I do not want children as a part of my life. As a child I had playfully **externalized** this reality and considered having children believing that I had no other option. Now that I have matured I regard this **anticipatory** identity as simply another option for my life, one that I believe I will not pursue.

I feel there are big issues at stake in our lives today. I have started learning about our government and how it really works in our capitalist society. I began to question not only my place in the world but what kind of a future the U.S. has with a government that lies and bullies others for solely the purpose of financial gain. Being that the United States was in a time of domestic peace for so long many citizens took for granted that we couldn't be touched, that we were safe. After September 11, 2001 all Americans seemingly stood up in a united front against terrorism. It was during this time that I truly began my questioning of all that I had been socialized to become. I started questioning what I could do in order to make this world a safer place for future generations to come. My entire life changed, though, when I started to realize that by forming this so called united front we were instilling hatred in the hearts of every United States citizen. The president instated the Patriot Act that in my opinion created this sense that it was now acceptable to racially profile a person as long as they "look" or "act" like a terrorist. Left up for interpretation by those in power, the rights of the entire Arab world was and is being threatened. After watching decisions such as these being made I was sickened by the state of our union and I finally realized that I wanted to be a catalyst for change and/or help others in an effort to make a better tomorrow.

Max Weber identified three types of authority: charismatic, traditional, and rational-legal authority. *Charismatic authority* is based on the charisma of a person—Jesus is a good example. *Traditional authority* is passed on through social traditions and customs, such as the passing of a kingdom from father or mother to offspring. Finally, there is *rational-legal authority*, based on socially defined and legislated rules of conduct for those elected for or appointed to government positions—the U.S. government with an elected president is an example. As Weber also suggested, however, one can question whether such an ideal-type of authority can actually exist in pure form. As an elected leader, the President can influence law making and is able to make major decisions about our world and country. However our president is not supposed to do anything unless it is in the best interest of the people. This is what "democracy" is about. However, we as a people have come to a point where we accept what we are told as truth without questioning its validity. To blindly accept what we know next to nothing about and allow someone to make major decisions for us is problematic. Simply put, if we allow someone else to make the major decisions in our lives, then when something goes wrong we can blame him instead of ourselves. I fight this idea with every fiber of my being. I believe that not only do we have the right but also the obligation to speak out against the decisions we do not agree with which are being made in our name. In his movie, *The Big One*, Michael Moore sets forth an outstanding example of this idea. Here is a man who challenges the world of corporate America. He questions why American corporations are moving their companies to places such as Mexico and Asia when profits are up and the company is doing well here in the United States. The film portrays a good example of how it is possible to question authority and fight some of the injustice in our world.

I aspire to dedicate my life to helping the cause of peace. I wish to see the end of wars. I would like to put pressure on political leaders to make decisions, which are just, and to hold them accountable for decisions that are not. I want to be part of social reforms to help ensure equality for all, not just those living inside the four walls of the White House. I feel as though many Americans suffer from what Marx calls *false consciousness.* They are able to justify the decisions the President is making because he is promising a brighter future for America and the world. However, most do not see how dangerous the world is becoming, based in part on the President's decisions. It is my hope that I will be able to help open the eyes of at least a few American citizens, so that they may be able to see the truth of the poor decisions the President has made while in office.

Considering the above and what I want to do in my life, I have been forced to confront my decision to not have children. I have made this decision based on experience. My family structure was not a strong one, and as a result, I saw many of the negative aspects of raising a family. In his paper "Defying the Sweatshop, Sociologically Speaking" (2002), Steve Sacco discusses why he decided to stop buying anything manufactured in a sweatshop. Sacco grew in up in a white-collar family where he learned the value of hard work. He discusses how different his parents were in raising him and then goes on to write about the school he went to. Finally he seems to conclude that he was lucky enough to be surrounded by the right combination of people who inspired him into learning about these sweatshops and ultimately end his personal endorsement of them. Like Sacco, I believe that I was lucky enough to run into the right group of people in my life who have inspired me to reach out and make changes. Friends, family, and teachers have all helped to shape who I am and not one specific event has led to my awakening.

Critical Theory, associated with the theorists of the Frankfort School such as Herbert Marcuse, Eric Fromm, Max Horkheimer and others, is premised on a few basic ideas. The first is that any belief you hold is influenced by society. The second is that people of intelligence should critically examine the world around them, as it will help them and others become aware of diverse viewpoints besides what is popularly expressed. Critical Theory speaks to me, for it provides me with a method to think about and live my life. I always argue the other side of an issue because I believe it opens the mind to new ideas. Critical learning is not only invigorating, but also very important to me. I intend to apply my critical thinking and social awareness when choosing and pursuing a career that I am passionate about and would make some difference in the world around me. I cannot ignore, but in fact feel obligated, to pursue a line of work that contributes to fighting injustice anywhere and everywhere. I am trying to plan and pursue the steps necessary to make my dream happen. My goal remains a socially uplifting career, one that is important enough to me that I put serious time and effort into achieving it. A college education has been the first hurdle of my journey. I am in college struggling to balance a full time job, classes, and a relationship, yet I refuse to let anything deter me from achieving my goal.

Phenomenological Sociology is concerned with taking prior assumptions, or assumed truths, and questioning them in order to better understand the way the world around us has been socially constructed. I was raised to believe that I should be a mother because it would give my life meaning—somehow make me whole. When I was a bit older, I began to question this idea, seeking to craft my own way of living. I thought about what my life would be like without the obligation raising a family would undoubtedly bring. I have weighed the advantages and disadvantages of being a mother, and have found the disadvantages to be too high for me. I feel my place is in the community helping to change legislation, helping to ease the burdens of those who are less fortunate, and in contributing to bring about improvement and change in social programs. I want to be the key in easing some of the major problems facing our communities, including other families and parents today, in hopes that the next generation will encounter a world that is a little better than the one I grew up in. I think that for me raising a family would greatly impede this ambition. Just as in the movie *The Matrix*, I feel as though I have been awakened to a made-up world that I thought was reality, and have rediscovered a real world that gives me more than just one option. Just as Neo took the red pill and chose to see the truth, I too have chosen to break out of my socially constructed world and carve my own direction in life.

There are some real consequences I may inevitably face because of my decision. I will not have the bond and lasting relationship many say comes with being a mother. I may have trouble finding a mate, since most people do want to have children at some point during their lives. I may also always wonder if I have made the right decision, but I suppose everyone asks themselves that at some point during their lifetime. I have considered all these consequences and have decided to take my chances. I feel I have made a rational decision for someone in my circumstances. I looked at all the options, and based on what I believe in and what makes the most sense in my own life, have made up my mind about not raising children. I will not have the financial obligation that comes with having children. I am able to continue my education (formal or informal) without the difficulties posed by raising a child. I will be free to go where I want, when I want, and how I want. I will never face the worries of being a good mother, or the potential loss of identity which sometimes can occur in the fast-paced society in which we live.

My best friend has a baby, and I have

watched her entire life change before my eyes. She suddenly does not have the freedom to go whenever she pleases, she is always tired, and her life seems caught up in the ever-infantile world of Elmo and teething rings. The conversations I have with her now are less intellectual and more related to her child's food and movements. These things are all very important to her, but seem foreign to me. My friend never really made a decision to have or not have children, she simply had her son. I don't think she thought very much about the choice she was making and whether or not it would be good or bad for her or her child either. In fact, I often wonder to what extent women become mothers because they consciously choose to have children, and to what extent they become mothers because they are moving forward in their lives in a predetermined way, just as in *The Matrix*. The matrix is supposed to symbolically represent a world where, unless awakened, those living in it are completely unaware of its artificiality. The point really is not that of becoming mothers; the point is to what extent we consciously make such an important decision about our lives. I believe that most Americans live their lives in this same way. What we all need is what Herbert Blumer calls **interpretation**. Somewhere between impulse and action, we should all crave conscious thinking and choice. With this idea in mind, my decision to not have children becomes based, in part, on my observation and consideration of my friend's experiences. I am interpreting her situation as limiting, and therefore it acts as a deterrent for me. More than that, I have given this decision the same conscious and attentive thought I give every important decision in my life.

Homans, when discussing his notion of ***distributive justice,*** states that "what matters to people is that reward should be proportional to investment and contribution" (Wallace and Wolf). The amount of work put into something, such as a job, should be adequately compensated. I believe that a mother works as hard if not harder than any career-oriented woman, yet the reward is not always guaranteed in the kind of society we live in. It is not guaranteed that children will love and respect their parents, and every parent runs the risk of not being compensated at all for the work they put into raising their children. I would much rather put my heart into something and be guaranteed some sort of compensation for it, even if the only compensation I get is of an intrinsic nature, of being able to say I worked hard and now I am at peace. I don't perceive mothers being guaranteed that sort of peace in their lives. I believe that if a child makes a poor decision, the mother will always blame herself as if she had failed in some way. I believe that distributive justice should apply to all, especially to mothers who perform essential work for society. Short of that, I want the education and hard work I put into social programs to bear results. I feel more assured of being successful in this way than I would if I was a mother. My hope is that the next generation will live in a better world than I did.

When I was a child, my mother stayed at home with my six siblings and me. I saw my mother lose herself in her role of a mother and a homemaker and become overwhelmed to the point of shutting down and under-compensating in order to survive. The depression then began to set in, and her entire identity is now completely distorted and barely recognizable. I often wonder if she regrets having children and whether or not she would have been happy with only a few, or perhaps even none at all. I suppose my biggest fear with having children is that I would lose myself as she has, and that is something I am not willing to risk happening. My mother's life was compromised due to the fact that she grew to see her situation as hopeless. She can't change her past actions, she can't make her children go away, and she can never go back to the way her life used to be. She was a different person, one I have never met and probably never will. Her feelings fell somewhere between wishing we had never been born and feeling responsible for harming our emotional well-being. The guilt she must have felt undoubtedly is still with her. Her response to her situation has been expressed through a withdrawal from society and a life lived in seclusion. In my mother's everyday life **drama,** the **front region** compelled her to act in public as a good mother—one who loved and was there for her children in every way because this is what she believed to be socially acceptable. She was taught that this type of life would give her some sort of meaning and direction for her life. In the **back region** of her life, however, she was simply not happy with her role as a mother, and as a result she became emotionally unavailable and incapable of being an effective mother. She has spent most of her adult life as an actor in a play, not truly knowing that she was acting at all. I watched this for my entire life and saw no result other than pain in being a mother.

Writing these lines have helped me discover feelings I did not realize I had. Growing up in a home with an emotionally unavailable mother who regretted having children was a scarring experience. I see now how quickly my mother spiraled out of control, until she had sunk so deep that it became impossible for her to lift herself out of her situation. I often wonder who my mother would have been, had she not given in to outside pressures to have children. I try to imagine if she might have been pursued her education and found the cure for cancer, or AIDS, or maybe could have been a great painter. Unfortunately, I'll never know what she could have accomplished. It is possible that she could have done many things, but her life was diverted and she suppressed her inner feelings until she became someone she could no longer respect. Being a mother was an admirable thing, but she was obviously not happy with it. As a result, she will never know what her future may have held.

I have reflected on all of the influences in my life thus far and have not seen anything that would make me interested in having children. Through his concept **the looking glass self**, Charles Cooley illustrated how we often know, and feel about, ourselves through our imagination of how others perceive us. I have seen my mother completely lose herself because of her children. I have seen my friend lose much of her freedom for her child. I have imagined myself in their shoes, and have felt fear. Such an experience changes completely how a woman views herself and the outside world. Suddenly, learning seems to cease and a woman's life is put on hold to raise her children. Only some of these women will ever accomplish any of their goals, and I am saddened by this thought. I wonder how it is that our **alienating** society has taught us that it is fine to stunt our education and halt our life dreams because a child has been brought into our world.

My decision is of course based on my own life experience. Those who have helped keep my spirit up, have kept me willing to put up a fight for myself and make a series of decisions to achieve important goals. I will not feel fulfilled to spend the most important years of my lifetime at home. I want to change lives and travel the world and give my life meaning. I cannot compromise my ideals if I want to accomplish them. Seeing my mother regret her decisions was a very sad thing, and I believe she made those decisions because she was socialized to believe that children would be the ultimate accomplishment she could have. She compromised her own life and sought to do the same to each and every one of her children. She will never be a whole person again. For this I am sad, mostly because it troubles me that she would sacrifice everything to create lives that I don't believe she ever really wanted in the first place. Unfortunately, I don't think her story is uncommon.

I have decided that rather than potentially ruin the life of another human being that has not even been born, I will focus on helping those who are already alive and in need, including myself. There are many in need of something more than what they have, and I believe it will be better if I direct my energies to those already living. The exact direction I will take in my life is yet to be determined as I am furthering my education. I do know that I will be working with the public. For some time, I have considered going into the Peace Corp. I know that whatever I choose, I will succeed. I will not allow myself to be forced into making a decision, which will cause me to lose myself. My life's goal is to live it to the fullest, and I believe that I am gaining the skills I need to achieve that goal.

It is my sincere hope that everyone will be fulfilled in whatever way they choose to be. I believe that anyone can find meaning in whatever life they consciously choose, whether it be with a family or a career. I feel, for the first time in my life, that I have a better knowledge of who I am and what I want to do with my life. Every experience I have had, whether good or bad, has contributed in some way in bringing me to where I am today. I have struggled along the way but feel my eyes have opened to all possibilities. I still have the youth to believe all things are possible, and the wisdom to know that nothing in life is easy but the hardest things are always the most valuable. My decision is based on the circumstances and experiences of my own life, and what I feel can best accommodate the fulfillment of my goals.

I understand that becoming a mother does not in and of itself prevent one from achieving important goals in life. After all there have been many mothers, of many children, whose contributions to society have been exemplary—provided that they found a way to strike a balance between their private, personal troubles in the sphere of their families and the public issues of their times to which they also deserved to make significant contributions as human beings:

> *"I could not, at any age, be content to take my place by the fireside and simply look on. Life was meant to be lived. Curiosity must be kept alive. One must never, for whatever reason, turn his back on life."*
> Eleanor Roosevelt

References

Farganis, J. (2000). *Readings in Social Theory: The Classic Tradition to Post-Modernism*. Third Edition. Boston: McGraw-Hill.

Lorber, J. (1994). "The Social Construction of Gender." *Reconstructing Gender: A Multicultural Anthology.* Boston: McGraw-Hill. 2003. p. 96-103.

Margulies, E. (2003). "Why I Smoke: Sociology of A Deadly Habit." *Human Architecture: Journal of the Sociology of Self-Knowledge.* Vol. II, No. 1.

Wallace, R.A. and Wolf, A. (1999). *Contemporary Sociological Theory: Expanding the Classical Tradition*. Fifth Edition. New Jersey: Prentice Hall.

Films

"The Big One." (1998). Miramax Home Entertainment.
"Erin Brockovich." (2000). Universal Pictures.
"The Matrix." (1999). Warner Bros.

Durkheim, Mead, and Heroin Addiction

Nancy O'Keefe Dyer

UMass Boston

The "**social fact**" of heroin use and abuse in the United States today is a particularly tragic and troubling one. In February 2000, The National Drug Intelligence Center reported the "hardcore addict" population to be between 750,000 and 1,000,000. Additionally, there are a large number of "occasional" or "casual" users of heroin. On the streets of Boston today, a bag of heroin costs around $10... less than one Oxycontin (which sells for at least $10 per milligram) or two mixed drinks in a "classy" establishment, and as much as a case of cheap beer. The World Socialist Web Site, in July 2000, printed an interesting statement which may serve as a launching pad for this discussion. Quoting a Public Health officer in Seattle, it reads: "Dr. Oxman thinks he is commenting on the relative cheapness of the drug when he says, 'In today's economy you can work a minimum-wage job and scrape up enough for housing and food and be a heroin addict,' but, in fact, he is pointing unwittingly to a harsh reality of American life. The main point is not so much that young people who work in a convenience store or fast-food restaurant—and see no better prospect in the offing—*can afford* to do drugs, but that so many feel they need to."

Why *do* they feel they need to?

If evaluated rationally, a risk/benefit analysis of heroin use should lead to its total and near immediate extinction. According to a 1997 National Institutes of Health "Research Report" entitled "Heroin Abuse and Addiction," short term medical complications of heroin use include constipation, inability to urinate, nausea/vomiting, lowered blood pressure (which can lead to fainting after using) and slowed respirations. Long term medical complications include "scarred and /or collapsed veins, bacterial infections of the blood vessels and heart valves, abscesses and other soft-tissue infections, liver or kidney disease, lung complications (TB, pneumonia)," and the risks of contracting Hepatitis B and/or C and HIV- not to mention the very real risks of overdose, coma and death.

Heroin withdrawal symptoms, though rarely fatal in themselves, are extremely uncomfortable. Symptoms include: sleepiness, tearing of the eyes, muscle aches and spasms, stomach cramps, hyperventilation, hypothermia, joint pain, vomiting, diarrhea, "goose bumps," anxiety and hostility. S.H., a dear friend who has used IV heroin for almost 30 years (and has withdrawn many times) describes another symptom—the feeling that his "skin is crawling—as if there are bugs and worms inside my skin and they are all moving at once. I can't get away from it and I can't stop it. It makes me want to rip all my skin off my own body." He can tolerate the nausea and vomiting, but one can truly *feel* his panic as he anticipates the moment when his skin will begin to crawl.

The "benefits" of heroin use are, to an extent, related to dose, route, and the purity of the drug used. The peak effects of intravenous heroin are felt within eight to thirty *seconds*. Effects of intramuscular injection are felt in five to eight minutes, while smoking or snorting produce peak effects in ten to fifteen minutes. The initial effect is a "rush" of warmth, well-being and euphoria, and the relief of physical pain, stress

---

Notice: Copyright of *Human Architecture: Journal of the Sociology of Self-Knowledge* is the property of Ahead Publishing House (imprint: Okcir Press) and its content may not be copied or emailed to multiple sites or posted to a listserv without the copyright holder's express written permission. However, users may print, download, or email articles for individual use.

and anxiety. Respirations and heart rate slow, and after the initial "rush," a period of sedation ("the nod") follows, often lasting several hours. In his book *Heroin*, Humberto Fernandez writes, "…all of these effects occur almost immediately, giving the user instant gratification. To the addict, (physical) ill effects… are a small price to pay for the analgesia, or elimination of physical and emotional pain that a dose of heroin provides…. It is no wonder that this euphoria is found to be so compelling psychologically and physically; after all, pain and pleasure are our most primal motivators. Thus, the compulsion to use despite adverse consequences is fueled by very basic brain functions, perhaps the most important elements to consider when trying to understand why someone would use such a dangerous, addictive substance" (Fernandez 57).

The social effects of addiction can easily be seen by walking through Boston Common, or Chinatown, or the areas near St. Francis House or Borders Books on a hot summer night, or worse, on a blisteringly cold winter one. Street addicts, whose **alienation** from family and loved ones and careers of crime and deviance have often left them homeless, are everywhere. Although many have long criminal records rendering them virtually unemployable, their first priority each morning is to "chase down" a fix, impacting their ability to maintain a job even if they can find one. Homeless addicts can be seen "stemming" for money, seeking out the "good product" of the day and a set of "sealed works" for a "safe" injection. This constitutes the most important work of the street addict's day- they "cop," "use," "nod," and wake up, knowing that they have to "cop" again, all the while manipulating friends and lovers, enemies and strangers to secure the money they need.

The obvious street addicts, of which my friend S. H. is one, are just one segment of the population of addicts. My friend M.S. is an example of another type: A daily user of IV heroin for over 25 years. M. S. maintained a successful construction business for many of those years. He had a home and plenty of money, so managing his habit was easier, less desperate and frantic, and less visible. Those who worked for him *didn't know* that he had a $250 daily habit— until he fell from a roof, shattering his pelvis. During the next seven weeks in the hospital, M. S. lived through multiple surgeries and an intensely painful heroin withdrawal. His secret was out, he felt guilty and humiliated, and many of his relationships with friends and employees were permanently destroyed. Nonetheless, on the day of his discharge from the hospital his two immediate priorities were to send a dozen roses to each of his favorite nurses and to "score some dope." He was addicted again before my roses arrived.

Much has been written and much research done in an effort to understand the phenomenon of drug addiction. The treatment modalities available—medical, behavioral, pharmaceutical, "Twelve-Step"— speak to the many theories that have arisen as a result of research done to date. Yet statistics on heroin use and abuse indicate remarkably low "cure" rates and an ever-increasing number of addicts and "casual" users. Perhaps the field has been waiting for my investigation of the ways in which Emile Durkheim and George Herbert Mead would view the phenomenon of addiction.

EMILE DURKHEIM

My effort to understand the way in which Emile Durkheim might explain heroin addiction is predicated on an understanding of two important Durkheimian concepts: collective effervescence and anomie.

Durkheim wrote extensively in the later years of his career about religion. In *The Elementary Forms of Religious Life*, Durkheim studied the "primitive" form of religious practice of the Aruntas in Australia. It was in the context of looking at their rituals and their totemic beliefs that Durkheim developed the idea of collective effervescence.

For Durkheim, **collective effervescence** describes the powerful feelings experienced by a group when in the throws of religious rituals. A description of these "awe-inspiring ceremonial occasions" can be drawn from Daniel Pals' *Seven Theories of Religion*: "In the middle of such throbbing assemblies, individuals acquire sentiments and undertake actions they never would have been capable of embracing on their own. They leave behind what is distinctively their own and merge their identities joyfully into the common self of the clan. In such ceremonies, they leave the everyday, the humdrum, the selfish; they move instead into the domain of what is great and general. They enter the solemn sphere of the sacred" (Pals 104). Durkheim himself describes the essence of these feelings in the *Elementary Forms of Religious Life*, "By what other name (than religion) can one call the state in which men find themselves when, as a result of collective effervescence, they believe they have been swept up into a world entirely different from the one they have before their eyes?" (Durkheim 1995:228)

It is instructive to note Durkheim's belief that religion ultimately represents nothing more—or less—than that society's worship of itself. It fulfills a basic need in human beings and in their societies. In Pals' *Seven Theories of Religion*, it is explained: "Religion's purpose is not intellectual but social. It serves as the carrier of social sentiments, providing symbols and rituals that enable people to express the deep emotions which anchor them to their community. Insofar as it does this, religion, *or some substitute for it*, will always be with us. For then it stands on its true home ground, preserving and protecting the very "soul of society" (Pals 111, emphasis added).

The second Durkheimian concept of which we need an understanding is "anomie."

In *The Division of Labor in Society*, Durkheim discussed the impact of industrialization and the division of labor on society and societal integration. Simple, pre-industrial societies, described as those with **"mechanical solidarity**," involved societies bound together by similarities and by the **collective conscience** of the group. The collective conscience consisted of the **"norms"** of that society—the unwritten but universally understood code of moral ethics and acceptable behaviors that directed and maintained life in the community. This "compass" was readily available to all members of the small, close-knit community. **"Organic solidarity"** is Durkheim's term for post-industrial society. Workers are often in competition with their fellow workers, leading to withdrawal from them with the eventual loss of connection between and among people. The small-knit communities gave way to urban areas densely populated with people from many different areas, each with his or her own moral and ethical code. As such there was no "collective conscience"—no universally understood code of morals and ethics. Under such circumstances, Durkheim believed a state of "normlessness" develops- a state he termed **"anomie."**.

It is not difficult to view our modern world as being in—or at least contributing to—a state of anomie. In "Addiction as a Social Construction: A Postempirical view" published in the *Journal of Psychology*, author Franklin Truan writes: "… modern society has become a mass of isolated individuals conforming to and **oppressed** by a central society which is **depersonalizing**, manipulative, and oppressive in character. Humans live without a positive relationship to the center of their own society. The center has become either fragmented or opaque, thereby cutting individuals off from an active and enhancing relationship to tradition and to a sense of community… hence, the phenomenon of the 'lonely crowd': consisting of masses of isolated and lonely individuals" (Truan, p. 493).

I believe that Durkheim would see the social problem of heroin abuse as resulting from the anomic state of modern society combined with the hunger of the people living in this state for those powerful experiences of collective effervescence.

People are suffering from loneliness and a sense of powerlessness. In addition to having lost the guideposts provided by the collective conscience, they have also often lost the community connections that provided them with opportunities to experience "rituals of collective effervescence." Alone, lost and empty, with no firm set of societal norms to guide them and no close community to protect them, the promise of "euphoria" may well be too tempting for some to refuse. An addict I know once said; "forget every explanation for this that you've ever read —it's all about the euphoria, honey—plain and simple."

Once in it, the drug subculture offers a sense of **community** and solidarity. There is a hierarchy. The members of the "clan" all know one another-—they eat the free dinners at the churches together, sleep on the streets together, end up in shelters and detoxes (and sometimes jail) together. For example, my friend S.H., a native of Rhode Island, appears to know every junkie in the city of Boston. Walking the city streets with S.H. is nothing short of a social event. Handshakes, hugs and introductions abound: "We were on the Island together…" "I know him from jail…" It's not like Beano on Saturday night back home, but it is a sense of community for those who desperately need one.

GEORGE HERBERT MEAD

Our examination of the way in which George Herbert Mead would view the issue of heroin addiction requires an understanding of his basic concepts—and the use of a little "creative license." First, the basic.

Mead believed that the "**self**' arose as a result of the **socialization** process. In *Mind, Self and Society* he wrote: "The self is something which has development; it is not initially there, at birth, but arises in the process of social experience and activity, that is, develops in the given individual as a result of his relations to that process as a whole and to other individuals within that process" (Mead 135). The self, then, develops as a result of interactions with the environment, from the earliest actions and reactions of parents to the larger social world of one's community and school experiences. Mead said the development of mind and the self occurred through three forms of activity—*language*, *play* and *the game*. Briefly, language involves the use of **gestures** and **significant symbols**, play involves the development of the ability to see events from the vantage point of another, and the game involves the further development of play to include being able to understand the position of many others in a situation. Regarding the game, Mead wrote in *Mind, Self and Society*: "What goes on in the game goes on in the life of the child all the time. He is continually **taking in the attitudes** of those about him, especially the roles of those who in some sense control him and on whom he depends… There are all sorts of social organizations… into which the child is entering, and he is playing a sort of social game in them… He becomes a something which can function in the organized whole, and thus tends to determine himself in his relationship with the group to which he belongs. That process is one which is a striking stage in the development of the child's morale" (Mead 160).

Finally, our discussion requires a brief mention of the **"me" and the "I."** Mead wrote that the "self" consists of two components: the "me," or the socialized self, is that aspect of the self that is aware of, and concerned with how others view and judge it, it is the "conscience," the internalized norms; the "I" is the spontaneous, creative, impulsive and sometimes unpredictable component of the self. The "me" and the "I" interact to guide and control behavior, with the "me" providing the control to keep the "I" in check.

Mead did not include in his writing any consideration of the potential effect of pathology in developing the "self." My understanding of his writing is that it assumes a healthy and adaptive relationship between the child and his "significant others" as the child's "self" develops. Using Mead's belief that the self is a blank slate that is "filled in" through actions and interactions with society, I believe that the quality of those interactions might be the basis for an explanation of heroin abuse based on Mead's concepts.

What are the subsequent effects of raising a child in an atmosphere of abuse or neglect? What are the consequences of sending children to board away from their home and community—or of leaving a child to roam freely within that community as a result of the lack of childcare—or of a simple lack of interest in the child? What kind of interactions would that child experience? What would the content of his "*game*" be? How does a poorly-developed or under-developed or totally **dysfunctional** "me" control an impulsive, unpredictable "I"? Mead wrote in *Mind, Self and Society* that while playing the *game*, the child "tends to determine himself in his relationship with the group to which he belongs" (Mead 160). If a child is abused, neglected or just plain ignored, what impact might that have on the way in which that child "determines himself"?

I believe that the consequences of such treatment are negative and quite profound. In "Becoming a Problematic Consumer of Narcotics" (2001) from *Substance Use and Misuse*, Ted Goldberg suggests that problematic consumers have "many of the following factors in their backgrounds: poverty, at least one parent with a high level of alcohol consumption, corporal punishment, serious conflicts in the home… unclear demands, inconsistent use of punishment… sexual abuse, overcrowded living conditions… these factors play an important role in the development of the individual's self image…" (Goldberg 1303). Later in the same piece, Goldberg writes, "In their early contacts with society, children who have been labeled by their parents exhibit the beginning stages of the provocative behavioral patterns recognized by everyone who has worked with marginalized people. Although the child's self-image is not firmly established, he can consciously break rules he is aware of, and in doing so provoke negative reactions which serve as a confirmation of what he believes he knows about what kind of person he is. The more frequently a child receives confirmation of his developing negative self-image, the more strongly established it becomes" (Goldberg 1312).

I believe that, if asked to examine the question of heroin abuse in society, Mead would feel the most appropriate place to start would be in the development of the "self." While his extensive writings on the relationship between the child and the parent(s) in relation to the developed "self" and the "socialized me" did not explore the possibility and consequences of pathology and dysfunction, this appears to me a logical extension of his work.

M.G., a friend who has abused every drug imaginable, recalls the experience, as a 5 year-old, of finding his father dead. Obviously, he didn't know what to do. Thirty years later, when Mark discusses his drug use and abuse, the story always begins with his having found his father, his inability to save him—and his mother's subsequent withdrawal and depression. In M.G.'s life, all roads lead back to his parents. Perhaps I now have a better idea of why that is so.

I will conclude this paper with a final excerpt from the Goldberg piece since it is the most powerful and the most fundamentally *true* description of the thinking—and the *life*—of an addict that I have read during my research. I shared it with a friend who, like me, has had a long painful relationship with a "problematic consumer" of heroin and she agreed—*this is what they do*. Goldberg writes:

> Due to labeling, problematic consumers of narcotics have drastically negative self-images, initiated prior to their starting to take illegal drugs. Others have judged them unworthy and they have accepted the ruling. They try to flee, for instance with the help of psychoactive substances, but they have already internalized the condemnation, and no-one can escape from what they bear within. Due to all the negative experiences problematic consumers endure, as an integral part of the life they lead on the narcotics scene, they confirm for themselves that they deserve to be severely punished: after all they destroy for others and have devastated their own lives. As time passes and the quantity and magnitude of negative life experiences escalates, they become all the more convinced that they do not deserve to exist. Their life-pattern increasingly becomes a process of insuring that justice is done. Others have condemned them, they have accepted the verdict, and they become their own executioners. BUT, at the same time, by stealing from them, frightening them, giving them a bad conscience, etc., problematic consumers wreak revenge on those who have passed judgment. (Goldberg 1314)

This has been a deeply personal and difficult project for me. So much of what I have read on the topic of heroin has hit "close to home"—too close, at times, for comfort. Ultimately, I prefer my "Durkheimian" answer to this question. Perhaps as a mother, I hate the thought of adding the layer of guilt to a parent's burden of responsibility that comes with the "Mead" response. Perhaps as a trusted friend and (at times) co-conspirator of S.H.'s parents, I know their love, patience, exasperation and desperation for their son, all of which I have shared, and can't bear the thought of even suggesting that they in any way contributed to his destruction. Ultimately, though, regardless of what causes it and perpetuates it, heroin addiction is a true tragedy.

REFERENCES

Choldin, H. (1978). "Urban Density and Pathology." *Annual Review in Sociology.* v9:91-113

Darke, S., and Ross, J. (2002). "Suicide Among Heroin Users: Rates, Risk Factors and Methods." *Addiction.* v97:1383-1394

Durkheim, Emile. *Suicide, A Study in Sociology.* (1951). New York, New York: The Free Press.

Durkheim, Emile. *The Division of Labor in Society.* (1984). New York, New York: The Free Press.

Durkheim, Emile. *The Elementary Forms of Religious Life.* (1995). New York, New York: The Free Press.

Fernandez, Humberto. (1998). *Heroin.* Center City, Minnesota: Hazelden Information Education,

Foster, J. (2000). "Social Exclusion, Crime and Drugs." *Drugs: Education, Prevention and Policy.* v7 n4:317-330

Goldberg, T. (2001). "Becoming a Problem Consumer of Narcotics." *Substance Use & Misuse.* v36 n9&10:1297-1322

Mead, George Herbert. (1963). *Mind, Self, and Society.* University of Chicago Press.

Merry, J. (1975). "A Social History of Heroin Addiction." *British Journal of Addiction.* v70:307-310

National Institute of Drug Abuse: *Research Report: Heroin Use and Abuse.* National Institute of Health Publication number 00-4165: October 1997.

Pals, Daniel L. *Seven Theories of Religion.* (1996). New York, New York: Oxford University Press.

Shilling, C., and Mellor, P. (1998). "Durkheim, Mortality and Modernity: Collective Effervescence, Homo Duplex and the Sources of Morality." *British Journal of Sociology.* v49 i2:193-210

Truan, Franklin. (1993). "Addiction as a Social Construction: A Postempirical View." *Journal of Psychology.* v.127 i5:489-500

Walsh, David. 2000. "Heroin overdose deaths on the rise in the U.S." World Socialist Web Site. July 2000 www.wsws.org

Anomie or Alienation?:
A Self-Exploration of the Roots of Substance Ab/use

Buddi Osco

UMass Boston

Substance abuse is a serious problem for millions of citizens in the United States, and throughout the world. Everyday, across the globe, individuals of different races, ethnicities, religions, cultures, and social classes struggle with the disease of drug addiction. Many people lay the blame for these problems on the individuals themselves, labeling them as criminals, deviants, or persons of weak moral character. Perhaps they even cite bad parenting, or other such factors. But what if the true source of the problem was greater? What if the problem lies not in the individual or their family at all, but in society as a whole? Or, rather, what if the problem lies in the individual's lack of a connection to the rest of society?

In this paper, I will attempt to apply Emile Durkheim's theory of anomie and Karl Marx's theory of alienation to the problem of substance abuse, using my own life experiences to illuminate the subject. Although I do not consider myself to be a substance abuser, I do feel that I am qualified to serve as the primary example because I use marijuana on an almost daily basis. I do not consider my marijuana-using behavior to be deviant; however, marijuana and its usage have been deemed illegal and, thus, unacceptable behavior in the society in which I live. That said, contrary to my personal beliefs, I do technically fit the societal label of "substance abuser."

Anomie is a social condition characterized by instability, the breakdown of social norms, institutional disorganization, and a separation between socially valid goals and available means for achieving them. It also refers to the psychological condition of futility, anxiety, and amorality afflicting individuals who live under such conditions. As Durkheim wrote in *Suicide: A Study in Sociology*, "no living being can be happy or even exist unless his needs are sufficiently proportioned to his means"(1951:246). Put another way, what Durkheim meant was that man has certain expectations for his life. If these expectations are not met by society, then this will result in the individual's feeling alone and detached from the rest of society. Furthermore, Durkheim said that individual's natural expectations are unlimited. It is society's purpose to lay down the law. As Durkheim wrote, "[society] alone has the power necessary to stipulate the law and set the point beyond which the passions must not go" (249). That is to say, it is society that must regulate people's needs and set limitations. If society tells us what goals we are capable of achieving and we are then unable to reach those goals, then a feeling of anomie is the result.

In modern society we are told that human potential is almost limitless. In the United States particularly we know of this belief as the "American Dream." Since childhood we are told that we can achieve any and all of our dreams as long as we put in the effort. But with passage into adulthood, we quickly learn that it is not hard work alone that fulfills our expectations. There are other factors beyond our initial control, such as race, economic standing, and social class, which determine our place

---

Notice: Copyright of *Human Architecture: Journal of the Sociology of Self-Knowledge* is the property of Ahead Publishing House (imprint: Okcir Press) and its content may not be copied or emailed to multiple sites or posted to a listserv without the copyright holder's express written permission. However, users may print, download, or email articles for individual use.

in life.

I come from a working-class family. My mother was raised in the rural Ireland. She lived in poverty, and came to America in search of a better life. My father was born and raised in the United States. He too lived in poverty as a child in the housing projects of Charlestown, MA. In a sense, they achieved the "American Dream," as they both graduated to a higher social and economic class. Likewise, they did so through their own hard work and merit, and without the assistance of a college education. As a teenager, seeing, learning, and realizing what my parents had achieved through their own persistence and valiant efforts, I only assumed that I too would someday do as they had done. Seeing as I had even more resources at my disposal than my predecessors, I naturally dreamed of surpassing the achievements of my own parents socially and economically. Instead, I have found that a society very much unlike the one that I was led to believe existed. I have discovered a world in which the "American Dream" is merely a pipe dream.

Unlike my parents, I was not raised in poverty. I was born and raised in West Roxbury, a middle-class neighborhood of Boston. My parents were wealthy enough to be able to send me to a parochial middle school. I attended the prestigious Boston Latin Academy High School, a public preparatory school in Dorchester, MA. I had always assumed that such schooling would eventually lead me to an equally prestigious college career. Instead, because of a lack of financial means, I was led to the University of Massachusetts in Boston—a commuter university characterized by my high school guidance counselor as a "safety school" to which one applies in the event one is not accepted to a better one.

At first, this turn of events did not subdue me. I still had very high hopes for my future. I wanted to major in communications with a focus on film or radio. I was disappointed to find that the university curriculum did not contain either field of study. But, nevertheless, I continued on with my pursuit of higher knowledge. In the back of my mind, I thought that, perhaps, eventually I could transfer to a different institution that would have the fields that I truly yearned to study. Obviously, this would never happen. Due to financial constraints, I was forced to change my future plans. I was forced to mold my dreams into something more realistic. Realistic in the sense that it was more attainable for someone of my social and economic stature. After three years at the university, I came to the sad realization that I was stuck in a dire situation. As Durkheim wrote, "reality seems valueless by comparison with the dreams of fevered imaginations; reality is therefore abandoned ..." (256). I discerned that because of circumstances beyond my control I would never achieve my life goals. And, more so, I realized that reaching the goals that I had so desperately strived for was nearly impossible in the first place—that, realistically, the very society that had peddled the idea of the "American Dream" to me in the first place was what made achieving it so difficult.

Although I was unaware at the time, what I was feeling was anomie. The situation did not make sense to me. I felt like I had been lied to by society. Just as Durkheim had described, there was a separation between socially valid goals and available means for achieving them. Psychologically, I was filled with anxiety and a feeling of futility because, as Durkheim wrote, "to pursue a goal, which is by definition, unattainable is to condemn oneself to a state of perpetual unhappiness" (248). And this is exactly where I found myself.

But the question is, did this condition of anomie contribute to my substance abuse? The answer, in my opinion, would be a resounding yes. Before this occasion, I would classify my marijuana use as strictly social. It was only after coming to the realization that my life was almost predetermined that I began using it on a much more frequent basis. And the reason that I was using it on an almost daily basis was to tide the feelings of anxiety. Without the distraction of marijuana, I would uncontrollably dwell on my feelings of helplessness. I needed something outside of my being to more or less forget, if only for a fleeting moment of time, my current state. In essence, I began to use marijuana more often because it was depressing to dwell on the fact that I was stuck in a dead-end situation. Marijuana became an escape from the everyday monotony that my life had become, and, in my mind, would surely remain.

Alienation is another social condition much like anomie, but which is a result of the division of labor in modern society. According to Marx, meaningful labor is what makes us human. That is to say that in order for our lives to be meaningful, we must have a fulfilling job in society. We must have a place in the grand scheme of things in order for us to feel like a member of society. Hence, the importance of labor. In essence, without a job we are useless. But more than that, our job must be something important to us. Our labor must make us feel as if we are contributing to society. Without this meaningfulness, we are left feeling outside of ourselves and, thus, outside of society as a whole.

In regards to my own life, I will use my current employment at a Barnes & Noble bookstore as the primary example. Before working at Barnes & Noble, I had had several other jobs in the retail industry. However, my past experiences had all felt as if I was simply pushing the products of the company. I did not connect with the merchandise, nor with the business. Furthermore, I had no desire to connect with either one. When I first began working at Barnes & Noble, though, I thought of it as a job in which I would be able to contribute to society. By this, I mean, that I would at least be promoting something that could potentially expand the knowledge of those who frequented the establishment. Although I would not actually produce any of the books that were to be sold, in my mind, just by selling the products I was still part of something that was productive to the general public. Moreover, I only assumed that the company would hold this same attitude, in at least some sense. Bear in mind that I did not expect to waltz into a utopia. But I did believe that they would show some semblance of a company that was, in some small way, dispensing knowledge to those who were thirsty for it. However, after working there for only a short time I was quickly exposed to a completely different attitude.

I found a business that was no different than any of those that I had been employed by in the past. Barnes & Noble is, in reality, nothing more than a multi-million dollar corporation that is simply interested in making money. They do not view their position as one in which they could possibly better society. Just like any other business in corporate America, they bow down to the almighty dollar. They view their products as just that. They are not contributing to society by providing books to the public. Instead, they are selling a product for profit. Nothing more, and nothing less. And, as such, I as an employee am viewed as nothing more than a possible commodity or expense. Just as Marx's theory of alienation had described, my employers have distorted my personal view of my labor. As Marx wrote in *The German Ideology,* "... as long as a cleavage exists between the particular and the common interest ... man's own deed becomes an alien power to opposed to him ..." (53). This "alien power" is very much how I have now come to view my job. I no longer believe that I am contributing to society. I feel no connection to my labor. There is no enjoyment to be had at my work, and there is no connection to be felt. It has simply become a means to an end. I go to work in order to earn money. There is no other way of evaluating the situation because that is the way that it is presented to me.

Furthermore, just as Marx's theory states, my job is also a competition between my fellow employees and myself. If the business is not being run well, we compete for the opportunity to serve the company—because, of course, when the company is not making money then it must cut costs and we, the employees, are seen as the primary expense. Hence, it is our opportunity to labor that is the first to be cut back. As a result, I view the other employees as an "alien power" as well. Sadly, I cannot think of them as friends or colleagues. In my mind, they are no better than the company for which we are employed. They are almost an extension of the company's mentality itself.

But do these feelings of alienation contribute to my drug abuse? I would have to respond negatively to this idea. My conflicted feelings toward my job and my employers do not seem to contribute to my marijuana use at all. Instead, my reaction to this alienation results in a rebellion toward my work that takes place in other forms. For example, when feeling no connection to my work, I might react by not giving much of an effort while working. Or I might react by showing up late, leaving early, taking overly long breaks, or perhaps taking more breaks than I am allowed. In the most devious case, I might steal a book every so often. In essence, yes, the feelings of alienation do lead to deviant behavior on my part, but the deviant behavior always manifests itself in the form of rebellion against the company. The point is that I am attempting to take out my aggression on the business that is causing the problem rather than on myself. This does, in some sense, feel justified in my mind.

In conclusion, I believe that although anomie and alienation do exist in my life, in my personal case anomie does contribute to my substance abuse while alienation does not. Although both conditions do produce reactions involving deviant behavior, the behavior manifests itself in different forms. With the feelings of anomie, there does not seem to be anyone to blame. I can point at society as a whole and blame it for my problems, but there is no one entity that I can take my feelings out on. Hence, unfortunately, my only option is to attempt to escape through the use of marijuana. With the feelings of alienation, on the other hand, there is an instigator that I can distinguish and release the tensions on to. Thus, my deviant behaviors are imposed upon my employer. However, I cannot say for sure that this would be the case for all individuals.

This is a topic that would probably be best investigated on an individual basis. Although I do believe that anomie could easily lead to substance abuse in many individuals, I certainly don't feel that it would lead to the same problems for everyone. Likewise, although my feelings of alienation do not cause me to abuse marijuana, surely this might be the case for some people.

References

Durkheim, Emile. (1951). *Suicide: A Study in Sociology*. Glencoe, IL: Free Press.
Marx, Karl and Frederick Engels. (1970). *The German Ideology*. London: Lawrence & Wishart.

Just Live:
The Trick Is, You Have A Choice

Savvas Fetfatsidis

UMass Boston

You would never know there was an entrance to a club on this street. All you could see is a crowd of about two hundred people pushing their way towards the same direction as if trying to save themselves from some catastrophe about to happen. Where the heck were all these people trying to go? They were trying to get into one of the most exclusive clubs in town. The only way to get into this place was if you knew someone or if you had money to bribe the doormen. The club catered to the tastes of all people from around the globe. It would not be surprising on any given Saturday night to hear songs from Brazil, Italy, India, France or Lebanon. Their motto was, "We are all one!"

At around 12 p.m., a man in a beige suit, smoking a cigarette, squeezed his way through to the door. He looked really sharp. There was a beautiful Latin woman holding his left hand as he hugged the doorman with his right arm, as if they were friends forever. He walked through the hallway shaking hands with every employee he saw. His table was waiting for him upstairs next to the Disc Jockey's booth. After greeting everyone he knew, he sat down with his woman awaiting the arrival of his friends, ordered two drinks and lit her cigarette. When the drinks arrived they both stood up and walked over to the edge of the balcony overlooking the huge dance floor swarming with people everywhere. As he kissed his girl, he felt like the luckiest man on the face of the earth.

Just a few years later, this same man at one o'clock in the morning on a Saturday night was sitting in the basement of his parent's house screaming to the God who created him, "Why the f--k am I alive? Tell me or I give up on you and the world!"

I am the man in this story.

In this essay I am going to explore the reasons that caused me to have a breakdown that memorable night after battling many months with what I labeled as "clinical depression." I will discuss how music not only helped me get over my "depression," but how it actually helped to make it worse. I will also connect my experiences to the ideas and theories of various important sociological figures throughout its history.

Let us begin with my life just a few years ago when everything seemed perfect. During that time my friends and I would religiously attend this club called M-80's every Saturday night. We went there so often that absolutely everyone knew us. To be even more precise, I knew everybody in there and introduced them to my friends. The reason I say this in such an arrogant way is because it made me feel very powerful being in the position to know the owners of the various huge clubs in Boston. I felt powerful being able to take care of everyone I knew trying to get inside, even if they were not twenty-one years old yet. Thomas Hobbes's theory that humans desire power certainly rang true during that time.

The Disc Jockey was a personal friend of mine. As stated earlier, the music he played at the club came from many different places throughout the globe. Greeks and Italians would sing along and dance to Lebanese and Turkish songs and vice versa.

The club was like a second home to all of us. **Durkheim** would say that we all held some type of a **collective consciousness**. Collective consciousness can be defined as the "totality of beliefs and sentiment common to the average members of society," (Adams 93) which in turn creates social solidarity or harmony. Most of the patrons were 1st generation born Americans, like myself, struggling with the pursuit of money in a place where everyone is supposedly equal. In the club, we were living this American philosophy. The music united all of us under one roof and under one God!

This music transcended into my car and home. As I drove and listened to the tape from the previous Saturday, I would reminisce on some of the highlights of the night and look forward to next week. "Music is powerful at the level of social groups because it facilitates communication which goes beyond words, induces shared emotional reactions and supports the development of group identity" (DeNora, 51). It was this connection and interest with the world around me that I thrived on. Working in my family's restaurant was not much of a burden back then because of my positive outlook and attitude.

I began to promote my own nights. Almost every night I would be at a different club, meeting more and more people, not to mention more and more women. I can honestly say that I was satisfied with the way my life was developing. I had money, friends, girls, and power… or so I thought!

When I turned twenty-one, something very life-changing happened to me. I had just broken-up with my longtime girlfriend, but I was still doing fine. On my birthday I threw a huge party on a boat. I partied all night with my friends and also managed to make some money as well. The owner of the boat asked me to take over Friday nights after seeing how many attended the night. I agreed foolishly without really giving any thought to what I was doing. The reason it was foolish was because for the very first time I would have a bar minimum, which meant that the bar must make three thousand dollars or I would have to pay the difference. Usually, my only expenses would be the Disc Jockey, flyer design and distribution. The two subsequent Fridays were the most terrible nights I had ever organized. On the first night only two people showed up, and on the second night only ten. I could not believe that nobody showed up. To add insult to pain, I owed almost six thousand dollars to a big Russian club owner. I was able to gather five thousand from my personal bank account, and I borrowed one thousand dollars from my parents.

I never promoted another night after that day. I began to feel uneasy about going out and showing my face to people who heard about my unsuccessful nights. It seemed like everybody had heard about my failure and embarrassment. In this business, consistency and trust is a key factor to success. Whenever I would run into people and they asked me if I were still promoting, I would tell them that promoting only gave me a headache and that I wanted to enjoy myself at a club from now on instead of work at one. This type of rationalization is what sociologists call **self-justification** when experiencing **cognitive dissonance**. (Aronson 146) In other words, failing at promoting, which is not consistent with the idea that a man should be successful (cognitive dissonance), caused me to create a different reason for quitting other than giving up (self-justification).

I started working in the family restaurant full time, and as time went by I was going out less and less. M-80's closed down due to too many liquor license infractions. Their motto changed from "We are all One," to "We are all None." Since those days I have yet to find a place where I felt such belonging and comfort except for this one place I will discuss momentarily. I was now between 22 and 23 years old, single and felt as if I was fifty. My daily routine was work, sleep, work, sleep, etc. I needed something, but I did not know what. I felt like I was in a vicious routine, lacking any real purpose in my life.

In retrospect, after reading Marx, I was able to at least categorize what was happening to me. I was experiencing **alienation**, which Karl Marx defines as the disconnectedness of an individual from his work because it is externalized and outside of himself. "Labour is external to the worker" (Tucker 32), and it is therefore not his own. He calls this "Estranged Labor." He is referring at this time to the negative effects of the Industrial Revolution and Capitalism, which totally changed the way that people lived and worked. Although this "Revolution" was a great success in terms of the national economy, there was an increased awareness and resentment of the negative aspects of industrialization. Before the Industrial Revolution the whole household was involved in production of goods, but now families no longer worked together. Stricter work habits were instituted as wage labor was introduced. Workers were now on a time schedule and looked at as surplus value. This is exactly how I was feeling, but now I realize that my attitude had a lot to do with it.

Although it is nearly impossible to determine, without a doubt, that my work was the major cause of my condition, it was even more impossible to say that it had absolutely no effect on me. When I was promoting I was in control of my responsibilities. I was creating something that I felt was really special. I was creating relationships with successful people from different industries and so on. At the restaurant I was only working for my parents serving the same exact customers day after day. My job eventually became a routine. I was working 12-hour days doing the same exact thing, and repeating "Thank you, have a nice day" about 300 times a day. I felt lost.

Out of the blue, a friend that I hadn't spoken to in a while invited me to an after hours club. This place opened at 6 a.m. on Sunday mornings until 11a.m. He gave me this pill known as Ecstasy, an amphetamine known to give a person the feeling of empathy and harmony within himself. I didn't know much about it at the time, but since my friend recommended it and everyone in this place was doing it, I decided to take one as well. All I can say is that I have never felt such an amazing feeling in my life. The techno music at the club felt like a genius inventor designed it specifically for me. I was one with the music and with everyone around me. Wherever I looked I saw people dancing, talking, touching, and kissing each other. There were no inhibitions. We were free in this place. We were able to let go of the rules and prejudices in our mind. I was convinced this was what life should be.

There were dealers in every corner of the club bluntly selling their merchandise, even in front of the bouncers and managers. This kind of relaxed atmosphere led me to believe that this drug could not be too bad for us. Which brings me to a very important question: If this place did not exist, would we have still taken the drugs? **Durkheim** might have said that we would probably not have taken the drugs if things were more **regulated**. In other words, if people started getting arrested in the club it would close down, so management would make sure not to let anyone deal or use inside the club. If there are no drugs, there are no drug users. I, on the other hand would disagree and say that I felt a need to escape my life. Whether I was going to use drugs, drink, smoke, fight someone, steal something or even kill myself, I would definitely have found a way to avoid living the way I was living.

Freud would probably say that I was living more in my **Superego** consciousness rather than balancing it with the Id. The Superego in humans controls the beliefs that are conditioned by society such as prayer, saying thank you when someone opens a door for you, staying quiet in a movie theatre and not driving past the speed limit. The **Id** is the exact opposite. It describes our instinctual character. A person is happier when he or she is in the Id because of the freedom associated with that state. He believes we should live in both of these states in order to be balanced. If we spend too much time in one particular state we crave the other and run the risk of becoming pathological.

Society and family have certain expectations for individuals, which I like to call power. This power is an invisible collection of norms, ideas, philosophies and prejudices that an individual learns throughout his life that puts pressure on him or herself to conform with the generally agreed upon way of life. I was conforming so often to the world around me that I craved the childhood feeling of just letting go and being myself. My use of drugs was the product of that desire.

We continued going to this club every Sunday morning for a whole year, every single week. After only a couple of times one pill did not work for me any more. I gradually increased my dosage every weekend until I reached ten to eleven pills per night. We began experimenting with other drugs too. One of my friends blacked-out in the parking lot and nearly broke his head. Another friend went into CVS to buy cigarettes and when he came out he sat in a stranger's car and told him to get out because he thought it was his own car. Despite all these signs of trouble we continued doing what we were doing.

Then, on Halloween night, my cousin passed out in the middle of the entrance line. We were taking mushrooms, a hallucinogen, that night. I quickly grabbed him with a buddy of mine and brought him to the car. He told us to go to club without him and that he was okay, so we did. If the same thing happened today I would stay with him in the car to make sure that he remained okay, but I am glad that I did not because something extraordinary happened to me inside the club that has forever changed me. I experienced the most powerful epiphany of my life up until that point.

I was sitting down inside the club just watching the crowd dance around. Everyone seemed hypnotized to the music and in their own world. They appeared extremely happy, but I began to feel that they really were not. I began picturing what type of life they had outside the club. I pictured how dysfunctional their families might be, and compared them to my life. I could not find a good reason why I was doing drugs. I came from the most loving family in the world. I was not like these people. I pictured how much my mother and father sacrificed for me. I pictured how much they loved me. Then I pictured them being in church praying for the family without a clue that their only son was out burning his brain somewhere. In the pit of my belly a feeling that I can only define as guilt and sadness began to rumble. I realized that I had taken my life for granted all this time. I am proud to say that I never did drugs again after that day. I have heard that most of those "friends" continue to obsessively party on the weekends. Their preferred party place is New York, where the clubs never close, and their preferred drug is now cocaine and crystal-meth. I really owe my life to my family.

Throughout the following year I was a complete and utter mess. Nothing made me happy. Yes, I made the decision to stop using drugs, but I didn't have anywhere else to go from that point. I even stopped going out because I was so used to being high when I was out that it wasn't exciting anymore. I forgot how to have fun. I now feel like I slept my way through that year. My memory ceases to find any important events that happened to me. I thought I would be lost forever. It was during this time that I had my first and only nervous breakdown. I remember looking at myself in the mirror shaking and thinking that I was going to die right then and their.

My journey back to the consciousness and sanity of reality began when I started to listen to music again. One of my sister's friends was having a birthday party for her son and asked me to play a few songs on the guitar for them. I was extremely excited because it had been a long time since I played in front of anyone. I immediately began listening to the radio to see what songs were in at the time. The song that really struck me the most was "Higher," from Creed. The song described the way I felt for a long time. The song soon became the anthem to my life. Music on a general level mirrors us as individuals and as part of a culture (Norberg 6). I became convinced that I was not the only one feeling this way. The song goes as follows:

> *"Higher"* (words and music by Creed)
>
> *When dreaming I'm guided to another world*
> *Time and time again*
> *At sunrise I fight to stay asleep*
> *'Cause I don't want to leave the comfort of this place*
> *'Cause there's a hunger, a longing to escape*
> *From the life I live when I'm awake*
> *So let's go there*
> *Let's make our escape*
> *Come on, let's go there*
> *Let's ask can we stay?*
> *Can you take me Higher?*
> *To a place where blind men see*
> *Can you take me Higher?*
> *To a place with golden streets*

To me, this song represents a celebration of escape from reality, such as sleep. As I listened to the song I drifted away imagining a different, magical, peaceful world where you can do anything you want, even fly. The scary part was that I could not help thinking that the feeling of escape they are singing about can be permanently obtained by death. This song held two contradicting functions in my life. One was that others shared my thoughts and feelings, which made the way I feel normal in a way, therefore comforting me. Two, it caused me to constantly crave an escape from the world. The more I dwelled on this unrealistic world the more distant I was becoming from the people around me. Nothing made sense. The world ceased to have a meaning for me. "Music can have a very powerful influence on our emotions, moods and behavior" (Hodges 36). According to Hodges, in Nazi Germany, music was carefully selected for use at mass rallies to generate appropriate patriotic emotions. I now believe that a similar phenomenon was happening to me with Creed's music.

I continued listening to Creed's music thinking that they would lead me to answers for the mysteries of my life. Another popular song called, "My Own Prison" is about being a prisoner within your own mind and body.

> *"My Own Prison"* (words and music by Creed)
>
> *A court is in session, a verdict is in*
> *No appeal on the docket today*
> *Just my own sin*
> *The walls are cold and pale*
> *The cage made of steel*
> *Screams fill the room*
> *Alone I drop and kneel*
> *Silence now the sound*
> *My breath the only motion around*
> *Demons cluttering around*
> *My face showing no emotion*
> *Shackled by my sentence*
> *Expecting no return*
> *Here there is no penance*
> *My skin begins to burn*
>
> *(And I said oh) So I held my head up high*

Hiding hate that burns inside
Which only fuels their selfish pride
(And I said oh) We're all held captive
Out from the sun
A sun that shines on only some
We the meek are all in one

This song is about wallowing in your own misery and sin. For a person who is depressed this song can have drastic effects on his mental health. Taken to heart, this song can spark a person to begin questioning himself and his actions to a compulsive level even if there is nothing wrong with him or her—like it did to me. There is no sign of hope or of resolution in the song, which meant that there was no resolution in my life. I was listening to this and other self-loathing songs that influenced my attitude for many months. I did not realize what was happening to me until a close friend told me sincerely that he thinks the music I listen to is really affecting me and that I should try listening to other genres.

I took my friend's advice and I began listening to different music, totally boycotting groups that sang about the abstract dimensions of the mind and life. One such group is called Vaya Con Dios. Most of their songs are upbeat and have a certain walking and finger-snapping rhythm to them.

"Nah Neh Nah" words and music by Vaya Con Dios

I got on the phone and called the girls, said
Meet me down at Curly Pearls, for a
Ney, Nah Neh Nah
In my high-heeled shoes and fancy fads
I ran down the stairs hailed me a cab, going
Ney, Nah Neh Nah
Ney, Nah Neh Nah
Ney, Nah Neh Nah
Nah Neh Nah

When I pushed the door, I saw Eleanor
And Mary-Lou swinging on the floor, going
Ney, Nah Neh Nah
Sue came in, in a silk sarong
She waltzed across as they played that song, going
Ney, Nah Neh Nah
Ney, Nah Neh Nah
Ney, Nah Neh Nah
Nah Neh Nah

It was already half past three
But the night was young and so were we, dancing
Ney, Nah Neh Nah
Oh Lord, did we have a ball
Still singing, walking down that hall, that
Ney, Nah Neh Nah
Ney, Nah Neh Nah
Ney, Nah Neh Nah
Nah neh nah

This song celebrates life! "Nah Neh Nah" symbolizes action itself, for the sake of itself. What the particular action is isn't important. What is important is that we continue moving (living). The lyrics combined with the strut of a cool beat cause me to bob my head to smile. I now understand that I do not need to question everything I do. After listening to other Vaya Con Dios songs like, "It Must be Love" and "I Don't want to Know" nothing bothered me for a whole month. I was productive, positive and enjoying every minute of it.

Originally this paper was going to only analyze the effect of music on the individual and society, but as I was writing I began thinking more and more about the last few years of my life, and how much I've grown and changed. Finally putting this journey into perspective turned out to be very important for me. I have learned that being aware of a problem is the first step in solving it, but we should not make the problems our life. I am now looking at the family restaurant in a much more positive way and have taken many responsibilities on my shoulders. One day that store will be my own family's bread and butter, so I will take care of it with all my strength.

I believe that in society people of similar statuses and backgrounds are most likely to experience certain similar struggles. Each person deals with those struggles in their own personal ways and at their own pace. For me, family, friends, work, music and love are the core influences of my character. It was important for my character to go through this mental and spiritual suffering. It helped me to become a better and stronger person. In each society there are powerful forces influencing us, so the more we know about society the more we can deal with it. The old proverb that says that "seek, and you shall find," is the truth. In any given situation you can find positive and negative aspects. The trick is to know you can choose between the two. Sometimes I still need to remind myself to just relax and enjoy the ride of life because one day it will come to an end.

References

Adams, Bert N. (2002) *Classical Sociological Theory*. Sage Publications, Inc. California.

Aronson, Elliot. (2003). *The Social Animal* 9th ed. Worth Publishers, New York.

DeNora, T. (2000). *Music in Everyday Life*. Cambridge: Cambridge University. Press

Emerson, Ralph Waldo. *Selected Essays*. (1982). Viking Penguin Inc. Canada. *Self-Reliance*, pg. 175 – 204

Freud, Sigmund. *Civilization and its Discontents*. (Part of the readings for Soc 341, Fall 2003, UMass Boston)

Fromm, Erich H. (1941). *Escape From Freedom*. Fitzhenry & Whiteside Ltd., Ontario, Canada

Hansen, C.H. & Hansen, R.D. (1991). Constructing personality and social reality through music: Individual differences among fans of punk and heavy metal music, *Journal of Broadcasting and Media*, 35(3), 335-50.

Hodges, D.A. & Haack, P.A. (1996). The influence of music on behaviour. In D.A. Hodges (ed) *Handbook of Music Psychology*, San Antonia: IMR press.

Norberg, Eric. (1996). *Radio Programming*. Published by Elsevier Science Burlington, Ma

North, A.C., Hargreaves, D.J. and O'Neill, S.A. (2000). The importance of music to adolescents, *British Journal of Educational Psychology, 70*, 255-272.

Scheel, K.R. & Westefield, J.S. (1999). Heavy metal music and adolescent suicidality: an empirical investigation, *Adolescence, 34* (134), 253-273.

Sloboda, J. A. (1999). Everyday uses of music listening: a preliminary study. In Suk Won Yi (ed) *Music, mind and science*. Seoul: Western Music Institute

Tucker, Robert C. (1978) *Economic and Philosophic Manuscripts of 1844, The Marx-Engels, Reader,* 2nd *ed*. W.W. Norton, New York.

Songs:

"Higher" by Creed
"My Own Prison" by Creed
"Nah Neh Neh" by Vaya Con Dios

"Asian":
Just A Simple Word

Kuong C. Ly

UMass Boston

"Asian"—just a simple word. Defined by Merriam-Webster Dictionary as "a native or inhabitant of Asia."[1] To others, however, the word "Asian" is widely portrayed and associated with docile model minorities, exotic strangers, and passive individuals from a distant shore far in the East. This state of being exotic has created this sense of false exoticism among society about Asians from the "exotic" East.[2] Asians, whose racial ethnicity may be from Asia but who live their lives in the United States, are viewed as Asian Americans with strong focuses on educational and academic pursuits as means of obtaining social equality in their new land. Often times, their struggles for social justice are gained privately as individuals instead of voicing their opinion in the public arena like African Americans and other minority groups. Although some Asian Americans fit the stereotypes that perpetuate the "model minority" myth, society needs to take a closer look at how these false assumptions end up hurting Asian Americans and dividing ethnic groups along with ignoring important issues facing Asian Americans in the United States.

Since the first Chinese immigrants arrived in California as railroad workers in the nineteenth century, Asians have made significant contributions to developing nationhood and expansion of democratic institutions in the U.S. As the years have gone by, the flood of Asians into the United States has increased tremendously. The racial formation of Asian Americans can be traced throughout United States's history. From the Chinese railroad workers to Japanese strawberry farmers, to newly arrived refugee "boat people" from Southeast Asia, the simple term Asian is no longer defined as "a native or in habitant of Asia," but also associated with a number of myths and **stereotypes**—"a standard mental picture that is held in common by members of a group and that represents an oversimplified opinion, prejudiced attitude or uncritical judgment."[3] These have in turn caused tremendous problems for the Asian American community and has caused me personally tremendous turmoil as a Cambodian American living in the United States.

In *The Karma of Brown Folk*, by Vijay Prashad,[4] the question "What does it feel like to be a solution?" was proposed to the Asian American community by the author.[5] The notion of the Asian Americans being the "model minority" has created a picture of a hard working, studious group of Asian Americans who excel in academics and attend the top universities throughout the United States. This term was first used in print by sociologist William Peterson in an article titled "Success Story: Japanese American Style" published in the *New York Times Magazine* in January of 1966. Peterson concluded that Japanese culture with its family values and strong work ethic en-

---

1. Merriam-Webster's Dictionary. Online. www.webster.com
2. Webster's Dictionary.
3. Webster's Dictionary.
4. Prashad, Vijay. *The Karma of Brown Folk*. Minneapolis, Minnesota: University of Minnesota Press. 2000
5. Prashad. P. viii

Notice: Copyright of *Human Architecture: Journal of the Sociology of Self-Knowledge* is the property of Ahead Publishing House (imprint: Okcir Press) and its content may not be copied or emailed to multiple sites or posted to a listserv without the copyright holder's express written permission. However, users may print, download, or email articles for individual use.

abled the Japanese Americans to overcome prejudice and to avoid becoming a "problem minority."[1] This idea that Asians are the successful minority has become so widespread that admission offices at colleges and universities across the country do not include Asian or Asian Americans in their diversity recruitment efforts or affirmative action policies because Asian Americans are overly represented at the top schools and universities in the United States, even though they remain a minority group in the public's opinion because they are a part of the population that makes up the majority—whites. Many will argue that Asian Americans should not be bitter about these ideas and perceptions that shine light on their accomplishments. But, at the same time, this model minority myth has thrown Asian Americans into a limelight that has cast a shadow on the disturbing numbers of Asian American males and females suffering from behavior problems, substance abuse, and mental health problems.[2]

On March 10, 2004, Diana Chen of Cupertino, California, a nineteen year old sophomore student at New York University, took her own life by taking the fatal plunge from her midtown Manhattan apartment. Investigators reported that Chen ended a one-year relationship with her boyfriend that night which may have ignited her unspeakable action.[3] A week earlier, on the 3rd of March, the body of a Massachusetts Institute of Technology (M.I.T.) student Daniel S. Mun was found in the Charles River after his disappearance earlier that December. Police official stated that Mun's death was indeed a successful suicide since Mun's body was fully clothed and wearing roller skates.[4]

Today, suicide has become the second leading cause of death among Asian American youths, yet many have neglected to discuss the issue openly in fear of breaking the stereotype of this "perfect" model minority. Very few teen outreach organizations that were established to help youths at risk of drug abuse, violence and other social behavior have reached out to the Asian American community because many are blinded by the "model minority" myth. In order to help Asian Americans who are in a position where they need professional assistance, the public needs to destroy the false ideas and misconceptions that the "model minority" myth has perpetuated. In addition to this, research shows that Asian Americans have the leading number of attempted suicides within the last few years and very few have been aware of this matter. With the pressure from parents, school and surrounding community placed on the shoulders of an Asian youth to succeed, many feel obligated to uphold the stereotypes created by society based on their racial identification and when they fall short of these expectations there can be several psychological problems that may lead them to do the unthinkable. No matter how successful individual Asian Americans are in society, we cannot ignore the problems they face. The question still remains, if Asian Americans are model minorities, are these actions—drug abuse, attempted suicide, depression—model behaviors?

When looking at the model minority myth, individuals must recognize that biologically, not all Asian Americans are born natural scholars. There is no scientific evidence proving that there is some special gene within Asians that allows them to have unprecedented intelligence compared to other racial groups. Asians are diversely different with a broad range of intelligence, occupation and wealth. There seems to be this false belief that all Asian immigrants are examples of "rags to riches" story because many immigrated to the United

---

1. Chin, Andrew. Origins. www.modelminority.com. 21 April 2001.
2. Chow, May. "Failing APA Youth." *Asian Week*, 19 March 2004
3. Chow. "Failing APA Youth."
4. Hemel, Daniel J. "Body of MIT Junior Found." *The Harvard Crimson*. 3 March 2004.

States and have been successful in establishing themselves in this new land they call home. However, we cannot ignore the countless number of Asians who still live in the slums and unsanitary conditions in urban dwellings in Chinatowns across the United States.

If we continue to perpetuate this misconception that Asians are science and math scholars in academia, society continues to corner Asian Americans to believe that if they do not fit these ideas set before them, then there is something "wrong" with them.[1] It is no surprise that adolescence is believed to be the hardest period in an individual's life. Social acceptance by one's school community or surrounding environment is extremely vital in an individual's self-esteem. But for many Asian American youths, school events and social functions may lead to a feeling of isolation and anxiety. Unaccepted by their peers and classmates, pegged as four-eyed science geek and returning home to a house where their parents can't accept "B"s for English papers can be quite hard for an Asian American youth.[2] It can get lonesome when you have unrealistic expectations placed on you by society and parents, such as being valedictorian, getting a 1600 on your SATs, becoming an accomplished violinist, obtaining a 4.0 GPA and getting into an ivy league university? What is the value of getting into Harvard, Yale, Princeton and the alike when depression runs rampant and more expectations of succeeding at university is thrown in your direction because you were born into a racial group that you could not control and more expectations of succeeding at your academics pursuits are placed upon you once you receive the ivy league acceptance letter that your parents, not you, have been waiting for?

The world can be extremely racist without knowing it. When people in the U.S. think about racism, discrimination, and prejudice, they refer to the African American struggles, years of slavery, Dr. Martin Luther King, and the civil rights movement. Most public schools annually celebrate African American history month and read works like W.E.B. Dubois's *The Soul of Black Folk* where the question of "what does it feel like to be a problem" is proposed.[3] When the month of May roles around, schools often neglect Asian American history month. Rarely do schools include Amy Tan novels in their curriculum or focus on the Chinese Exclusion Act that regulated Chinese immigration into the United States or the bombing of neutral Cambodia during the 1970s. Everyone forgets the Japanese internment camps set up by the United States government, but remembers the Japanese attack on Pearl Harbor, the loss of "American" lives during the Korean War, and the number of innocent U.S. soldiers who died in the Vietnam war—a war that the U.S. should not have involved themselves in. Yet, the Vietnamese are the "evil" communist, a negative orientalism in the eyes of the general public and to those who served in the war. So, while model minority myth seems to say that Asian Americans are model citizens in the United States, how come we are rarely celebrated for our accomplishments both as a "racial" group and as "ethnic" individuals?

Part of the model minority myth and part of what society has conceived of Asian Americans in addition to the exoticism and academic scholars is the idea that Asians don't have a voice—they are passive individuals. White society has pegged Asians as model minorities because unlike other racial groups like African Americans, we have accepted many of the injustices placed upon us like the Japanese Internment camps created during World War II and the Chinese Exclusion Act implemented in 1886. Many newly arrived immigrants

---

1. Prashad. P.4
2. Chow. "Failing APA Youth."

3. Prashad. P. vii

have this attitude that America is not their land and therefore they feel as if they do not have a voice in American society and culture. They came "here to work hard and make money, and not to interfere in political matters."[1] The establishments of African American history month and the implication of African American literature in school curriculums were the result of persistence and vocal protest for change by the black community at large. However, many Asians do not feel that it is their place to voice their opinion; therefore, they have often been ignored and rarely celebrated as a community.

When people think of the word "Asian," countries like China, Japan, Korea and Vietnam and model minority myths pop into their mind. What many often ignore is the simple fact that Asians are much more than that. There are many other nations that make up Asia. In addition to racial stereotypes, there are also very many ethnic stereotypes within the Asian community; these ethnic stereotypes also help break and mold the model minority. What if you are Asian in every sense of the word but completely ignored by your own racial group? What if your ethnicity is often viewed as the ugly duckling—the black sheep of the Asian community? This is something that is unknown to the American (white) society, but the Asian community is fully aware of it. To the eyes of other minorities and white society, you appear to be just another smart and successful Asian, but to your own racial community, you have contributed nothing. This is what it is like to be me, a Cambodian American with two identities.

Today, the nation of Cambodia remains one of the poorest countries in the world. After years of civil war and turmoil, bombed by the United States during the 1970s after false accusation of siding with North Vietnam, followed by four years of genocide under the Khmer Rouge, in addition to military invasion and occupation by Vietnam in the 1980s, Cambodia is often viewed as a deteriorating country on the verge of collapse by other Asian countries. When American society views the Far East, they often think of the "four rising tigers"—nations like Japan with rising economic power in a world context. Many ignore the fact that most of Asia remains poverty stricken, "third world" nations like Cambodia. When the United States opened its door to Cambodian refugees, several families immigrated to the United States bringing with them the blood that flowed through the "killing fields"—a word coined for the Khmer Rouge regime that slaughtered two million Cambodians from 1975-1979. Unlike the boat people of Vietnam, the people of Cambodia spent four years under the rule of Pol Pot, a communist dictator whose "re-education" program consisted of destroying Cambodia's culture, society and institutions. Any sign of wealth or education led to death. Two million out of Cambodia's six million population were unjustly slaughtered. Sadly, this dark past has followed refugees who immigrated to the United Sates.[2] This largely contrasts with several other ethnically Asian groups like Japanese, Koreans and Chinese who came to this country searching for new opportunities and a better standard of living. These groups did not flee their native land the same way that many Cambodians had to in order to live.

Fearful of what succeeding in education may cause, several Cambodian American youths are rarely pressured by their parents to pursue a college degree after graduating from high school. In fact, Cambodian Americans have the highest percentage of high school dropouts, and the lowest percentage of college graduates. This, of course, contradicts the model mi-

---

1. Prashad. p.106

2. Flaccus, Gillian. "The Killing Fields of Long Beach." A. 13 February 2004.

nority myth and stereotypes that have been placed on the Asian American community by society. Unlike broader society, the Asian American community is fully aware that Cambodians do not excel in academia like most Asian Americans, which have caused tension between Cambodians and other Asian groups. Several Asian Americans have also bought into the notion of the "model minority" myth and believe that the community should perpetuate this "positive" stereotype so that we can prove to society that indeed we are the "rags to riches" racial group who have established themselves in the United States. Asians and Asian Americans who enjoy the stereotypes coined by society on Asians believe that Cambodians are disrupting the validity of the reputation and insist that Cambodians catch up to the rest of the Asian community by being successful. However, the Cambodian community has ignored other Asian groups because many of them are struggling to feed their kids and make enough money to pay the rent—education just isn't a priority when many are struggling to keep their kids away from gangs and violence.

From October 2003 to February 2004, six Cambodian Americans died violently in Long Beach, California. Violence is not uncommon in the Cambodian American community since hey first immigrated here in the 1970s.[1] Long Beach, California has one of the largest Cambodian communities in the United States and has had several shootings within recent months that led to the death of six Cambodian American men. These shootings open a window into this fragile refugee community undergoing the hardship of generation gap between parents and children, which is only made worse by the legacy of Cambodia's past and the public's complete denial that an Asian community has not flourished the same way that the model minority myth has suggested and taught us all to believe.

Unlike other Asian groups who immigrated to the United States in hopes of better opportunities, the life experiences of Cambodian American parents who fled the bloody killing fields and their American-born children differ so tremendously that most families are unable to overcome the cultural divide—which in turn has caused many Cambodian youth to turn to drug and violence, seeking refuge in the brotherhoods of gangs. Cambodian parents who grew up in Cambodia are often so busy working to provide for their kids that they are unable to look after the actions of their children. Cambodian refugees came to the United States with nothing, many of whom were women who lost their husbands and were forced into blue color jobs that prevented them from looking after their children. Even among those whose husbands survived the genocide, both parents had to work in order to provide for their children. Cambodian youth who were born and raised in the United States often view their parents' work as neglectful of their existence and turned to gangs as a way to seek a "family."

In addition to all this since there is very little verbal communication between parents and children, the parents speak Khmer but not English and the children speak English and often times broken Khmer. Rarely is the general public aware of this problem because they see Cambodians like other Asian immigrants who came to this country and not the dark history and struggles that have followed Cambodians who flee oppression. Those who are aware of the harsh reality for the Cambodian community have pegged Cambodians as the Asian community outcast for not succeeding in the ways that other groups have. Even those in other racial groups who are aware of the problem and the Asian community at large are unwilling to offer a helping hand, causing many Cambodians to relocate to

---

1.Flaccus. "The Killing Fields of Long Beach."

Long Beach, California and Lowell, Massachusetts—the two largest Cambodian American communities in the United States rigged with urban violence and drugs. These areas where Cambodian Americans are building their new lives are often poverty stricken districts where most kids end up turning to a life of violence and drugs similar to the life that had been place before Little B in the Elaine Brown's "The Condemnation of Little B."[1] The reason why the Asian American community does not recognize Cambodian Americans as part of their racial group is due to class conflict. Because so many Cambodian Americans do not pursue education like other Asian Americans, they often have blue-collar jobs that pay very little. The successful Asian Americans often question why Cambodian Americans struggle to catch up with the rest of the Asian community, and because of class conflict, Cambodian Americans are often not included in the racial formation of Asian American identity in the United States.

Throughout my life, I'm face with several questions of "What does it mean to be Asian?" and "How do you define being Asian?" "It's only a word" is what I tell myself. But, I know that it is so much more than that. The racial side of my mind tells me I should break the Asian American mold of model minority myth and challenge the general public's opinion of Asian Americans by becoming a blue-collar college dropout, or by carrying out the struggle for social justice by voicing the need to bring down the false stereotypes of "model minority" that society has built. But by doing so, I'm only validating the stereotypes that the Asian American community has placed on my Cambodian American ethnic identity. So, the ethnic part of my mind tells me that I should break the mold placed on Cambodian Americans by getting a college education and pursuing the model minority myth. Does that mean that by doing so the racial side of my mind has won, or does that mean that the ethnic side of my mind has triumphed? The battle between which of the two molds I should be breaking remains, and I'm still torn as to what it means to be "Asian"—after all *it's just a simple word*. Or is it?

REFERENCES

Brown, Elaine. *The Condemnation of Little B: New Age Racism in America*. Boston: Beacon Press. 2002.

Chin, Andrew. Origins. www.modelminority.com. 21 April 2001.

Chow, May. "Failing APA Youth." *Asian Week*, 19 March 2004

Flaccus, Gillian. "The Killing Fields of Long Beach." A. 13 February 2004.

Hemel, Daniel J. "Body of MIT Junior Found." *The Harvard Crimson*. 3 March 2004.

Merriam-Webster's Dictionary. Online. www.webster.com

Prashad, Vijay. *The Karma of Brown Folk*. Minneapolis, Minnesota: University of Minnesota Press. 2000

---

1. Brown, Elaine. *The Condemnation of Little B: New Age Racism in America*. Boston: Beacon Press. 2002.

Defining the Other

Jorge Capetillo-Ponce

UMass Boston

"Everything is what is not."

—G. W. F. Hegel

I

Throughout human history, we find a continuous struggle to define the other, the foreigner, the unknown, the opposite of we or I. And, as the above quote from Hegel indicates, what they are, that we are not, helps define the frontiers of personal and group identity.

In the earliest written accounts, in ancient civilizations like Sumer, Akkad, Egypt, China, India, Mexico, we find stories of battles, of fighting "other" people, as well as accounts of commerce and marriage with people from "other lands." Through this interaction with the other, with the stranger, humans have gradually defined themselves, assigning to both themselves and others distinguishing and unique racial, cultural, and socio-political characteristics

They are further distinguished from one another by language, art and religion. Over time, such concepts as race, ethnicity, community, nationalism—among many others—emerged to explain certain aspects of our obsessive concern with the other. These concepts have been used to explain the "sense of belonging" we see in groups, in neighborhoods, in institutions, in primitive tribes, in nations. Sometimes these concepts have also been utilized to explain or foster legitimacy and identity among individuals and/or groups, and sometimes to create divisions and conflict.

Christianity inherited the structure of classical antiquity of defining other peoples by a rank of valuation based on its geographical proximity to a center of civilization such as Rome, Athens, Constantinople or Alexandria. For the "civilized" groups of the ancient Roman world, the closer or contiguous "others" were considered "barbarians," because they spoke a language that sounded like "bar-bar" to the Romans. But while not considered quite human, these barbarians were still identifiable through their engagement in such social exchanges as commerce and war. Beyond the land of the barbarians, lived the unknown "monstrous races." As we can see in drawings from the Middle Ages and early Renaissance, they were depicted as people with their faces in their belly, with many arms or legs, with only one eye on the forehead, or, in general, with features very close to those of animals.

With the triumph of Constantine as sole emperor of Rome in the fourth century A.D., Christianity became the official religion of the late Roman Empire, and the Roman trichotomy of civilized, barbarians, and monstrous humans was transformed gradually to the religious trichotomy of the faithful (that is, the Christians), the unredeemed, and the unredeemable. Muslims—many Islamic societies until the 17th and 18th centuries were as developed or more than European nations—Slavs, Vikings, Franks, and Germans, were considered heretic but redeemable. That is, their acceptance of the word of God would upgrade their category to faithful or Christian, because members of the unredeemed category had a soul and thus could be transformed.

This was not the case for the category

of monsters, now the unredeemable. Members of this category of religious otherness were not fully human simply because they lacked a soul and could not be converted into Christianity. It was applied to the horseback people that invaded Christendom from the east, such as Mongols, Huns, and Tartars. In fact, the conquests and raids dating from late antiquity up to the time of Gengis Khan and his descendants, were considered by the Christians of the Middle Ages as attacks on the faithful by evil forces. Interpretation of events at that time was based solely on biblical grounds. Thus, these evil strangers were associated with the descendants of Cain, or of Noah's son Ham who had sinned against his father and against God.

Within this unredeemable, monster-like category were also inserted black Africans. The medieval belief that they had no soul constituted one of the key reasons why there was little resistance to black slavery until much later.

Here it is important to underline that at the very beginning of the conquest of the New World, the American natives or Indians were also enslaved by the Spanish. But in this case an enlightened Dominican priest, Fray Bartolomé de las Casas, defended the natives and actually took the case to the Spanish court and eventually to the Vatican. The debate between Fray Bartolomé and another learned Spaniard, Ginés de Seplveda, was a famous one, with the final result being that Indians were recognized as having a soul, and thus redeemable. Still, while Fray Bartolome had won his case, and Indian slavery was banned in Spanish America, it was not the same case with African blacks, who were brought as slaves by the millions in the following centuries to Spanish, Portuguese, French, and English-dominated areas of the American continent.

II

There were other categories of otherness in Europe. Through the accounts of travelers like Marco Polo, far-away nations such as China and India became partially known. They were considered civilized but unknown peoples. They were enigmatic people. This started to change in the fifteenth century, when the era of voyages of discovery began in Portugal, inspired by the Portuguese prince Henry the Navigator. And soon enough, the "discovered" others began to realize that discovery was synonymous to colonization and submission.

But the Europeans were not the only ones to produce categories of the other. In fact, all communities and nations have a similar view, considering themselves as the center of humanity—what social scientists call ethnocentrism. One good example is the Chinese, who for many centuries were, indeed, the wealthiest, most populous, and powerful state on earth. One great example of this ethnocentrism is the that in the sixteenth century the Italian missionary Mateo Ricci brought to China a European map of the world showing the new discoveries in America. The Chinese were glad to learn about America, but one point in the map offended them. Since it split the earth's surface down the Pacific, China appeared off at the right hand edge and the Chinese thought of themselves as literally "The Middle Kingdom."

The Hindus, for their part, developed an intricate and hierarchical method to divide their own society into different segments or castes. But they also developed a special category, the Mlecchas, that was applied to the uncivilized barbarians living outside their land. In fact, no pious Brahmin (the highest caste in India) dared set foot on the land of Mlecchas, because they had a fear of physical and cultural contamination.

Another example is that for the medieval Muslim the world looked very different from what it did to the Christians, or the Chinese, or the Hindus. Most Muslims believed that Mohammed's birthplace, Mecca, was the center of the earth's surface, and Muslim maps showed precisely that location for the holy city. We still see this idea of Mecca and Medina holding a special place in the world, in the pilgrimage to those cities—or *Hajj*—that every good Muslim should embark upon at least once in a lifetime. It is also important to note that Muslims had their own categories of the other, based also on religion. They called Christians and Jews *ahl-al-kitab* or "people of the book" who, even though had a lower status, were differently treated in comparison to peoples and groups belonging to other religions.

III

For many centuries, the biblical texts, and the accounts of classical authors from Greece and Rome, continued to provide the main paradigms for the interpretation of other peoples and cultures. With the gradual secularization of Europe during the Renaissance and the Enlightenment, a more scientific approach was developed. One example is Linne's theory, that categorized human races as follows:

- Americans: reddish, obstinate, regulated by custom
- Europeans: white, gentle, and governed by laws
- Asians: yellow, sever and ruled by opinion
- Africans: black, crafty and ruled by caprice.

This classification exhibited some enduring characterizations of raciology. It implied a certain bias in physical traits, temperament, and political-moral behavior. By the 19th. century, these bases were being inserted into scholarly treatises that interpreted national histories as accounts of struggles between races; with victors showing a racial superiority over the vanquished. By this time too, there were a few centuries of experience with black slavery and Indian semi-slavery, which further reinforced the sentiment of unquestioned white European superiority.

Of course there were exceptions to this trend. Even during the time of the Roman Empire, Tacitus saw Rome corrupting the barbarians. During the Enlightenment, Rousseau held similar views when he idealized the primitive man. Some even joined the other, like the Spaniard Gonzalo Guerrero, who at the beginning of the conquest of Mexico by Hernn Cortés, joined the Mayans in their efforts to fight the *conquistadores*. But the dominant view of European superiority gradually spread, through the pervasive economic and political structures of colonialism, to most of the world, and even more rapidly with the technical advances in communication and printing.

This tendency to see history as a struggle of races for dominance was aided by such natural sciences as biology. One example is a theory developed by Franz Von Gall, called "phrenology," which proposed that mental activity had a physical base in the brain which in turn shaped the skull of the specific individual. This approach, which tried to correlate cranial morphology with racial characteristics, was being widely used at the turn of the 20th century, as we can see in Conrad's novel *Heart of Darkness*, where the central character, Marlowe, is submitted to such a test by a Belgian doctor in Congo.

The 19th century produced various racial theories, that led gradually in the twentieth century to the Nazi "racial science" with the results that we all know. Only after WW II, with the crushing defeat of fascism and nazism, did these theories start to assimilate the idea that any attempt to explain cultural forms on a purely biological basis is doomed to failure.

De/Reconstructing Utopianism:
Towards A World-Historical Typology

M.H. (Behrooz) Tamdgidi

UMass Boston

We often find ourselves debunking utopianism because of the historical shortcomings of Marxism, despite realizing that Marxism itself, in its classical writings at least, never claimed to be a utopian doctrine in the first place. For the founders of "scientific socialism," in fact, being both scientific (as Marxism claimed to be) and utopian was a contradiction in terms. If anything, it would be more logical to explore the problems of Marxism with regards to its claimed scienticity than its alleged utopianism—if we intend to pursue a dialectical critique of the inner consistency of the doctrine, that is. For the contemporary critics of Marxism and utopianism, however, one seems to have been a failure because it has been the other.

Underlying the above controversy over whether Marxism was scientific or utopian (with the former implying a positive attribute, and the latter a negative one—regardless of whether sympathetic or critical stands are taken vis-à-vis Marxism) is the commonly assumed typological dualism of science vs. utopianism itself. Frederick Engels, of course, famously immortalized this typological dualism in his 1880 work, *Socialism: Utopian and Scientific*, in order to legitimize the newly arisen doctrine as a "scientific" enterprise in contrast to its "utopian" precursors. Consequently, we still have a hard time treating Marxism as being both utopian and "scientific," which of course would make the attribution of its failures to the two aspects that much harder. It has to be one *or* the other—an instance of either/or formal logical dualism which seems to run counter, in fact, to the dialectical logic Marxism prided itself to have materialistically reinvented. The long-inherited binary structures of our knowledges seem again to pose a difficulty here.

Is it possible that the real problem is with the way the problem itself has been posed—that the boundaries of science and utopianism are fuzzier than they appear to be? To be sure, those who are still interested in making efforts towards a just global society have found the identification of utopianism with Marxism to be an obstacle, to say the least. It may therefore be useful to make an effort at deconstructing our taken-for-granted positions on the matter and revisit the plethora of definitional and conceptual fuzziness and inconsistencies surrounding utopianism in the hopes of making a clearer stand on the subject.[1]

My aim in this paper is to deconstruct utopianism as a world-historical social movement, and reconstruct a typology of utopianism that allows the interpretation of the historical debunking of utopianism by Marxism (or vice versa) as an expression partly of internal rifts among various types of utopianism, partly of gradual departure of Marxism from utopianism in its classical lifetime, and partly of the "false" con-

---

1. This paper is a revised version of an excerpt from the second chapter of my previous work, "Mysticism and Utopia: Towards the Sociology of Self-Knowledge and Human Architecture (A Study in Marx, Gurdjieff, and Mannheim)" (2002).

Notice: Copyright of *Human Architecture: Journal of the Sociology of Self-Knowledge* is the property of Ahead Publishing House (imprint: Okcir Press) and its content may not be copied or emailed to multiple sites or posted to a listserv without the copyright holder's express written permission. However, users may print, download, or email articles for individual use.

sciousness of the movement about its own dual identity vis-à-vis utopianism and science due to ideological-political exigencies. Using the proposed typology of utopianism, in other words, I will argue that Marxism's efforts to distinguish itself from utopianism (and vice versa) had as much to do with ideological rhetoric as with substance and lack thereof. What explains the ideological aspects of the controversy has to do with self-promotion in light of the perceived failures of the other types. But this does not mean Marxism was not utopian in a certain sense; it was a specific type of it in contrast to others (as will be explained later). But it gradually lost its utopian message as it "matured," which should legitimately raise the question whether its failures were due to its specific form of utopianism and/or its gradual departure from utopianism altogether.

I will argue below that Marxism failed its own ends both because of the limits of its specific approach to utopianism, and because of its gradual abandoning of utopianism altogether,[1] eventually embracing a non-utopian, "realpolitik," antisystemic mode preoccupied more with shattering (or running) the existing social institutions than with creatively building alternative ones in their midst, a way proven more effective in previous successful historical "transitions." The failures of the practical types of utopianism or departures from the utopian mode altogether have also been met, on the opposite end of the contrast, by the self-limiting of the contemporary utopian tradition to its literary and science-fiction types, which has had the opposite, but similar, effect of abandoning the applied utopian pursuits of a just global society. One way or another, the above developments have served the ideological-political function of preserving the status quo in micro and macro social spacetimes—a function or interest to which the Mannheimian sociology of knowledge may trace the origins of the typological confusions surrounding utopianism in the first place. The historical result has been the gradual throwing away of the baby of utopianism in general with the bath-waters of failures of specific types of it.

Marxism represented a new, "scientific," type of utopian movement in contrast, on one hand, to the philosophical and religious varieties preceding it, and on the other hand the briefly revived humanist type (as somewhat represented by utopian socialists) which was soon frozen in embryo by Marxism's own ideological-political rhetoric and ascendance in the world-wide opposition to capitalism. What I intend to point out is a need to go beyond the polemics and the rhetoric of these movements in order to develop a typological framework of utopianism which accounts for the historical failures of Marxism due in part to the shortcomings emanating from its specific utopian type and partly due to its gradual departure from the utopian typology altogether. The point is to redeem the value of utopianism as a specific strategy for social change in contrast to the antisystemic mode characterizing the dominant form of opposition movements to capitalism during at least the past two centuries.

MARXISM AND UTOPIANISM

Historically, there has been a curious attitude on the part of both Marxist and utopian currents to deny their common lot.

---

1. Consideration of the distinction between the young and old Marx, and multiplicities of Marxisms is important in this regard. It is this dual nature of Marxism as a utopian and an antisystemic movement that explains Karl Mannheim's classification of Marxism as both an ideology and a utopia in his classic *Ideology and Utopia* (1936). In other words, the dual positioning of the movement did not have to exist if it was not due to the intrinsic duality which the movement came gradually to develop in the transition from the young to old variants of Marx's thought. For further details on this, see Tamdgidi 2002, 2003.

The case of Marxism's efforts to dissociate itself from utopianism is well known and does not need much elaboration. Considering itself a "scientific socialist" doctrine, Marxism from its very beginnings built its self-identity on a clear polemical program of dissociating itself from utopianism in general, and "utopian socialism" in particular.[1] But the other side of the equation, often overlooked, seems to be as perplexing as the other.

Five bibliographers in English language on the utopian literature (Haschak 1994; Negley 1978; Beauchamp 1977; Lewis 1984; Sargent 1979, 1988) hardly mention or include Marxism (some not even the "utopian socialist" literature) in their commentaries and resource lists on utopianism. The problem, judging from the standpoint of these bibliographers' own explicitly stated criteria, seems to be more than a matter of impracticality of listing the enormous amount of literature on Marxism. Nor does this seem to be due to the limitations emanating from the boundaries imposed by the bibliographers on their own subject matter. The very definition of utopianism offered by these compilers, which basically seems to limit utopianism to the so-called "utopian literature" or at best to sources on isolated experimental "utopian societies or communities," defies inclusion of Marxist literature in their works. Consider, for example, this statement by Glen Negley, a major bibliographer of the utopian literature:

> The Declaration of Independence or the Communist Manifesto may be said to be an expression of profound political and philosophical ideals, but neither is a utopia. (Negley 1978:xii-xiii)

The attitudes on both sides cited above, nevertheless, are in sharp contrast to approaches employed in other encyclopedic entries (e.g., Kateb's entry in *Encyclopedia of the Social Sciences*, 1968, 16:267-70,[2] or his entry in *The Encyclopedia of Philosophy* 1972, 8:212-215), or in major scholarly works on the subject (Manuel and Manuel 1979;[3] Mumford 1941;[4] Mannheim 1936;[5] Kateb 1972; Kumar 1991[6]) in which Marxism is treated as an integral part of utopianism in general. The more recent *Encyclopedia of Utopian Literature* (Snodgrass 1995), also,

---

1. Marx and Engels wrote in the *Manifesto of the Communist Party* ([1848] 1978:498-499): "The significance of Critical-Utopian Socialism and Communism bears an inverse relation to historical development. In proportion as the modern class struggle develops and takes definite shape, this fantastic standing apart from the contest, these fantastic attacks on it, lose all practical value and all theoretical justification. Therefore, although the originators of these systems were, in many respects, revolutionary, their disciples have, in every case, formed mere reactionary sects. They hold fast by the original views of their masters, in opposition to the progressive historical development of the proletariat. They, therefore, endeavor, and that consistently, to deaden the class struggle and to reconcile the class antagonisms. They still dream of experimental realization of their social Utopias, of founding isolated *"phalansteres,"* of establishing "Home Colonies," of setting up a "Little Icaria"—duodecimo editions of the New Jerusalem—and to realize all these castles in the air, they are compelled to appeal to the feelings and purses of the bourgeois. By degrees they sink into the category of the reactionary conservative Socialists depicted above, differing from these only by more systematic pedantry, and by their fanatical and superstitious belief in the miraculous effects of their social science."

2. "Perhaps Marxism is the only utopian, or quasi-utopian, body of thought that large numbers of men have actually tried to translate into practice. But Marxism is not the only version of utopianism that has worked to generate the feeling that the real world is profoundly imperfect and that some sort of change, even small, and not even in a utopian direction, is a pressing necessity" (Kateb 1968:269).

3. "Despite the persistence with which they belabored some contemporary utopians, essential parts of the *Critique of the Gotha Program* were in fact the answer to a utopian inquiry that Marx himself had initiated ... A hundred years after it was written, the *Critique of the Gotha Program* can be most effectively illuminated if it is restored to the utopian landscape in which it was originally planted" (Manuel and Manuel 1979:699).

includes entries on "Marx," "Engels," and "The Communist Manifesto." Kateb's commentary in his 1972 piece in *The Encyclopedia of Philosophy* (1972) regarding the need to view Marxism as a part of the western utopian tradition hardly needs further elaboration:

> Those philosophies of history which culminate in a vision of achieved perfection are a third type of utopia. These are the theories of inevitable progress created by men like Condorcet, Hegel, Spencer, and Marx. Hegel and Marx especially would have fought against inclusion in the utopian tradition ... For all that, their writings have been taken by others as utopian. No list of the major sources of utopian literature would be acceptable without them and the other theorists of inevitable progress. (Kateb 1972:213)

Even if the shared terrain occupied by utopianism and Marxism are acknowledged, however, the estrangement between the two movements must itself be accounted for. Why do Marxists and utopists deny their common lot?

An immediate explanation that comes to mind may perhaps be found in the perceptions by adherents in each current of the failing and/or discredited nature of the theories and/or practices affiliated with the other current. Marx and Engels explicitly criticized their utopian predecessors in terms of the speculative nature of their doctrines and/or of the isolated scope of the communal experiments they carried out in the context of the reality of a globally expanding capitalist mode of production. In order to advance their own political and organizational agenda in the interests of the working class to create a world communist society, in other words, founders of scientific socialism had to clearly dissociate themselves from the failed movements which had actually prefigured and nourished their own past.

The reverse process of estrangement, that of the traditional utopians' dissociating themselves from Marxism, of course surfaced later. The reality of increasing failure of the Marxist movement to abide by its own principles, let alone of setting an example for an alternative communist society, soon led traditional utopian writers, communal experimenters, or simply those interested in utopianism as a literary genre only, to either dissociate their own utopian interests from the failing experiments of the world communist movement, or to attack the existing order and/or Marxist social experiments by developing a specifically new genre of utopian literature. The emerging dystopianism in the twentieth century, a lit-

---

4."In his Socialism: Utopian and Scientific, Frederick Engels made a plea for a realistic method of thought, which limited itself to a here and now, as against what he derided as the utopian method, the attempt on the part of a single thinker to give a detailed picture of the society of the future. Yet at the present time it is easy to see that if the utopian socialism of Owen has been ineffective, the realistic socialism of Marx has been equally ineffective; for while Owen's kind of socialism has been partly fulfilled in the cooperative movement, the dictatorship of the proletariat rests upon very shaky foundations, and such success as it has had is what it would be like as to anything else" (Mumford 1941:242-43).

5."Even the socialist-communist mode of thought and experience which, as regards its origins, may be treated as a unity, is best understood in its utopian structure by observing it as it is attacked from three sides ... It represents not merely a compromise but also a new creation based upon an inner synthesis of the various forms of utopia which have arisen hitherto and which have struggled against one another in society" (Mannheim 1936:239-240).

6."Marx and Engels, it is true, went out of their way to deny that the future socialist or communist society would be a closed or completed system. So much could be admitted, however, without necessarily affecting the perception of the basically utopian quality of their vision of the future socialist society" (Kumar 1991:60).

erary movement focusing on the evils of modern society, used the medium of utopian literary style to criticize not only the existing capitalist order but also the dehumanizing nature of social realities emerging from the realpolitik conduct of Marxist, socialist, and communist movements across the globe. As Kumar has pointed out,

> [a]ll the major anti-utopias of the twentieth century have been so dependent on actual contemporary societies as sometimes to run the danger of merely seeming descriptions of them. Zamyatin's *We* and Koestler's *Darkness at Noon* rehearsed and projected the forms and thought structures of the new Soviet society. George Orwell's *Animal Farm* and *Nineteen Eighty-Four* similarly drew on the theory and practice of the Soviet Union... (Kumar 1991:66)

The above discussion is meant to highlight the debated nature of the relationship between Marxism and utopianism, questioning taken-for-granted assumptions that general consensus exists regarding their identity and/or difference. To explore the debate further, however, we need to delve more carefully into the definitional landscape surrounding the utopian thought and movement.

UTOPIA AND UTOPIANISM

What exactly is utopianism?

"Utopia," which is derived from the word "topos" (place) in Greek and phonetically plays on the Greek words "eu" (good) and "ou" (no), has the double-meaning of a good place that does not (yet) exist[1] (Sargent 1988; Kumar 1991; Kateb 1976). Of course the term, invented by St. Thomas More in 1516 in his classic satirical novel by the same name, inherited a preexisting tradition that goes back in the west, from a literary standpoint, to Plato's *Republic* at least, and in the East to the earliest religious and mythological beliefs and texts. Therefore, from a general point of view the search for a good place that does not (yet) exist can be regarded as an aspiration of all humanity across all times and places. The fact that the term "utopia" was coined in the west in relatively recent times should therefore not distract us from recognizing that the reality which the concept denotes is much older and much wider in origin, and the concept itself embodies or signifies the human desire to move beyond the existing social status quo and to live an ideal life.

---

1. In his *Ideology and Utopia* (1936), Karl Mannheim presented a typology of modern utopian mentalities that included the Orgiastic Chiliasm of the Anabaptists, the liberal-humanitarian idea, the conservative idea, and the socialist-communist idea. The conservative notion of utopia, Mannheim suggested, is that of utopia already achieved in the sense that the social status quo represents the perfect or ideal society achieveable from the point of view and interests of dominant social forces. This is in contrast to the other three forms which involve seeking an alternate social reality in the here-and-now (Chiliastic), as a result of socio-political progress and state action (liberal-humanitarian), or socio-economic revolution (socialist/communist). Acknowledging the usefulness of the typology, I think Mannheim's attribution of a utopian status to the conservative perspective as reiterated above obfuscates the consistency of the definition of "utopianism" as a search for ever new social conditions that do not (yet) exist. In other words, the notion of utopianism by definition involves transcendence of the social status quo and is by nature a critical outlook (which to be sure can be of both reactionary or progressive kinds, i.e., can be conservative for its regressive seeking of social conditions lost in the past, or progressive for its seeking of social conditions not yet achieved). The point here is that a reference to existing social conditions as achieved utopias, is a contradictory statement that diminishes the definitional value of the concept as denoting a desire and/or action for social transformation beyond the status quo—whatever that may be. This is a good example of how in the course of both ideological and scholarly debates the conceptual distinctiveness of utopianism has been diluted.

There was, however, a specific meaning attached to "utopia" as More practiced it, and that was the belief in the good life's being realizable on this earth through the initiative of ordinary human beings. It was this creative humanist bent in the Morean version that may explain why his particular name, term, and attitude became in time the standard bearer of what modern world understands by utopianism. In fact, it was this earthly scope of Morean utopianism effected through the action of ordinary human beings creatively building and running a new communal arrangement, that distinguished it both from the earlier religious and philosophical (Platonic) forms, and what gave impetus to the later scientific variety which found its classic form in Marxism.

Therefore, qualifying the utopian nature of various movements merely based on their practical orientation or the spatiotemporal scope of their experimentation is misleading. The imagined/practical attitudes or the spatiotemporal scope of envisioning/implementation of the movement's project may provide a subclassificatory scheme for types of utopianism as a whole, but they should not enter into the determination and definition of whether a movement is utopian or not. For instance, utopianism has sometimes been envisioned and/or practiced in a limited spatiotemporal scope—say an inner experience, an interpersonal relationship, a communal organization, a particular societal or even civilizational project—rather than generalized as a global, transhistorical movement encompassing the whole humanity. Certainly, this was one sense in which Marx debunked his utopian predecessors or contemporaries. For him, the good life could only be a global reality. However, this does not make the local experimentations any less real—perhaps less effective, but not less *real*. Likewise, simply a proclamation, or a theoretical clause, in the most militant of antisystemic manifestos asserting the global nature of the emancipation project does not make the movement espousing that viewpoint any less utopian. So the distinction between a utopian and non-utopian movement cannot really be a matter of the spatiotemporal scope of social experimentation and/or projected transformation. We need to look elsewhere to define what utopianism actually introduced into the discourse on the means and the ends of achieving the good life.

How is utopianism distinguishable from the "antisystemic" modes of social movement behavior? After all, all movements struggle for a "nowhere," or an aspired goal that has not yet been realized or fulfilled—how can it be otherwise? Nor can the distinguishing feature of utopianism be that it merely deals with speculative and mental constructions of an ideal life, rather than making efforts at practical realization of those goals. There have been many practical utopian movements and communal experimentations often using scientific tools and knowledges in their endeavors. And conversely there have been many "antisystemic movements" that have not gone beyond mere declarations and manifestos of protest against their adversaries. Moreover, just because utopian efforts have failed, or been identified with "unrealistic" social aspirations, cannot be a distinguishing feature of utopianism. Obviously, many "antisystemic movements" (let alone, mainstream political mobilizations) have also failed in bringing about the good life. Failure per se, in other words, cannot enter our efforts at defining and understanding what is distinctive about utopianism as a social movement. So what is it that actually distinguishes the utopian movement from all others?

Utopianism can be most generally defined as a movement in human thought and/or action to bring about an ideal life *beginning in the here and now*. In the antisystemic mode, the attention is on fighting the adversary, building a self-identity around that fight, while the goals for which the fight is waged are relegated to the background and projected into a future to be created once the fight is won. There is an inherent gap and alienation between means and ends in the antisystemic mode of bringing about social change. In contrast, in the utopian mode, building the alternative vision in the thought and/or realities of the here-and-now is the primary focus of the movement. The utopian movement changes the world by the examples of its alternative imaginations, visions, experimentations, and self-constitutions of what the world can or should be, not by promises and decrees declared in the midst of antisystemic fervor.

To begin with, the spatiotemporal and social *relativism* of the utopian aspiration must be taken into account. The standards for a desired "perfect" life have of course been always geographically and historically relative and changing. A utopian desire or demand raised at a particular historical conjuncture may become, once and if realized, the status quo with respect to new utopian demands and aspirations. Likewise, a utopian desire in one place may not be shared by others in other places. Besides, socially, the utopian demands raised by a particular class or strata, seeking goals or changes that best suits its own interests (often wrapped in the universalistic language of "for the good of all"), may in fact be considered reactionary, regressive and simply undesirable from the standpoint of other social classes or strata. Obviously, "utopia" as a universal term must always be historically contextualized. Utopianism always involves a search for a good life by and relative to the interests and visions of a specific historical agency at a particular place and time.

Utopianism may be further qualified as a movement that is concerned with the design and construction of alternative historical realities beginning in the *here and now*. Whether such a concern becomes limited in one or another utopian movement to the speculative and mental domain, whether such a concern is not actually intended to be practically implemented by the utopian movement, or whether such ideal constructions are actually implemented but in practice fail, are secondary as far as the general definition above is concerned. In contrast to reactive modes of antisystemic behavior that concentrate on building a movement that instrumentally focuses on the destruction of the old order in order to reach a good life projected into the future (be that future distant or near, illusively or "realistically" conceived), the utopian attitude involves making efforts, whatever their scope, towards imagining, theorizing and/or practically realizing that future goal in the here and now.

If this is what makes a utopian project utopian, then how can Marxism be utopian? After all, Marx, while being convinced of the necessity and the possibility of a future ideal society, refused to provide a blueprint of it (except for brief philosophical and/or political tracts), and instead directed workers' attention to the struggle against capitalism as personified in the bourgeoisie. Should we not then agree with the founders of scientific socialism that what they were advancing was not utopian, but scientific?

In what follows, by introducing a typology of utopian movements as a whole, I will argue that the difference between Marxism and other forms of utopianism is partly a matter of typological differentiation within utopianism and partly a result of departure of the Marxism from that typology in its development during Marx' lifetime. Marx and Engels, despite their rejections of utopianism, and reluctance to draw up blueprints for the future society, nevertheless to an extent practiced in a different form what utopian movements (according to the above definition) engage in—namely, seeking the utopian society beginning in the here and now by building a communist party and movement adhering to certain principles of communal living projected to become universal in at least the early developmental stages of communist society. Marx and Engels's repeated calls to see communism not as a blueprint for a "future society" but as an actual movement taking place in the midst of the present "under our own eyes" merely represented the *modus operandi* of a different, a "scientific" type, of utopianism which legitimated itself "scientifically" based on assumptions of what were thought to be inevitable "objective" movement of class society towards a classless state. In Marx's view the incessant participation, in the here and now, of the proletarian-communist movement in an objectively given and inevitable building of workers' unions, of proletarian communist parties, of an international association of proletarian parties, of proletarian states, etc., towards achieving the immediate goal of a world-wide communist revolution were simply historically necessitated stages of progress towards attaining a utopian society.

However, at the same time, built into Marx and Engels's doctrine, was a self-imposed denial of the utopian nature of their movement, ideologically serving the function of dispelling doubts about the scientific nature of their views and misassociations with what was perceived to be failing utopian efforts in the recent or distant past. Therefore, while Marxism drew powerful inspirations from utopianism (hence Engels's regarding, say, French socialism, as one of its sources) it also sought to distance itself from it for the purpose of self-promotion. This attitude which lies at the root of the antisystemic form of the movement, in contrast to its utopian content, served the purpose of postponing not only the blueprints, but also the practice, of the utopian imaginations which initially inspired the movement. This antisystemic strategy became in time framed by the doctrine of class struggle which came to be regarded as the means towards the idealized classless society under communism. The central thesis guiding this non-utopian, antisystemic, movement strategy towards utopian ends was based on the revolutionary nature of the proletariat as an oppressed class whose emancipation will, as the theory claimed, would bring about the self-abolition of itself as a ruling class in the postrevolutionary period and the emancipation of the society as a whole. To end all classes, in short, a class-based antisystemic strategy had to be pursued.

For further clarification of this point, let me proceed with introducing a typology of utopianism.

TYPES OF UTOPANISM

A general typology of utopian movements can be developed based on three basic criteria: 1-The perceived **agency** that is considered to be the primary determinant for the realization of the utopian project (ordinary humans, distinguished elites, supernatural forces, objective natural/historical laws); 2-The **attitude** adopted for the pursuit of the utopian project (reflective, literary, experimental, transformative); and 3-The **scope** of imagination and/or realization of the utopian vision (intrapersonal, interpersonal, communal, societal, environmental, or cosmic).

Figure 1 (next page) shows the way in which the general typology of utopian movements may be conceptualized along the three criteria listed above. Notice that the combination of five agencies (considering the two subtypes of scientific utopianism as separate categories), four attitudes, and six agendas provide a total of at least 120 different ideal-types (in terms of various tracks along the agency, attitude, and agenda criteria). Of course, our numerical suggestion here is only illustrative, and by no means do I mean to rigidify the three

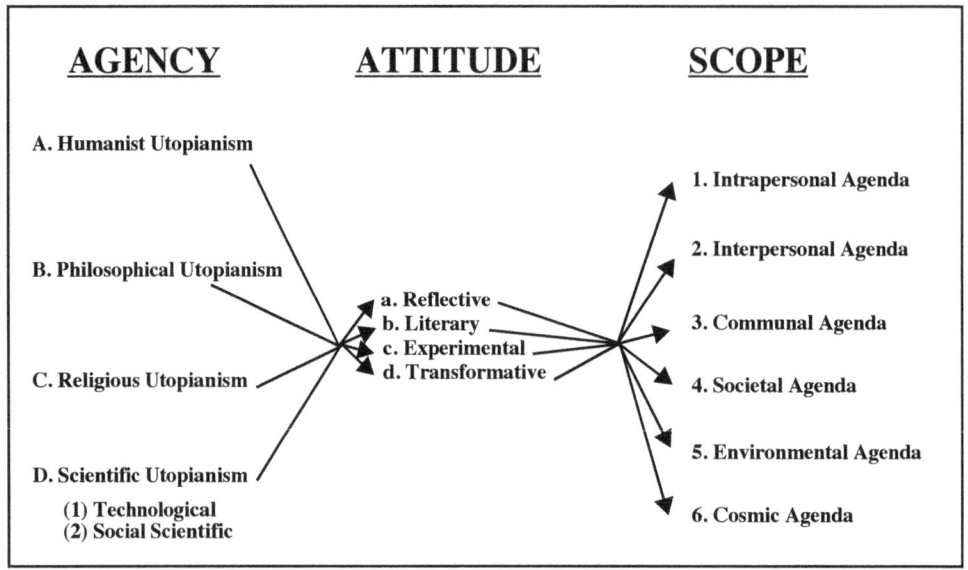

Figure 1: Types of Utopian Movements

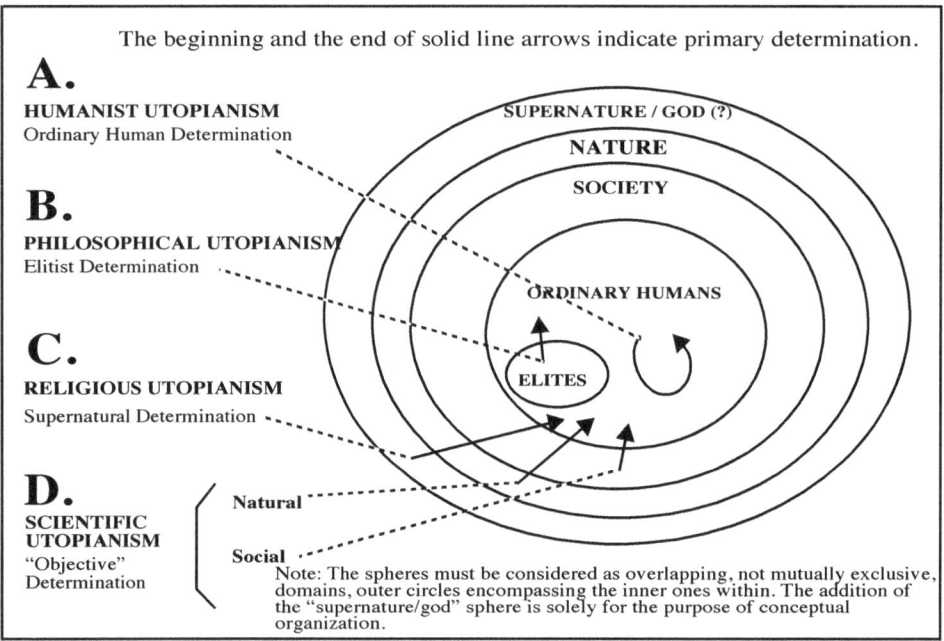

Figure 2: Typology of Utopianism Considered in Terms of Part-Whole Schema

major criteria and their sub-classifications into arbitrary numerical formulations. What I would like to convey here is that the classificatory scheme suggested here allows us to consider the rich totality of the varieties of forms utopian movements may take in historical context. It must also be noted that an actual historical utopian movement may display a multiplicity of types and trends in itself, with one perhaps being predominant at a time. Whether a predominant type can be identified in each historical case of utopianism cannot of course be ascertained in an a priori manner, for one or any combination of the ideal (agency/attitude/scope) types may develop (and thus be discovered) in one or more phases or stages of any given utopian movement. In fact, actual historical movements may evolve from one type or subtype to another while sublimating remnants of the older varieties.

Type A utopian movements are those in which ordinary humans determine the utopian project. In this type, the arts and the creative impulses drive the efforts to build the good life. The other three types may be considered alienated forms of humanist utopianism, in that the determining factor in the realization of the project in these other forms shifts away from ordinary humans themselves and becomes associated with outside forces, be they a group of elites, supernatural forces beyond, and/or objectively pre-ordained natural/historical laws.

Type B utopian movements are those in which one or more "distinguished" individuals, elites, wise men, "philosopher kings," geniuses, etc., are seen as determinants of the utopian project. Type C utopian movements are those in which the primary determinant of the origins, development, and/or realization of the utopian project is perceived to be supernatural forces. The determination may not be always positive and supportive of the utopian project, though; God may be perceived, for example, to have created this world for suffering and trial, the actual utopia being realizable not in this world but in the promised hereafter. Type D utopian movements are those in which the primary determinants of the utopian project are perceived to be the "objective forces" operating in nature in general and/or in history in particular. In these movements the objective "laws of motion" of nature and history, and not supernatural forces such as God, or ordinary or distinguished humans, enable or retard progress towards an ideal life.

The difference between the humanist and elitist (A and B) on one hand and the "social scientific" type (B2) on the other hand, can be considered in terms of the distinction between agencies. Humanist and elitist movements, despite their differences, emphasize the role played by the human agency, creativity or knowledge/will, to bring about the good life, whereas the social scientific utopists emphasize the inherent laws of motion objectively operative in society as determining factors, which then allow human actors to play (or not) their historical roles as catalyzers (or fetters). In scientific utopianism, the role of human or elite agencies is downplayed and subordinated to the dictates of the limits and/or opportunities posed by objective natural and/or historical conditions. In Marx's words, expressing the scientific utopian model, men do make their own history but not under conditions of their own choosing, but through aligning their actions with the objective laws governing society.

With regards to the four broad agency types, it is important to consider their relationship in a dynamic, rather than rigid and mutually exclusive, manner. A particular type A may not negate the role played by elite, god, or nature/history agencies in the utopian project, but consider that their influences are, or are meant to be, processed through the will and creativity of ordinary human agencies. Perceiving ordinary humans as being equally invested with the extraordinary powers of the elite, of god(s), or of natural/historical progress, is an example. Type A, B, or D movement may also be "religious" in the sense that they may not deny the existence of God, but for various reasons consider divine intervention not primary for the realization of the utopian project—they may in fact adopt the argument that it was divine intent to leave it to the ordinary humans, to distinguished individuals or prophets, or natural or historical evolution to guide humanity towards the good life. The same may be considered for type A or B movements that may not deny the relevance and effect of objective natural, social, or divine forces, but maintain the significance of human volition and action—as *natural* and/or *historical* forces themselves—in the pursuit and success of the utopian project.

In general, the typology of utopian movements presented above may best be conceived in terms of a part-whole modality rather than conceptualized in the pattern of mutually exclusive movement types (see Figure 2, previous page). In other words, each type does not exist apart from domains singled out by other types. The totality is operative for each type; however, in each a particular sphere of reality is perceived to be more important and determinant than the other. From the standpoint of humanist utopianism, to say that ordinary humans are masters of their own destiny does not necessarily contradict the notion that history, nature, or even supernatural forces are at work, if human powers are perceived to be also those of society, nature, and divine spirits. The power of the elite may also be considered to be an alienated form of ordinary human powers. So are the powers attributed to nature, history, or even the supernature, which can be interpreted as alienated forms of ordinary human powers. Only when these alienated powers are divested from their human origins and projected as "other" forces beyond the power of human understanding, will, and action, do distinct forms of utopianism become clearly distinguishable.

To proceed with the second criteria of subclassification of each of the above major types, we may consider subtypes a, b, c, and d as being based on what **attitude** the utopian movement takes with regards to the realization of the utopian vision. In type a, the utopian project is a reflective experience, individually or collectively, in sensation, feelings and imagination, not even communicated to others perhaps, or at most existing in oral forms of expression—not yet finding its way into literary or practical realms. By acknowledging type a, we are basically recognizing that just because a utopian vision is not written down, expressed in objective form, or realized in historical context, does not mean that it does not exist. Utopian visions are often reflective at first, and only in subsequent development become expressed in literary or practical forms.

In type b, the utopian project is expressed or systematized in literary or art forms, making it possible to be communicated to others via objectified writings and artifacts. This is a crucial step, for it allows the utopian project to be communicated across time and space regardless of the intentions of its originators. The literary utopias may themselves take various forms, of course, ranging from the most fantastic and fictional to the most precisely formulated, constitutional, and programmatic tracts intended for implementation.

Type c attitude involves experimentation, in practical terms, with the utopian ideas, visions, or theories in every day life. But this is only "experimental" in nature, that is, the primary purpose is not to commit oneself to transforming reality as an end in itself, but changing reality is pursued only to further develop and elaborate on the utopian idea, vision, or theory.

In type d attitude ("transformative"), finally, the aim is to make persistent and continuing efforts towards the realization of the utopian project in reality.

Again in the above attitude typology, the various tracks must not be conceived in isolation from one another. Often, especially in the later types, all the elements of the (preceding) types may be present, but one may be predominant at any given time and place. Moreover, the attitude typology must be considered in its multiple variations with respect to the agency typology. Each of the agency typologies may adopt one or more of the utopian attitudes.

The **scope** typology sub-differentiates utopian movements based on which domain the utopian movement primarily focuses on for bringing about change. Type 1 is intrapersonal, and denotes the inner life of the individual. Note here, for example, that based on the attitude typology, this inner personal utopianism may take reflective, literary, experimental, or transformative forms. For instance, an individual may not only envision a utopian ideal for and by her/himself, but proceed with writing down or expressing in various art forms specific plans of realizing that vision in her/his individual life, and actually proceed to do so.

For Type 2 (interpersonal) utopianism the primary focus of utopian reflection, writing/expression, experimentation, and/or transformation is the interpersonal space, of specific relationships with another person. Type 3 (communal) utopianism acquires a strong organizational dimension considering that individuals are influenced by the type of social organization in which they live. In other words, type 3 introduces elements of social externalization and structuration of the utopian project beyond the immediate dyadic intentions of interpersonal actors. In this case, conscious and persistent effort is spent on the development of alternative objective social structures and organizations alongside fostering of new behavioral patterns.

Type 4 (societal) is concerned not just with the affairs of the narrow utopian commune, but the latter is used as a means or an example for a wider societal (ethno-national, civilizational, or global) utopian project for which the utopian vision is developed. Type 5 focuses on the environmental context within which the utopian project is to be realized. It is one thing to conceive of the utopian project in terms of human species, another to consider the latter as part of the biosphere as a whole, including consideration of all other life forms. Type 6 involves primary concerns with the cosmic dimension and implications of the utopian vision.

Notice here that in the scope typology, there is not an assumption of a particular intellectual and/or practical *attitude* towards the utopian project. A utopian vision, for instance, may involve cosmic preoccupations without necessarily involving any practical steps to realize it, one way or another—most science fictions of outer space variety are in this category. In the latter case, though, one may also find a cosmic utopianism which involves practical steps, regardless of how strange they may be (mass suicide to spiritually link up with a passing comet!). That is why I have separated the attitude typology from the scope typology to allow more flexible intermixing of various subtypes within and across the major agency typologies. In each of the latter, the concern with the particular domain of utopian vision may be reflective, literary, experimental, or transformative at a give time or place for a given utopian movement. Any utopian movement may experience one or another of the various agency, attitude, or scope typologies in the course of its life cycle. For the purpose of clarification, the possible alternative tracks of the utopian movement can be considered using arrow tracks in Figure 1 (above).

IMPLICATIONS OF THE TYPOLOGY

The inclusive model of utopianism as

explicated above moves beyond a classificatory system that is based solely on what can be readily "observed" as a utopian movement. The literary utopias or utopian communities investigated by scholars are then treated as only a fraction of the world-historical utopian movement as a whole. In the new typology, the "silent utopias" in everyday lives of ordinary people which never find expression in any tangible literary or communal forms are treated as being as much a part of the unfolding global story of utopianism as the more visible and "classical" forms.

What Wallerstein has called (1998) "utopistics" or "efficacious" utopianism, a distinction also made somewhat similarly by Mannheim (1936) in terms of utopias that aim to "shatter existing society," may be considered as the specific type involving social scientific agency and experimental/transformative attitudes in the scheme considered above. But these, as in the case of Marxism, also display tendencies for postponing creative efforts in building the future society in the here-and-nows of the present. The projection of utopia to a future apart from making efforts, no matter how small, in building it by example in the midst of the present, would be seen as a departure from the utopian mode of bringing about social change and as proximity to the antisystemic social movement variety. Antisystemic social movements, as noted above, may be defined as those more preoccupied with shattering the present as the means of the movement, at the expense of making greater efforts at building the ends of the movement in the here-and-now.

For the purpose of this investigation, the determination of whose utopia is more "efficacious" and "shattering" than others is considered to be a subjective matter, depending on which historical agency proclaims or judges the case. Any utopist may claim her or his approach to be the most effective from the particular vantage point of her or his own interests and purposes in pursuing the project. Likewise, a non-efficacious or non-shattering utopia may not necessarily be of any lesser value or significance than those espoused to be more realistic. Many of the more efficacious utopianisms of the modern times had their beginnings in fictive utopian literature (St. Thomas More's *Utopia* is the best example), and many of the dystopian literature of twentieth century have had significant impact on the critical historical and social consciousness of a large international audience (George Orwell's *Nineteen Eighty Four* is a good example). It may thus be more fruitful to treat all forms of utopianism as diverse exercises in utopianism, and relegate judgments regarding their efficaciousness and substantive realism to the investigation of such theories and/or practices, rather than dismissing one or another utopian project on an a priori basis.

My proposed typology incorporates existing classifications of utopianism, but goes beyond them in providing a more inclusive picture of human efforts on a global scale in search of the good life. This typology treats utopianism broadly as a world-historical movement, of which only a particular branch may be attributable to the western tradition, while regarding the scientific variety as a western artifact, or a "western" concept and movement (Kumar 1991) by pointing out the notion of utopia as a naturally and/or historically pre-ordained goal towards which humanity is making "progress" in an "evolutionary" process. The typology incorporates religious "precursors" of utopianism as being themselves a particular type of utopianism. What is useful in the suggested typology is the distinction made between humanist and philosophical/elitist utopianism on one hand, and the religious and scientific types on the other. To elaborate on this let me turn to the question with which I began this paper.

Besides what I consider to be the original historical type of utopianism, namely humanist utopianism, which relied on creativity and artfulness of ordinary humans to bring about a good life, there have been three major types of utopianism in world-history, adopting, respectively philosophy, religion, and science as the paradigms from which to derive their utopian visions and/or practices. The splitting of humanist utopianism into its three alienated forms may be seen as corresponding to the splitting of ancient civilizations into diverse forms of classical political, medieval religious, and more recent modern economic empires.

Philosophical utopianism is best represented by the Platonic search for the good society as formed and guided by the philosopher kings. Although religious sentiment and vision may be considered to have existed in all early utopias, including humanist and philosophical ones, it is with the rise of cultural/religious empires that religious utopianism gains its classic form. Given that most of the earliest civilizations and classical political empires had developed in the non-western regions of the world (Egypt, India, Persia, Mesopotamia), it is not surprising to see that religious utopianism is predominantly and classically eastern in origin ("east" is used here in its broadest meaning of what is non-west).[1] Jewish, Christian, and Islamic forms of religious utopianism and mysticism took their classical shape during the long medieval period. Scientific utopianism of both technological-bourgeois and socialist types, originating in the west in the course of the so-called Renaissance, Reformation, Enlightenment, and the Industrial Revolution, were of course best represented by various types of bourgeois utopianism and Marxism. More's *Utopia* or Omar Khayyam's *Rubaiyat*, may be considered heretical utopian movements in thought that do not easily fit in philosophical, religious, or scientific utopianisms, and have much more affinity with the humanist variety that emphasizes the value of ordinary human agency in bringing about the conditions for the good life. When they emerged, these heretical utopianisms heralded a return to humanist utopianism in reaction to the failure of orthodox religious efforts; however, despite their openness to skepticism and secularism, they may not easily be classifiable also under the scientific variety that emerged later. Omar Khayyam in particular was skeptical as much about the claims of science as about the claims of orthodox religion and philosophy—despite being himself publicly a scientist/astronomer, a religious man, and a free-thinking philosopher. Works by More (who was beheaded by religious orthodoxy), or eastern utopists such as Omar Khayyam, and certain other utopian literature and communal experiments emphasize, along with their acknowledgment of religious morality and/or use of scientific imagination and knowledge, the role of creative and willful action by ordinary humans in favor of utopian landscapes. As such they may be considered precursors of a humanist utopian renaissance that does not shy away from incorporating the contributions of philosophical, religious, and scientific utopianism within the framework of a new humanist utopianism. Humanist utopianism may therefore be considered both eastern and western in origin.

---

1. For similar use of the East-West distinction see Abdel-Malek (1981a/b): "For studies in the human and social sciences in the contemporary Orient--tentatively defined here as Asia and North Africa, but which also encompasses the whole North African continent as well as other areas in the central and southern-eastern part of the Western hemisphere—must address themselves primarily to this very transformation which the Orient is undergoing in a changing world" (1981b:192); "The structuralist-functionalist networks in the human and social sciences were busily elaborating their 'neo-Marxist' theories of 'center' and 'periphery', where the 'center' was, of course, the West, and the 'periphery', needless to say, the sphere of the nations of the Three Continents--in a word, the Orient" (1981b:193); "... the emergence of the Orient, the access and emergence on to the contemporary scene of the Three Continents of Asia, Africa and Latin America" (1981a:177).

By pointing out the spatial origins of various types of utopianism, I do not mean to suggest that each type has been confined to its original birth-place. On the contrary, all types of utopianism in time have often become global in scope. The global scope of each type, however, should not necessarily prevent us from ignoring their spatial points of origin. Christianity, for example, which is claimed often to be a "western" religion, is obviously an eastern religion (taking the eastern shores of the Mediterranean sea as a cut off point) which only later spread throughout the west and world as a whole. Most world religions are eastern in origin, despite the fact that most have now institutionalized themselves globally. In contrast, Marxism which is a global socialist ideology and movement, clearly originated in the west and built itself primarily on the economic, political, and philosophical sources that were European in origin. Its global expansion to the east (such as China, for example) should not prevent us from recognizing its western origin.

The break with religion in the paradigmatic structure of scientific utopianism is clear. The bourgeois ideology of "separation of church from state," to which Marxism also adhered, provides a historical demonstration of this defining feature of western utopianism. Western utopianism in the form of the bourgeois ideology of "progress" is the dominant type of utopianism today. Even Marxism adhered to and operated within the utopian ideology of progress which is the cultural *raison detre* of the modern capitalist world-system as well. The emphasis in western utopianism on experiment and practice on one hand and the predominance in modern times of this type of utopianism on the other hand are the two mutually reinforcing aspects of its character.

The policy of downplaying the other three major philosophical, religious, and humanist forms of utopianism, shared by both the bourgeois and socialist forms of western utopianism, emanates from their perceived and claimed hegemonic status in the global political arena. Although as a western doctrine Marxism has itself been regarded as the latest, the farthest advancing, and failing, global experiment in utopianism, the "success" of bourgeois utopianism characterized by the ideology of progress can hardly be sustained today even according to the data generated by global financial institutions (such as the World Bank and the IMF). The deepening gap between the rich and the poor across the globe and within nation-states, the worsening problems of hunger, housing, and environmental degradation, the outbreak of modern plagues and diseases such as AIDS, etc., and the inability of the system to eradicate them, are more than mere statistical data, but facts of everyday life for a majority of the world's population.

UTOPIANISM BEYOND MARXISM

While the typology presented above clarifies in what sense Marxism may be regarded as a utopian doctrine (i.e, as a scientific variety of it based on the predetermined action of natural/historical objective laws), it also points to the extent to which Marxism also departed from utopianism as a whole by embracing an anti-systemic mode preoccupied more with fighting a class enemy than with building the alternative cultural, political, and economic structures in the midst of the existing society. In his comparative study of several urban social movements (1983), Castells has stressed the degree to which the success of social movements historically has depended on their efforts in articulating the cultural, political, and economic dimensions of their aspired communal life in the existing reality than in declarations and demands to be made from the State. Building the alternative social arrangement, even in a minor scale, in the here and now, in other words, is a much more powerful strategy for social change than promises made in the most militant manifestos and declarations.

The danger of drawing the wrong lessons from the experience of Marxism, however, is to associate its wrongs with utopianism as a whole—a mistake that obviously pleases the conservative trends in the social and political establishment. Critical theorists and activists have found much inspiration in Marxism to the extent that they have been able to decipher the utopian message found in the early writings of the young Marx. Some of the self-critical reflections of Marx may have found its way to Engels's correspondence (Marx and Engels 1975), but perhaps not sufficiently to transcend the economistic structure of mature Marxism and a dialectical return to the utopian spirit in Marx's early writings in which neither idealism, nor materialism, but humanism was declared to be the riddle of human history resolved.

The typology presented above is only a preliminary effort at clarifying the meaning and forms of utopianism as a world-historical social movement. By distinguishing various types of utopianism from one another, the typology allows us to refrain from doing away with a social movement simply because of the failures of particular approaches to it in world-history—especially so, if such failures actually emanate from ideas or practices not belonging to the typology altogether. In essence, utopianism has been about desiring and/or making efforts towards optimally better worlds that do not (yet) exist—and doing so beginning in the here and now, by the example of how we think, feel, imagine, and act while conducting our everyday lives.

The debunking of utopianism as a whole has been a significant ideological and political feat for the guardians of the status quo across world-historical time and space—paved in modern times with the good intentions of antisystemic movements who have internalized the ideology in their movement rhetoric and agenda. How could the desires and/or movements for radical social change in favor of optimally better human conditions be more effectively extinguished, other than through declaring any efforts made towards such ends altogether fantastic, unrealistic, and impractical:

> Where the critics of the utopian method were, I believe, wrong was in holding that the business of projecting prouder worlds was a futile and footling pastime. These anti-utopian critics overlooked the fact that one of the main factors that condition any future are the attitudes and beliefs which people have in relation to that future." (Mumford, 1922: 298)

References

Abdel-Malek, Anouar. 1981a. *Social Dialectics: Civilizations & Social Theory.* Albany: University of New York Press.

Abdel-Malek, Anouar. 1981b. *Social Dialectics: Nation & Revolution.* Albany: University of New York Press.

Arrighi, Giovanni, Terence K. Hopkins, and Immanuel Wallerstein. 1989. *Antisystemic Movements.* London: Verso.

Arrighi, Giovanni, Terence K. Hopkins, and Immanuel Wallerstein. 1992. "1989, The Continuation of 1968." *Review* 2:221-242.

Beauchamp, Gorman. 1977. "Themes and Uses of Fictional Utopias: A Bibliography of Secondary Works in English." Pp. 55-63 in *Science-Fiction Studies* 4.

Castells, Manuel. 1983. *The City and the Grassroots: A Cross-Cultural Theory of Urban Social Movements.* Berkeley: University of California Press, and London: Edward Arnold.

The Encyclopedia of Philosophy. [1967] 1972. Paul Edwards, Editor in Chief. 8 volumes. New York: Macmillan Publishing Co., Inc. & The Free Press.

Encyclopedia of the Social Sciences. 1981. Guilford, Conn.: Dushkin Pub. Group.

The International Encyclopedia of the Social Sciences. 1968-. Sills, David L. and Robert King Merton, eds. New York: The Macmillan Company and The Free Press.

Harvey, David. 2000. *Spaces of Hope*. Berkeley: University of California Press.

Harvey, David. 2001. *Spaces of Capital*. London: Routledge.

Haschak, Paul G. 1994. *Utopian/Dystopian Literature: A Bibliography of Literary Criticism*. Metuchen, N.J., & London: The Scarecrow Press, Inc.

Kateb, George. [1963] 1972. *Utopia and Its Enemies*. Schocken Books.

Kateb, George. 1968. "Utopias and Utopianism." Pp. 267-70 in *The International Encyclopedia of the Social Sciences*, edited by David L. Sills, vol. 16. New York: The Macmillan Company and The Free Press.

Kateb, George. [1967] 1972. "Utopias and Utopianism." Pp. 212-215 in *The Encyclopedia of Philosophy*, vol. 8. New York: Macmillan Publishing Co., Inc. & The Free Press.

Kumar, Krishan. 1991. *Utopianism*. Minneapolis: University of Minnesota Press.

Mannheim, Karl. 1936. *Ideology and Utopia*. Translated by Louis Wirth and Edward Shils. New York: Harcourt Brace and Company, Harvest Books.

Manuel, F. E. and F. P. Manuel. 1979. *Utopian Thought in the Western World*. New Jersey: Humanities.

Marx Karl and Frederick Engels. 1975. *Selected Correspondence*. Moscow: Progress Publishers. Third revised edition.

More, Sir Thomas [1516] 1965. *Utopia*. New York: Penguin Books.

Mumford, Lewis. 1941. *The Story of Utopias*. New York: Peter Smith.

Negley, Glen. [1977] 1978. *Utopian Literature: A Bibliography with a Supplementary Listing of Works Influential in Utopian Thought*. University Press of Kansas.

Sargent, Lyman Tower. 1979. *British and American Utopian Literature, 1516-1975: An Annotated Bibliography*. G K Hall & Co.

Sargent, Lyman Tower. 1988. *British and American Utopian Literature, 1516-1985: An Annotated Chronological Bibliography*. Garland Pub.

Snodgrass, Mary Ellen. 1995. *Encyclopedia of Utopian Literature*. Santa Barbara, California: ABC-CLIO.

Tamdgidi, Mohammad H. 2001. "Open the Antisystemic Movements: The Book, the Concept, and the Reality" *Review*, XXIV, 2:301-338.

Tamdgidi, Mohammad-Hossein. 2002. "Mysticism and Utopia: Towards the Sociology of Self-Knowledge and Human Architecture (A Study in Marx, Gurdjieff, and Mannheim)." Ph.D. Dissertation, Binghamton University (SUNY).

Tamdgidi, Mohammad H. 2003. "The Three Component Parts and Errors of Marxism" Presented to the "Marx and Progress" panel of the *Rethinking Marxism*'s Fifth Gala Conference of *Rethinking Marxism*, November 2003.

Tucker, Robert, C., ed. 1978. *The Marx-Engels Reader*. 2nd edition. New York: W. W. Norton & Company.

Wallerstein, Immanuel. 1998a. *Utopistics: Or, Historical Choices of the Twenty-First Century*. New York: The New Press.

Contributors & Abstracts

Ayan Ahmed, graduated from UMass Boston in Spring 2004 with B.A. in Sociology and a minor in Psychology. She enrolled in Soc. 341, Elements of Sociological Theory, section 2 (Tamdgidi), during the Spring 2004 semester. **Paper Title**: *The Complexity of Naive Acceptance of Socially Manipulated Beliefs*. **Abstract**: This is a paper about self-evaluation and exploration. I struggle to understand myself in relation to my beliefs and how those beliefs were derived from society, parents and teachers as a whole and not through self reflection and education. I strive to recognize the manipulations I suffer through the hands of others in general and through my own self. Most importantly, I try to appreciate through the readings (or commentaries) of such scholars and philosophers as Freire, Ghazali, Durkheim, and Gurdjieff the nature of society and how individuals become oppressed by abiding with what others have prescribed—hence becoming "beings for others" as opposed to "beings for themselves." Finally, I try to lay bare the complexity associated with trying to break free from manipulation and habituation and the irony in which one, having realized manipulation and habituation at the conscious level, is still driven subconsciously to embrace those very conditions one was seeking to avoid.

Keilah Billings, is a junior joint-majoring in Sociology and Psychology at UMass Boston. She enrolled in Soc. 341, Elements of Sociological Theory, section 3 (Tamdgidi), during the Spring 2004 semester. **Paper Title**: *Questioning Motherhood: A Sociological Awakening*. **Abstract**: The idea of having a child is one that seems to go against my nature. Forming families seem to be the reigning desire for most women and men as they grow older and more mature, and the need to procreate seems to grow more and more prevalent. This need for procreation rips through a woman as a freight train through its rails. Having a child is a natural process that many people feel is a major part of their lives' design. To me, the idea of having a child is more of a threat; an end to the independence I have worked so hard to achieve. I am afraid that it would mean the end of who I am today, and I fear that being a mother would turn me into someone I do not want to be. Because of all this, I feel that making the decision to have a child would mean sacrificing my very being. So when I choose not to have children, I am going against the social norms I have been taught my whole life.

Jorge Capetillo-Ponce, is Assistant Professor of Sociology at UMass Boston. **Paper Title**: *Defining the Other*. **Abstract**: G. W. F. Hegel said: *"Everything is what is not."* Throughout human history, we find a continuous struggle to define the other, the foreigner, the unknown, the opposite of we or I. And, as the quote from Hegel indicates, what they are, that we are not, helps define the frontiers of personal and group identity.

Chris DaPonte, is a junior joint-majoring in Criminal Justice and Sociology at UMass Boston. She enrolled in Soc. 341, Elements of Sociological Theory, section 3 (Tamdgidi), during the Spring 2004 semester. **Paper Title**: *Will I Marry*

Her? **Abstract**: Recently, the issue of gay couples' rights to marry has raised much controversy. Over 60% of the population does not believe that gay couples should have the right to marry, but those that agree and disagree with gay marriage are all voicing loud protests against one another. President Bush is currently attempting to pass a Constitutional Amendment defining marriage as a union between a man and a woman. Most proponents of this amendment hold marriage as a sacred religious ceremony. Ritual, as defined by Randall Collins is a "'stereotyped sequence of gestures and sounds'… that make emotions more intense, and commit them more strongly to views of reality…" (Wallace and Wolf, 148). Those who are against gay marriage hold this view of a sacred ritual with family and friends. It is something that little girls spend years longing for. What they are not seeing, however, is that marriage does not end after the ceremony, and that the ceremony doesn't have to be about a white dress and a church.

M. D., is an undergraduate student at UMass Boston. **Paper Title**: *Body Image: A Clouded Reality.* **Abstract**: I think body image has become a social dilemma in our society. Eating disorders are too common among women, and I put 100% of the blame on society. But how did our society become so clouded that we actually believe that someone who looks as though they haven't eaten in months is beautiful? In the past, women like Marilyn Monroe were considered beautiful, and being full-figured was praised. I would give anything to live in a society where that was the case, as I'm sure many women today do. We know what eating disorders do to the body, so why do we continue to torture our bodies? We as a society need to take a step back and look at what we have become: A materialistic, image-obsessed society that praises beauty more than it praises knowledge, love, and life. We are made up of individuals all with a false consciousness of what we really want. I think our society has a clouded image of what is beautiful. Women all over the world are killing themselves to conform their bodies to society's standards. Instead of praising women for being healthy, we criticize them and place pressure on them to be like what they see on television, in films, or on the runways. Eating disorders are growing problems which many seem to brush aside, assuming those afflicted by the problem will take care of themselves. The only way to change the growing rate of eating disorders is to change the way our society functions as a whole.

Nancy O'Keefe Dyer, is a senior majoring in Social Psychology and minoring in the Study of Religion at UMass Boston. She enrolled in Soc. 341, Elements of Sociological Theory, (section taught by Professor Jorge Capetillo-Ponce) during the Fall 2003 semester. **Paper Title**: *Durkheim, Mead, and Heroin Addiction.* **Abstract**: Much has been written and much research done in an effort to understand the phenomenon of drug addiction. The treatment modalities available—medical, behavioral, pharmaceutical, "Twelve-Step"—speak to the many theories that have arisen as a result of research done to date. Yet statistics on heroin use and abuse indicate remarkably low "cure" rates and an ever-increasing number of addicts and "casual" users. Perhaps the field has been waiting for my investigation of the ways in which Emile Durkheim and George Herbert Mead would view the phenomenon of addiction.

Savvas Fetfatsidis, is an undergraduate students majoring in Sociology at UMass Boston. He enrolled in Soc. 341, Elements of Sociological Theory, (section taught by Professor Jorge Capetillo-Ponce) during the Fall 2003 semester. **Paper Title**: *Just Live: The Trick Is, You Have A Choice*. **Abstract**: Originally this paper was going to only analyze the effect of music on the individual and society, but as I was writing I began thinking more and more about the last few years of my life, and how much I've grown and changed. Finally putting this journey into perspective became very important for me. I have learned that being aware of a problem is the first step in solving it, but we should not make the problems our life. I believe that in society people of similar statuses and backgrounds are most likely to experience certain similar struggles. Each person deals with those struggles in their own personal ways and at their own pace. For me, family, friends, work, music and love are the core influences of my character. It was important for my character to go through this mental and spiritual suffering. It helped me to become a better and stronger person. In each society there are powerful forces influencing us, so the more we know about society the more we can deal with it. The old proverb that says that "seek, and you shall find," is the truth. In any given situation you can find positive and negative aspects. The trick is to know you can choose between the two. Sometimes I still need to remind myself to just relax and enjoy the ride of life because one day it will come to an end.

Michelle B. Jacobs, graduated in Spring 2004 from UMass Boston with a B.A. in Criminal Justice and a minor in Sociology. She enrolled in Soc. 341, Elements of Sociological Theory, section 3 (Tamdgidi), during the Spring 2004 semester. **Paper Title**: *Obsessed with Impression Management: A Critical Sociology of Body Image in Capitalist Society*. **Abstract**: The issues with impression management that we have in society today are perpetuated through the media and how it portrays body image. Just as my family affected me, society and media are influenced by the capitalist/consumer society. It is made so that we all have a certain role to play and a certain way to look and if we do not fit into that then we do not get as far in the social world as one who may be ideal in the looks department. They reap the social rewards that society has to offer. Big corporations feed on this and make the public even more needy of the ideal body image by throwing it in their faces everyday on the television and the magazines. Writer Allen Ginsberg once said; "Whoever controls the media—the images—controls the culture" (Maclean's 1). This is a very true statement. Society is based on looks and the capitalist society that we live in does not promote realistic beauty ideals or cater to the average woman. We all have issues with our bodies whether it comes from being bombarded with these wafer thin images portrayed in magazines or from the family we were raised in. At both micro and macro social levels, obsession with body image is a social dilemma we will all face in our lifetime.

Jennifer M. Kosmas, is a junior majoring in Social Psychology and minoring in Women's Studies at UMass Boston. She enrolled in Soc. 341, Elements of Sociological Theory, section 3 (Tamdgidi), during the Spring 2004 semester. **Paper Title**: *The Roots of Procrastination: A Sociological Inquiry into Why I Wait Until Tomorrow*. **Abstract**: Whenever I have an assignment due, even my friends become nervous for me because they know what it entails. I tell even the closest of all my friends that I complete my papers on time, because I am all too familiar with the disappointment and disbelief reinforced when they find out I have done this late yet another time. Procrastination seems to generally be associated with things such as laziness, bad habits, lack of responsibility, etc. College students are famous for it. While some do it more often than others, there is no one who is not guilty of it every now and then. And why not? Who would really rather write a research paper over some other immediately enjoyable activity? But when looked at more deeply, procrastination can become a problem for some, and even begin to interfere with one's normal functioning. It is even connected with other things such as depression and anxiety. Exploring my issues concerning procrastination with the help of various sociological theories, I come to realize where they may have stemmed from and why I might behave in such ways. With this knowledge, I hope to be able to change this ever-present factor in my life.

Kuong C. Ly, is an undergraduate student at UMass Boston majoring in Sociology. He enrolled in Soc. 321, Racial & Ethnic Relations, (section taught by Anna Beckwith), during the Spring 2004 semester. **Paper Title**: *"Asian": Just a simple Word*. **Abstract**: Throughout my life, I'm face with several questions of "What does it mean to be Asian?" and "How do you define being Asian?" "It's only a word" is what I tell myself. But, I know that it is so much more than that. The racial side of my mind tells me I should break the Asian American mold of model minority myth and challenge the general public's opinion of Asian Americans by becoming a blue-collar college dropout, or by carrying out the struggle for social justice by voicing the need to bring down the false stereotypes of "model minority" that society has built. But by doing so, I'm only validating the stereotypes that the Asian American community has placed on my Cambodian American ethnic identity. So, the ethnic part of my mind tells me that I should break the mold placed on Cambodian Americans by getting a college education and pursuing the model minority myth. Does that mean that by doing so the racial side of my mind has won, or does that mean that the ethnic side of my mind has triumphed? The battle between which of the two molds I should be breaking remains, and I'm still torn as to what it means to be "Asian"—after all *it's just a simple word*. Or is it?

Lynne K. Marlette, graduated in Spring 2004 from UMass Boston with a B.A. in Sociology and a minor in Asian American Studies. She enrolled in Soc. 341, Elements of Sociological Theory, section 1 (Tamdgidi), during the Fall 2003 semester. **Paper Title**: *Honesty, Trust, and Love—In* That *Order: A Reflective Sociological of My Emotional Kaleidoscope As An Adoptee*. **Abstract**: This is a self exploratory paper sparked by a question that has loomed in my head for some months now; "Should I take antidepressants?" Through analyzing my thoughts and emotions leading to the depressing state, I explore my early childhood experiences as an adopted child from Korea and explore a more recent, emotionally charged break-up in that context. I use the knowledge gained in order to draw conclusions regarding how to change and lead my life.

Marie Neuner, is a junior at UMass Boston, majoring in English and minoring in Sociology. She enrolled in Soc. 341, Elements of Sociological Theory, section 2 (Tamdgidi), during the Spring 2004 semester. **Paper Title**: *Who Are "I"? A Sociology of My Traditional, Modern, and Postmodern Selves*. **Abstract**: This paper investigates my multiple selves, in particular the conflict between my traditional and modern self-identities. Through phenomenology, my inability to strictly adhere to one set of beliefs is treated as problematic in order to understand how society influences the development and nourishment of each self. By uncovering the oppressive nature of universal truths in our postmodern society, the pressure to choose among metanarratives is deemed unnecessary. Postmodernity is discussed as a hybrid mode combining both tradition and modernity and not as a complete departure from them. Ultimately, the postmodern era in which we live, if fostered, can allow greater personal freedom from society's oppressive frameworks and a personal reclamation of power.

Buddi Osco (pen name), is an undergraduate student at UMass Boston. He enrolled in a course taught by Professor Jorge Capetillo-Ponce at UMass Boston. **Paper Title**: *Anomie or Alienation?: A Self-Exploration of the Roots of Substance Ab/use*. **Abstract**: Substance abuse is a serious problem for millions of citizens in the United States, and throughout the world. Everyday, across the globe, individuals of different races, ethnicities, religions, cultures, and social classes struggle with the disease of drug addiction. Many people lay the blame for these problems on the individuals themselves, labeling them as criminals, deviants, or persons of weak moral character. Perhaps they even cite bad parenting, or other such factors. But what if the true source of the problem was greater? What if the problem lies not in the individual or their family at all, but in society as a whole? Or, rather, what if the problem lies in the individual's lack of a connection to the rest of society? In this paper, I will attempt to apply Emile Durkheim's theory of anomie and Karl Marx's theory of alienation to the problem of substance abuse, using my own life experiences to illuminate the subject.

Guadalupe Paz, graduated in Spring 2004 from UMass Boston with a B.A. in Psychology and a minor in Sociology. She enrolled in Soc. 341, Elements of Sociological Theory, section 1 (Tamdgidi), during the Fall 2003 semester. **Paper Title**: *The Effects of Immigrant Experiences on the Bifurcation of Women's Consciousness*. **Abstract**: As human beings, we are fascinating evolving creatures capable of influencing our surroundings and being influenced by it as well. The central issue that has emerged in my life is the constant pull between two cultural standards. My Hispanic culture pulls me towards being a housewife and the influence of the American culture pulls me towards being a working mom. Ultimately my goal is to explore how both have influenced the way I perceive myself as an immigrant woman in this country.

D. M. Rafferty, is a junior joint-majoring in Sociology and Psychology at UMass Boston. She enrolled in Soc. 341, Elements of Sociological Theory, section 3 (Tamdgidi), during the Fall 2003 semester. **Paper Title**: *My Life's Tapestry: Casting Theoretical Lights on the Social Threads That Tie Me Down*. **Abstract**: I view my life as a large and ever changing tapestry. I am cut from a bolt of very strong, durable, and coarse working class material. Being born female certainly factored into the pattern of this design. However, woven deeply in my foundation are also threads of limitation resulting from the classist and sexist attitudes that still persist in today's society. Socio-economic class and gender roles constitute the two most influencing social stratifications that have shaped the outlines of my life. Reviewing personal experiences in light of the classical, contemporary, and postmodernist theories in sociology will hopefully reveal new hues and textures in the ever changing tapestry that is my life.

Annie Roper, is a junior joint-majoring in Sociology and Psychology at UMass Boston. She enrolled in Soc. 341, Elements of Sociological Theory, section 1 (Tamdgidi), during the Fall 2003 semester. **Paper Title**: *From Alienation to Exploration: Breaking Free From the Iron Cages of My Life.* **Abstract**: The social experience of alienation has affected most of my life. I grew alienated from my core self when I attended Catholic schools and I've been working on changing that ever since. Those rules were hard to live by and they took their toll on my life, leaving me with social scars. I went from living what amounted to a child's utopian life to one like prison, where I attended school and met bureaucracy, discipline and repression. My imagination was stifled, my creativity crushed, and my expectations became nil. Alienated and demoralized, I became a factory worker. I smoked pot, worked and drank. I abandoned free thinking for years, repressing memories and drinking and drugging to keep away pain and fear. My social worldview narrowed to tunnel vision—with only a bottle in sight before me. It is only now that I am facing my demons in this paper. I'm allowing my sociological imagination a free rein: I'm finally putting my personal troubles into broader perspective in reference to family, society and my place in the world.

Elizabeth J Schumacher, graduated in Spring 2004 from UMass Boston with a B.A. in Social Psychology. She enrolled in Soc. 341, Elements of Sociological Theory, section 2 (Tamdgidi), during the Spring 2004 semester. **Paper Title**: *Alice in the Gendered Sports Fan Wonderland: A Sociological Inquiry.* **Abstract**: C. Wright Mills encouraged people to develop a sociological imagination in order to "place themselves in social context and identify how public issues affect them at the personal level, arguing that people need to know the source of their difficulties in order to make sense of their lives (Disch 2)." I believe that gender, in many cases, may be the source of such difficulties. Disch goes on to stress the importance of empowerment through the challenging of the patriarchal system. She states that, "without seeing the complexity of human experience and the complexity of human oppression, we cannot begin to address the real needs of human beings caught in systematically oppressive social structures (Disch 14)." Though the feminist movement has vastly improved the situation of women, many challenges and obstacles still endure. Over the past century, substantial progress has been made in the opportunities afforded to women in voting rights, education, and job possibilities, but many social issues still need to be improved. In this paper I will discuss the obstacles women continue to face in their efforts to be seen as equals in the sports world as fans.

M.H. (Behrooz) Tamdgidi, is Assistant Professor of Sociology at UMass Boston. **Paper Title**: *De/Reconstructing Utopianism: Towards a World-Historical Typolo-*

gy. **Abstract**: Marxism represented a new, "scientific," type of utopian movement in contrast, on one hand, to the philosophical and religious varieties preceding it, and on the other hand the briefly revived humanist type (as somewhat represented by utopian socialists) which was soon frozen in embryo by Marxism's own ideological-political rhetoric and ascendance in the world-wide opposition to capitalism. What I intend to point out is a need to go beyond the polemics and the rhetoric of these movements in order to develop a typological framework of utopianism which accounts for the historical failures of Marxism due in part to the shortcomings emanating from its specific utopian type and partly due to its gradual departure from the utopian typology altogether. The point is to redeem the value of utopianism as a specific strategy for social change in contrast to the antisystemic mode characterizing the dominant form of opposition movements to capitalism during at least the past two centuries.

www.ingramcontent.com/pod-product-compliance
Lightning Source LLC
Chambersburg PA
CBHW080401030426
42334CB00024B/2962